Legalines

Editorial Advisors:
Gloria A. Aluise
Attorney at Law
Jonathan Neville
Attorney at Law
Robert A. Wyler
Attorney at Law

Authors:
Gloria A. Aluise
Attorney at Law
David H. Barber
Attorney at Law
Daniel O. Bernstine
Attorney at Law
D. Steven Brewster
C.P.A.
Roy L. Brooks
Professor of Law
Frank L. Bruno
Attorney at Law
Scott M. Burbank
C.P.A.
Jonathan C. Carlson
Professor of Law
Charles N. Carnes
Professor of Law
Paul S. Dempsey
Professor of Law
Jerome A. Hoffman
Professor of Law
Mark R. Lee
Professor of Law
Jonathan Neville
Attorney at Law
Laurence C. Nolan
Professor of Law
Arpiar Saunders
Attorney at Law
Robert A. Wyler
Attorney at Law

LABOR LAW

Adaptable to Thirteenth Edition of Cox Casebook

By Charles N. Carnes
Professor of Law

Supplement in Back of Book

BAR/BRI

EDITORIAL OFFICES: 111 W. Jackson Blvd., 7th Floor, Chicago, IL 60604
REGIONAL OFFICES: Chicago, Dallas, Los Angeles, New York, Washington, D.C.

SERIES EDITOR
Linda C. Schneider, J.D.
Attorney at Law

PRODUCTION MANAGER
Elizabeth G. Duke

SECOND PRINTING—2005

Copyright © 2003 by BarBri, a Thomson business. All rights reserved. No part of this publication may be reproduced or transmitted in any form or by any means, electronic or mechanical, including photocopy, recording, or any information storage and retrieval system, without permission in writing from the publisher. Printed in the United States of America.

Legalines®

**Features Detailed Briefs of Every Major Case,
Plus Summaries of the Black Letter Law**

Titles Available

Administrative Law	Keyed to Breyer
Administrative Law	Keyed to Strauss
Administrative Law	Keyed to Schwartz
Antitrust	Keyed to Areeda
Antitrust	Keyed to Pitofsky
Civil Procedure	Keyed to Cound
Civil Procedure	Keyed to Field
Civil Procedure	Keyed to Hazard
Civil Procecure	Keyed to Rosenberg
Civil Procedure	Keyed to Yeazell
Conflict of Laws	Keyed to Currie
Conflict of Laws	Keyed to Hay
Constitutional Law	Keyed to Brest
Constitutional Law	Keyed to Choper
Constitutional Law	Keyed to Cohen
Constitutional Law	Keyed to Rotunda
Constitutional Law	Keyed to Stone
Constitutional Law	Keyed to Sullivan
Contracts	Keyed to Calamari
Contracts	Keyed to Dawson
Contracts	Keyed to Farnsworth
Contracts	Keyed to Fuller
Contracts	Keyed to Kessler
Contracts	Keyed to Murphy
Corporations	Keyed to Choper
Corporations	Keyed to Eisenberg
Corporations	Keyed to Hamilton
Corporations	Keyed to Vagts
Criminal Law	Keyed to Johnson
Criminal Law	Keyed to Kadish
Criminal Law	Keyed to LaFave
Criminal Procedure	Keyed to Kamisar
Decedents' Estates & Trusts	Keyed to Dobris
Domestic Relations	Keyed to Clark
Domestic Relations	Keyed to Wadlington
Evidence	Keyed to Waltz
Evidence	Keyed to Weinstein
Evidence	Keyed to Wellborn
Family Law	Keyed to Areen
Federal Courts	Keyed to Wright
Income Tax	Keyed to Freeland
Income Tax	Keyed to Klein
Labor Law	Keyed to Cox
Labor Law	Keyed to St. Antoine
Property	Keyed to Casner
Property	Keyed to Cribbet
Property	Keyed to Dukeminier
Property	Keyed to Nelson
Property	Keyed to Rabin
Remedies	Keyed to Re
Remedies	Keyed to Rendelman
Sales & Secured Transactions	Keyed to Speidel
Securities Regulation	Keyed to Coffee
Torts	Keyed to Dobbs
Torts	Keyed to Epstein
Torts	Keyed to Franklin
Torts	Keyed to Henderson
Torts	Keyed to Keeton
Torts	Keyed to Prosser
Wills, Trusts & Estates	Keyed to Dukeminier

All Titles Available at Your Law School Bookstore

THOMSON
BAR/BRI

111 W. Jackson Boulevard, 7th Floor
Chicago, IL 60604

SHORT SUMMARY OF CONTENTS

		Page
I.	**HISTORICAL BACKGROUND AND INTRODUCTION**	1
	A. Historical Background	1
	B. The Present Scope and Coverage of National Labor Legislation	17
	C. National Labor Relations Board-Organization and Procedure	20
II.	**ESTABLISHMENT OF THE COLLECTIVE BARGAINING RELATIONSHIP**	23
	A. Protecting the Right to Self-Organization	23
	B. Selection of the Bargaining Representative	51
III.	**COLLECTIVE BARGAINING**	68
	A. Negotiating the Collective Bargaining Agreement	68
	B. Subjects of Collective Bargaining	78
	C. Other Issues Involving Collective Bargaining	87
IV.	**STRIKES, BOYCOTTS, AND PICKETING**	91
	A. Introduction	91
	B. Employee Concerted Actions Under the NLRA	91
	C. Constitutional Limitations	101
	D. The National Labor Relations Act	107
V.	**ADMINISTRATION OF THE COLLECTIVE AGREEMENT**	128
	A. Introduction	128
	B. Nature of the Agreement and of the Grievance Process	128
VI.	**SUCCESSORSHIP**	161
	A. Succession of Unit, Representational Status, and Survival of the Bargaining Agreement upon Change of Ownership of the Business	161
VII.	**IMPACT OF THE ANTITRUST LAWS ON UNION CONCERTED ACTIVITIES**	165
	A. Legitimate Union Activities Exempt from Antitrust Laws	165
VIII.	**FEDERALISM AND LABOR RELATIONS**	169
	A. The Role of State Law in Labor-Management Relations: The Preemption Doctrine	169
	B. Representation, Bargaining, and Concerted Activities	174

Labor Law - i

IX.	RECONSIDERING THE NLRA AND THE FUTURE	181
	A. The Context Then and Now	181
	B. Changes in Context	181
	C. Gap Between Employee Preferences and the Extent of Organization	181
	D. Labor Law Reform	182
X.	THE INDIVIDUAL AND THE UNION	183
	A. Union Duty of Fair Representation	183
	B. The Individual and Her Grievance	187
	C. Devices Insuring Union Security	190
	D. Union Hiring Halls	195
	E. Benefits for Union Officials	196
	F. Discipline of Union Members Under the NLRA	197
	G. Judicial Supervision of Union Discipline	201
	H. Election of Union Officers	209
	I. Corruption in Unions—Landrum-Griffin Titles II, III, and V	214

TABLE OF CASES 217

TABLE OF CONTENTS AND SHORT REVIEW OUTLINE

	Page
I. **HISTORICAL BACKGROUND AND INTRODUCTION**	1
A. **HISTORICAL BACKGROUND**	1
1. Pre-Civil War Period	1
a. The beginnings	1
b. Criminal conspiracy doctrine	1
2. Civil War to World War I—The Growth of National Unions and Labor Unrest	1
a. The growth of unions	1
b. The 1880s—The Knights of Labor—confederations of local and national bodies into a larger unit	1
1) Origin	1
2) Growth	2
3) Decline	2
c. 1880-1914—The American Federation of Labor—the growth of a national craft union	2
1) Origin	2
2) The major tenets of the AFL philosophy	2
3) Growth of the AFL and strong resistance	2
3. Judicial Reaction to the Growth of Unionism—The "Labor Injunction"	2
a. Introduction	2
1) Permanent injunction	3
b. The Restatement of Torts	3
c. The ends or purposes test	4
d. Use of the Sherman Act against unions	4
1) Introduction	4
2) Sherman Act applied	5
3) "Local" strikes	5
4. The Clayton Act	5
a. Introduction	5
1) Objectives	6
2) Jurisdiction	6
b. Ineffectual in practice	6

		1) Introduction	6
		2) Secondary boycotts may be enjoined	6

5. The Norris-LaGuardia Act ... 7

   a. Background ... 7
   b. Reasons for the Norris-LaGuardia Act ... 7

      1) Judicial problems ... 7
      2) Yellow dog contracts ... 7
      3) "Objectives" test ... 7
      4) Vicarious liability ... 7
      5) Procedural objections ... 7

   c. Provisions of the Act ... 8

      1) Employee rights ... 8
      2) Agreements contrary to Act unenforceable ... 8
      3) Limitation on injunctions ... 8
      4) Findings required for injunction ... 8
      5) Negotiation and mediation ... 9

6. Effect of the Antitrust Laws ... 9

   a. Early law—*Danbury Hatters Case* ... 9
   b. Clayton Act ... 9
   c. Limitations on the scope of the Sherman Act ... 9

      1) Sit-down strike not a "combination" in restraint of trade ... 9
      2) Jurisdictional disputes—The Sherman and Norris-LaGuardia Acts ... 10
      3) Applicability of Norris-LaGuardia Act to secondary picketing ... 11

7. Constitutional Protections ... 12
8. The Wagner Act (NLRA) of 1935 ... 13

   a. Background—the era of encouragement for labor ... 13

      1) Introduction ... 13
      2) The Railway Labor Act (1926) ... 13

         a) Background ... 13
         b) 1934 amendments to the Act ... 13
         c) Air carriers ... 14

   b. Basic provisions of the Wagner Act ... 14
   c. Constitutionality of the NLRA ... 15
   d. Formation of the CIO ... 15

9. The Taft-Hartley Act (LMRA) of 1947 ... 15

   a. Background ... 15
   b. The effects of Taft-Hartley ... 15

		1) Injunctions	15
		2) Restored governmental neutrality	16
		3) Collective bargaining	16
		4) Outlawed the "closed shop"	16
		5) Federal court jurisdiction	16

    10. The Landrum-Griffin Act (LMRDA) of 1959 16

        a. Background 16
        b. Basic provisions of the Act 16

B. THE PRESENT SCOPE AND COVERAGE OF NATIONAL LABOR LEGISLATION 17

    1. The Railway Labor Act 17

        a. Jurisdiction 17

            1) Air carriers 17
            2) Rail carriers 17
            3) Employee groups 17

        b. Coverage of employees 17

            1) Factors considered 17
            2) Employees not directly involved in transportation 17

        c. Handling disputes 17

            1) Section 6 17
            2) Section 10 17

    2. The National Labor Relations Act (NLRA) 17

        a. Jurisdiction 18

            1) Introduction 18
            2) Labor dispute 18
            3) Commerce 18
            4) Affecting commerce 18
            5) NLRB jurisdictional discretion 18

                a) Basis for policy 18
                b) Jurisdictional guidelines 19

        b. Coverage of employers and employees 19

            1) Employers covered 19

                a) Inclusions 19
                b) Exceptions 19

            2) Employees covered 20

Labor Law - v

		a)	Inclusions	20
		b)	Exceptions	20

    C. **NATIONAL LABOR RELATIONS BOARD—ORGANIZATION AND PROCEDURE** 20

        1. Organization of the Board 20

            a. Panel 20
            b. Delegation of powers 20
            c. The General Counsel 20

        2. Primary Functions of the Board 21

            a. Representation cases 21
            b. Unfair labor practice cases 21

II. **ESTABLISHMENT OF THE COLLECTIVE BARGAINING RELATIONSHIP** 23

    A. **PROTECTING THE RIGHT TO SELF-ORGANIZATION** 23

        1. Protection Against Employer Interference, Restraint, and Coercion 23

            a. Restricting activities on company-owned property—solicitation and distribution rules 23

                1) Solicitation by employees 23

                    a) Defined 23
                    b) Restrictive rules 23
                    c) Off-duty employees 23
                    d) Employee solicitation 24

                2) Solicitation or distribution by nonemployees 25

                    a) Distribution on employer premises by nonemployees 26

                3) The "captive audience" doctrine 27
                4) Duty to provide list of employee names and addresses 27

                    a) Employee lists 28

                5) Anti-union speech 29

                    a) "Laboratory conditions" test for reelection orders 29
                    b) Board considerations 30

                6) Noncoercive speech cannot be used as evidence of other employer violations 30

		7)		Coercive statements not protected	30
			a)	Employer's assertion of legal rights	30
			b)	Employer's prediction of adverse consequences	30
			c)	Statements held coercive	30
			d)	Nonfactual statements	31
			e)	Predictions based on facts	31
			g)	Predictions not based on facts	31
			h)	Employer can cease business	31
			i)	Employer can cite history	31
		8)		Misrepresentations	31
			a)	Board screening of electioneering	32
			b)	Latest position	32
		9)		Inflammatory appeals	33
			a)	Interrogation	33
		10)		Interrogation of employees	34
			a)	Anti-union environment	34
	b.			Coercive atmosphere defined	34
	c.			Economic coercion and inducement	35
		1)		Changing employee benefits to influence election	36
			a)	Application	36
		2)		Union unfair practices	37
		3)		Employee benefits	37
			a)	Representation election realities	37
2.				Employer Domination or Assistance	37
	a.			Test	37
		1)		Employer consultative committees	38
		2)		Negotiation with a union prior to formal recognition proscribed	40
	b.			Methods of determining unlawful domination or support	40
		1)		Solicitation of membership	41
		2)		Undue assistance	41
		3)		Use of company facilities	41
		4)		Domination through union by-laws or constitutional provisions	42
		5)		Employer choice between rival unions	42
3.				Employer Discrimination on the Basis of Union Membership	43

Labor Law - vii

	a.		Proving discrimination	43
		1)	Degree of proof required	43
		2)	Examples of employer discrimination	43
			a) Discrimination in hiring or firing	43
			b) Discrimination in tenure, terms, or conditions of employment	43
	b.		Union security agreements	44
	c.		Discriminatory discharge	44
		1)	Examples	44
	d.		Discriminatory lay-offs	44
	e.		Other justifications irrelevant	44
	f.		Scope of review of NLRA cases	45
		1)	"Substantial evidence" standard in a "mixed motive" case	45
		2)	Proof in "mixed motive" or "pretext" cases	46
		3)	Compare—section 8(a)(1)	46
		3)	The "runaway" shop	46
		4)	Closing down a department	46
	g.		Discriminatory demotions and transfers	47
	h.		Shutting down operations	48
	i.		Status of supervisors under the Act	49

4. Remedies for Violation of the Right to Organize 49

	a.	Cease and desist orders	49
	b.	Orders for affirmative action	49
	c.	Discrimination in the hiring of employees	49
	d.	Temporary injunctions	50
	e.	Prerequisites for injunctive relief	50
	f.	Range of NLRB remedies	51
	g.	Ordering recognition of union	51
	h.	Runaway shop remedies	51
	i.	Coercion and discrimination cases—back pay	51

B. SELECTION OF THE BARGAINING REPRESENTATIVE 51

1. Introduction 51

	a.		Employer refusal to bargain—section 8(a)(5)	51
		1)	Immediate duty to bargain	52
		2)	Uncertain cases	52
	b.		Election proceedings	52
	c.		Decertification	52
	d.		Restrictions of section 9 rights	52

				1)	Substantial interest requirement	52
				2)	Grounds for denying an election	52

                    a) Unremedied unfair labor practices ... 52
                    b) Election bar ... 52
                    c) Certification bar ... 52

        e. Contract bar—effect of a valid collective bargaining agreement ... 53
        f. Removal of the contract bar ... 53

            1) Introduction ... 53
            2) Invalid provisions ... 54
            3) Premature extension ... 54
            4) Defeating purposes of NLRA ... 54

2. Determining the Appropriate Bargaining Unit ... 54

    a. Introduction ... 54
    b. Board discretion ... 54
    c. Multi-employer bargaining ... 54

        1) Joint negotiations required ... 54
        2) Separate employer units ... 54

    d. "Community of interest" ... 55
    e. Single-plant vs. multi-plant units ... 55

        1) Early history ... 55
        2) Considerations ... 55
        3) Rule of discretion ... 55

            a) Application—Single versus multi-location unit ... 55

        4) Hospital unit standards by rule ... 56
        5) Rule valid ... 57

    f. Multi-employer bargaining ... 58

        1) Withdrawal from a multi-employer unit ... 58

    g. "Coalition" bargaining ... 59

        1) Introduction ... 59
        2) Employer must bargain ... 59

3. Representation Elections ... 59

    a. Introduction ... 59
    b. Review ... 59
    c. Meaning of a "majority" ... 60
    d. Eligibility to vote: economic strikers ... 60
    e. Unfair labor practice strikers ... 60

4. Review of Representation Proceedings ... 60

			a.	Introduction	60

                a. Introduction 60
                b. Effect 61
                c. Relief in equity 61
                d. Application of jurisdiction 61

        5. Alternates to Board-Conducted Elections 62

            a. Introduction 62

                1) Fair election unlikely 62
                2) *Cumberland Shoe* doctrine 63
                3) Criteria for bargaining orders 63
                4) Union never had majority 63
                5) Bargaining order not warranted 64
                6) Duration of the representative's authority 64

            b. Where successor acquires business other than by
                merger or purchase of assets 66

                1) Unfair labor practice proceedings 66
                2) Presumption concerning preferences of strike
                    replacements 66

III. **COLLECTIVE BARGAINING** 68

   A. **NEGOTIATING THE COLLECTIVE BARGAINING
       AGREEMENT** 68

       1. Scope of Union Negotiating Authority 68

           a. Individual contracts superseded on matters covered
               by collective agreement 68
           b. No exceptions 68

       2. Individual Contracts Permitted Where Not in Conflict
           with Collective Agreement 68

           a. No justification for refusal to bargain 68

       3. Section 9(a) Supersedes Section 7 Rights of
           Individual Employees 69

           a. No individual bargaining of discrimination claim 70

       4. Limitations on Union Authority and Majority Rule 71

           a. Exclusion of employees 71
           b. Duty to employees 71
           c. Decertification 71
           d. Landrum-Griffin Act 71
           e. Membership 71
           f. Nonmandatory subjects 71
           g. Additional safeguards 71
           h. Racial discrimination by union 71

			1)	Duty owed to all employees in unit	71
	5.	The Duty to Bargain in Good Faith			72
		a.	Statutory policy behind the "good faith" requirement		73
		b.	The "good faith" standard		73
		c.	Deadlocked negotiations		73
		d.	Present intent to agree		73
		e.	Subjective intent		73
		f.	"Bad faith"		73
		g.	Look to conduct of the parties		73
		h.	Inferences of "bad faith"		73
			1)	Content of proposals	73
				a) Employer retains full authority	73
				b) Employees lose benefits	73
			2)	Conduct or tactics in negotiations	73
				a) Dilatory tactics	74
				b) Demands that union drop pending charges	74
				c) "Take it or leave it" proposals	74
			3)	Inference of bad faith from subject matter	74
		i.	Duty to disclose information		75
		j.	Balancing against the interests of others		75
		k.	Work slowdown not bad faith		76
		l.	Unilateral change in employment conditions		77
		m.	"Boulwarism"		78
		n.	Remedies in the event of failure to bargain in good faith		78
			1)	Board-ordered bargaining	78
			2)	Compensatory relief	78
			3)	Refusal unfair but not flagrant	78
			4)	No forced agreements	78
B.	**SUBJECTS OF COLLECTIVE BARGAINING**				78
	1.	Permissive, Compulsory, and Illegal Subjects of Bargaining			78
	2.	Compulsory Subjects			79
		a.	Retirement plan benefits		79
			1)	Manner of payment	79
		b.	Work assignments		79
		c.	Grievances		79
		d.	Safety rules and practices		79
			1)	Early practice	79
			2)	Occupational Safety and Health Act	79

					a)	Incorporating OSHA standards	79
				e.	Management functions clause		80
			3.	Permissive Subjects			80
				a.	Examples		80
				b.	Cannot be prerequisite to mandatory subjects		81
				c.	Cannot be condition for overall agreement		81
				d.	No duty to bargain on policy objectives		81
					1)	Rationale	82
				e.	Management prerogative and union participation		82
					1)	Unit work by supervisors	82
					2)	In-plant food service	82
				f.	Other topics		82
					1)	Subcontracting	82
					2)	Decision to terminate business	83
					3)	Transfer of operation	84
					4)	Modification of retirees' benefits	86
	C.	**OTHER ISSUES INVOLVING COLLECTIVE BARGAINING**					87
		1.	Bargaining, the Strike, and Impasse Resolution				87
				a.	Statutory provisions		87
				b.	Strike threat overcoming impasse		87
		2.	The Effect of Strike on Duty to Bargain				87
				a.	Introduction		87
				b.	Subcontracting to maintain operations		87
		3.	Bargaining Remedies				88
				a.	Party cannot be compelled to accept mandatory contract provision		88
				b.	Board cannot write contract for parties		89
IV.	**STRIKES, BOYCOTTS, AND PICKETING**						91
	A.	**INTRODUCTION**					91
		1.	Interference with Concerted Activities				91
		2.	Constitutional Limitations				91
		3.	The National Labor Relations Act				91
	B.	**EMPLOYEE CONCERTED ACTIONS UNDER THE NLRA**					91
		1.	Protected Activity				91

			a.	Employer responses to "concerted" activities	91
			b.	Unorganized and single employee activities may be "concerted"	91
			c.	Collective bargaining claims as concerted action	91
			d.	Political appeals as concerted activity	92
		2.		Discharge and Reinstatement of Strikers	93
			a.	Reinstatement depends on category of strikers	93
			b.	Economic strikers	93
				1) Abolishment of jobs	94
				2) Degree of activity	94
				3) Filling vacancies	94
			c.	Unfair labor practice strikers	94
			d.	Limitation on reinstatement rights	94
			e.	Tactic	94
		3.		Unprotected Employee Conduct	94
			a.	Disciplining employees	94
			b.	Employee discharge for disloyalty	95
			c.	Employer refusal to rehire strikers	96
			d.	Employer discrimination against strikers	96
			e.	Employer lockout	97
			f.	Employer burden to show legitimate objectives	98
			g.	Strikers applying for reinstatement	99
			h.	Employee refusals to cross picket lines	100
			i.	Employer discipline of union officials	100
C.	**CONSTITUTIONAL LIMITATIONS**				**101**
	1.			Introduction	101
			a.	Due process	102
			b.	Freedom of expression	102
	2.			The Right to Strike	102
			a.	A qualified right	102
			b.	Unlawful strikes	102
				1) Determination	102
				2) General rule	102
				3) Violation of federal statute	103
	3.			Sources of Claimed Constitutional Right to Strike	103
			a.	First Amendment	103
			b.	Fifth Amendment	103
			c.	Fourteenth Amendment	103
			d.	Thirteenth Amendment	103

		4.	The Right to Picket	103
		5.	Regulating the Means by Which Picketing Is Carried Out	103

    a. Obstructing entrances 103
    b. Mass picketers 103
    c. Isolated misconduct 103
    d. State injunction against picketing 104
    e. Secondary picketing 104

  6. Handbilling at Shopping Mall 104
  7. Exclusion of Pickets from Shopping Mall 105
  8. Shopping Center Organizational Picketing 107

D. THE NATIONAL LABOR RELATIONS ACT **107**

  1. Union Unfair Labor Practices Affecting Organization 107

    a. Section 8(b)(1)—restraint or coercion 107

      1) Unlawful activities 107
      2) Prohibited activities 107

        a) Physical coercion 107
        b) Economic coercion 107
        c) Other forms of unlawful coercion 108
        d) Picketing 108

      3) Employee coercion 108

    b. Organizational and representational picketing 108

      1) Legality 108
      2) Limitation in the NLRA 108

        a) Uncertified union 108
        b) Board priority 109
        c) Problems 109

      3) Petition for certification not filed within thirty-day limit 109
      4) Publicity or informational picketing 110

        a) Interruption of deliveries 110

  2. Secondary Pressure—Regulation of Boycotts 111

    a. Activities proscribed 111
    b. Illegal objects 111
    c. Judicial interpretation of section 8(b)(4) 111

      1) Introduction 111

        a) No broad rules 111

	2)	Refusal to cross a picket line	112
	3)	The "primary action" proviso	112
	4)	Publicity other than picketing	112

        a) Picketing of secondary employer 112
        b) Handbilling 112

    5) Actions other than boycotts 113

        a) Secondary situations 113
        b) Primary situations 113
        c) Note 113

    6) Changes made by the Labor-Management Reporting and Disclosure Act of 1959 113

d. Contractor-subcontractor relationships in construction industry 113

    1) Introduction 113
    2) Picketing entire site is illegal 114

e. Application of section 8(b)(4) to specific problems involving secondary pressure 114

    1) Common situs situations 115

        a) Conflicting interests involved 115
        b) *Moore Dry Dock* rules 115
        c) Picketing subcontractor of employer 116

    2) "Separate gate" cases 116

        a) Gate used by employees of independent contractor 117
        b) Relatedness of work 118

f. Exceptions to section 8(b)(4) 118

    1) Requests not to cross picket lines 118
    2) The "publicity proviso" 118

        a) Limitation 118
        b) Secondary picketing of retail store 118
        c) Who is a "producer" 119
        d) "Means other than picketing" 120

            (1) Rationale 120
            (2) Impact—product boycotts by picketing 130

        e) What constitutes a "product" boycott 120
        f) Main product picketing 120

g. Hot cargo clauses 121

			1)	Background	121
			2)	Section 8(e)	121
			3)	"Work preservation" versus "work acquisition"	121
			4)	Subcontracting provisions that protect jobs	122
			5)	Clothing and construction industry provisos	123

      3. Jurisdictional Disputes 123

          a. Introduction 123

               1) Failure of employer to conform 124

          b. "No raid" agreements 124

               1) Express agreements 124
               2) Employer agreement 124
               3) NLRB functions under section 10(k) 124
               4) NLRB settlement of jurisdictional disputes 124
               5) Enforcement of work-assignment awards 125

                   a) Board resolution 125
                   b) Private resolution 125

      4. Featherbedding and Make-Work Arrangements 126

          a. Definition 126
          b. NLRA provision 126

               1) Example 126
               2) Requiring local performers to appear with national performers 126
               3) "Setting bogus" 126

      5. Violence and Union Responsibility 127
      6. Remedies for Union Unfair Labor Practices 127
      7. Jury Trials 127

V. ADMINISTRATION OF THE COLLECTIVE AGREEMENT 128

  A. **INTRODUCTION** 128

      1. Grievance Discussions 128
      2. Arbitration 128
      3. Judicial Resolution 128

  B. **NATURE OF THE AGREEMENT AND OF THE GRIEVANCE PROCESS** 128

      1. The Collective Bargaining Agreement 128

          a. The object of the agreement 128
          b. Nature of the collective bargaining agreement 128
          c. Who is involved 128

2.		The Grievance Procedure	129
	a.	The hierarchy	129
	b.	Defining the "grievance"	129
	c.	Providing for the procedures	129
	d.	What the grievance procedure can do	129
3.		Grievance or "Rights" Arbitration	129
	a.	Introduction	130

- 1) Widespread Use — 130
- 2) Arbitration Clauses — 130
- 3) Procedure — 130

	b.	Review of arbitrators' decisions	130
	c.	The duty to arbitrate	130
	d.	Complexity of issues	131
	e.	Discipline and discharge	131

- 1) Discipline of employees — 131
- 2) Discharge for drug use — 131
- 3) Arbitrary distinctions among employees — 132
- 4) Two views on the discipline question — 132
- 5) Guides for decision — 133

	f.	Subcontracting	133

- 1) Introduction — 133
  - a) Disengagement — 133
  - b) Competing forces — 133
- 2) The requirement of good faith — 133
  - a) Application of good faith requirement — 133
  - b) Implied good faith clauses — 134
  - c) Established company practices — 134
  - d) Management prerogative — 134

	g.	The effect of past practice and public law	134

- 1) Introduction — 134
- 2) Past practice — 134
- 3) Public law — 135

4.		Judicial Enforcement of Collective Bargaining Agreements	136
	a.	Federal court jurisdiction under Taft-Hartley section 301	136

- 1) Congressional intent — 136
- 2) The right to sue — 136

	b.	Judicial enforcement of agreements	136

Labor Law - xvii

		1)		Prior law	136
		2)		Exhaustion of remedies doctrine	137
		3)		Court may compel specific performance of agreement to arbitrate	137
			a)	Federal court power to fashion remedies	137
	c.	Recourse to private judicial machinery			138
	d.	Judicial enforcement of "no strike" agreements			138
		1)		Jurisdiction of state courts	138
			a)	Statutes of limitations	139

5. Judicial Enforcement and the Review of Arbitration Awards 139

    a. Introduction 139

        1) Determination of arbitrability 139
        2) Rationale 139
        3) District court assessment of merits 139
        4) Narrow reading of matters exempted from arbitration 140
        5) Arbitration after corporate statutory merger 141
        6) Presumption of arbitrability 142

            a) Expiration of the CBA 142

        7) Successor's duty to arbitrate 144
        8) Court enforcement of arbitrator's award 144
        9) Setting aside awards on the basis of "public policy" 145

6. Injunctive Relief Available 146

    a. Introduction 146

        1) Forum shopping after *Sinclair* 147
        2) Federal courts can issue injunctions 147
        3) Rationale—Taft-Hartley "repeals" ban on injunctions 147
        4) Enjoining a strike violating "no-strike" clause 147

    b. Showing required to obtain injunctive relief 148
    c. Individual damages 148
    d. Union damages 148

7. The NLRB's Role During the Term of the Agreement 149

    a. Union jurisdictional disputes 149
    b. Contract enforcement and unfair labor practices 149

        1) Rationale 149

			a)	NLRB jurisdiction not exclusive	149
			b)	Interpreting terms of agreements by the Board	149
			c)	Employee violations	150

       2) Suits by individuals 150
       3) Remedies in breach of contract suits 150

           a) Damages 150
           b) Injunctions 150

       4) Role of the NLRB 150
       5) NLRB deference to arbitration 150
       6) Board need not agree with arbitrator 151

           a) Board's present position on deference to arbitrators 151
           b) Deference to settlement agreements 152
           c) Deference in representation cases 152
           d) Title VII discrimination cases 152
           e) The *Collyer* doctrine 153
           f) Scope of the *Collyer* doctrine 153
           g) 1973 NLRB guidelines 153
           h) 1977 retrenchment 153
           i) Present status of doctrine 154
           j) Deferral by the courts to arbitration 154
           k) Application 155

    c. Modifying or terminating an existing agreement—Union-employer bargaining 156

       1) Basic rule 156
       2) Qualifications 157

           a) Certification of another union 157
           b) No duty to bargain where subject covered by existing agreement 157
           c) Subjects not covered in contract 157

    d. Unilateral adoption of drug and alcohol testing 158
    e. Partial transfer of operations for economic reasons 159
    f. The collective bargaining agreement and bankruptcy 160

VI. SUCCESSORSHIP 161

A. SUCCESSION OF UNIT, REPRESENTATIONAL STATUS, AND SURVIVAL OF THE BARGAINING AGREEMENT UPON CHANGE OF OWNERSHIP OF THE BUSINESS 161

  1. Survival of the Agreement and Representational Status 161

    a. Duty of new employer to bargain—"contractual successorship" 161

       1) Assumption of existing contract 161

			2)	Surviving corporation in statutory merger	161
	2.	Survival of Bargaining Status But Not the Agreement			161
		a.		Retention of some of the work force	161
		b.		Circumstances which will destroy the duty to bargain	161
	3.	The Effect of Delay			162
	4.	Successor's Responsibility for Prior Employer's Unfair Labor Practice			163
	5.	Successor Employer's Duties Under Prior Employer's Bargaining Relationship			163
	6.	Double-Breasted Employers			164

VII. IMPACT OF THE ANTITRUST LAWS ON UNION CONCERTED ACTIVITIES ... 165

A. LEGITIMATE UNION ACTIVITIES EXEMPT FROM ANTITRUST LAWS ... 165

1. Concerted Labor Union Activities Are Legitimate ... 165
2. Accommodation of Antitrust and Labor Policies ... 165
3. Illegal Combinations ... 165
4. Present Judicial Interpretation of the Exemption ... 165

   a. Union conspiring to eliminate competition ... 165
   b. Issues related to conditions of employment ... 166
   c. Extending the labor law exemption ... 167
   d. Union-subcontractor agreements ... 167

      1) Prohibiting dealings with nonunion subcontractors ... 167
      2) Setting rules for nonunion independent contractors ... 168

VIII. FEDERALISM AND LABOR RELATIONS ... 169

A. THE ROLE OF STATE LAW IN LABOR-MANAGEMENT RELATIONS: THE PREEMPTION DOCTRINE ... 169

1. In General ... 169
2. Preemption Doctrine ... 169

   a. Scope of federal power ... 169
   b. Theories ... 169
   c. State court attempt to exercise jurisdiction ... 169
   d. Matters of "peripheral" federal concern ... 170

      1) "Purely internal union matters" ... 170
      2) Emphasis on conduct in question ... 170

   e. Matters where state regulation will promote, rather than impede, federal labor policy ... 171

			1)	Union duty of fair representation	171
		3.	Statutory Exceptions		171
			a.	Damages for unlawful strikes or boycotts	171
			b.	Action for breach of collective bargaining contract	171
			c.	Where the NLRB refuses to exercise jurisdiction	171
				1) State court tort actions	171
				2) State trespass against picketing	172
				3) Activity unregulated by the NLRA	173

B. REPRESENTATION, BARGAINING, AND CONCERTED ACTIVITIES ... 174

1. State Qualifications for Union Officers ... 174
2. State Court Injunction Affecting Wage Clause ... 175
3. State Regulation of Minimum Benefit Standards ... 175
4. State Plant Closing Law ... 176
5. Preemption of Contract Breach Actions ... 176
6. State Unemployment Benefits for Strikers ... 176
7. Permanent Replacements and State Regulation ... 177
8. Enforcement of Rights Under Bargaining Agreements ... 178
9. State Refusal to Process State Claims ... 179
10. Retaliatory Lawsuits ... 179
11. State Regulation of Activities of Supervisors ... 179

IX. RECONSIDERING THE NLRA AND THE FUTURE ... 181

A. THE CONTEXT THEN AND NOW ... 181

1. Labor Force Organization ... 181

B. CHANGES IN CONTEXT ... 181

1. Economic ... 181
2. Demographic ... 181
3. Employer Practices ... 181
4. The Law ... 181

C. GAP BETWEEN EMPLOYEE PREFERENCES AND THE EXTENT OF ORGANIZATION ... 181

D. LABOR LAW REFORM ... 182

1. Strengthening the NLRA ... 182

    a. Prompt elections ... 182
    b. NLRB injunctions ... 182
    c. Use of bargaining ADR ... 182
    d. Counterindications ... 182

2. Allowing Wider Variety of Management/Employee Interaction ... 182

		3. Employee Participation Committees	182
		4. Nonmajority Union Representation	182

X. THE INDIVIDUAL AND THE UNION 183

A. UNION DUTY OF FAIR REPRESENTATION 183

1. Introduction 183

   a. The LMRDA 183
   b. Duty owed to all employees in unit 183
   c. Racial discrimination cases 183
   d. Inevitable differences 183
   e. Punitive damages 183
   f. Fair representation and the NLRB 184

      1) Discrimination 184
      2) Remedies 184
      3) Statute of limitations 184

2. What Constitutes "Breach" of Duty of Fair Representation 184

   a. Rationale 184
   b. Examples 185

      1) Unfair labor practices 185
      2) Invidious or arbitrary classification 185
      3) Sex discrimination 185
      4) Intimidation 185
      5) Political expediency 185
      6) Duty of fair representation in bargaining 185

3. State or Federal Action Proper 187

B. THE INDIVIDUAL AND HER GRIEVANCE 187

1. Right to Adjust Directly with the Employer 187
2. Right to Union Representation at Investigatory Interviews ... 187
3. Employee's Right to Judicial Relief Against Employer 187

   a. Exhaustion of contract remedies required 187
   b. Contract action against employer 187

4. Employee's Right to Judicial Relief Against the Union 188

   a. Action to obtain admission to the union 188
   b. Apportionment of damages 189
   c. Exhaustion of internal union procedures 190

C. DEVICES INSURING UNION SECURITY 190

1. Federal Regulation of Compulsory Union Membership Arrangement 190

		a.	Background	190
		b.	Present law	191
		c.	Types and legality of compulsory union membership agreements	191
			1) Closed shop	191
			2) Preferential hiring	191
			a) Required union membership	191
			b) Hiring halls	191
			3) Union shop	191
			a) Grace period	191
			b) Full membership not compulsory	191
			4) Agency shop	191
			a) Agency shop agreement in right-to-work state	192
			5) Maintenance of membership	192
		d.	Enforcement of union security clauses in the agreement	192
		e.	Authorization to negotiate union security agreements	193
	2.	State Regulation of Compulsory Membership Agreements—"Right to Work" Laws		193
		a.	Present legislative response	193
		b.	State courts decide validity	193
	3.	Union Members May Not Be Compelled to Make Political Contributions		193
	4.	Adequacy of "Escape" Clauses		194
	5.	Adequate Procedures for Escape		194
D.	**UNION HIRING HALLS**			**195**
	1.	Background		195
	2.	Union Unfair Labor Practices		195
		a.	Union coercing employer to discriminate in employment	195
			1) Nondiscriminatory exclusive hiring hall	195
		b.	Unfair financial practices	196
E.	**BENEFITS FOR UNION OFFICIALS**			**196**
	1.	Superseniority		196
		a.	Permissible and impermissible seniority discrimination	196

F.		DISCIPLINE OF UNION MEMBERS UNDER THE NLRA		197
	1.	Union Restraint and Coercion of Employee Rights		197
		a. Power of union to adopt and enforce internal rules		197
		b. Fines for failure to honor strike		197
		c. Fine for violating union rule		198
		d. Resignation from union		200
		e. Fine for attempting to resign		200
		f. Union discipline of supervisory members		200
G.		JUDICIAL SUPERVISION OF UNION DISCIPLINE		201
	1.	Limitations on Union Discipline		201
		a. Background		201
		b. LMRDA Title I—"labor's bill of rights"		201
		1) Equal rights		201
		a) Union jobs protection under the LMRDA		201
		2) Removals of union elected officers		202
		3) Freedom of speech and assembly		203
		a) Responsibility of members toward the union		203
		b) Replacement of union officials		203
		c) Balancing		203
		c. Judicial review of union disciplinary proceedings		204
		1) Scope of judicial review		204
		2) Federal courts and judicial review		204
		3) Dues, initiation fees, and assessments		205
		4) Protection of the right to sue		205
		a) Limitation against employer interference		205
		5) Due process safeguards against improper disciplinary actions		205
		6) The common law and disciplinary actions		205
		7) Exhaustion of internal remedies required		206
		a) Common law exceptions		207
		b) "May" rather than "must" exhaust		207
		c) Exhausting internal remedies		207
		d) The federal courts and exhaustion		208
H.		ELECTION OF UNION OFFICERS		209
	1.	Common Law Background		209
		a. Refusal to hear complaints		209
		b. Limited jurisdiction		209

	2.	Landrum-Griffin, Title IV	210
		a. Rights of union members under Title IV	210
		1) Voting	210
		2) Frequency of elections	210
		3) Secret ballot	210
		4) Nomination	210
		5) Eligibility for candidacy	210
		6) Notice of election	210
		7) Dissemination of campaign literature	210
		8) Membership lists	210
		9) Observers at the polls	210
		10) Election expenses	210
		11) Compliance with union constitution and by-laws	210
		b. Enforcement provisions	211
		1) No preelection remedy	211
		c. District court jurisdiction	211
		d. Requirement of reasonable qualifications	211
		e. Mootness	212
		f. Procedure	212
		1) Finding of "probable cause" as prerequisite to lawsuit	212
		a) Statement of reasons for not suing	212
		2) New elections	213
		3) Judicial power to invalidate elections—the "nexus" requirement	213
		a) Effect	213
		b) Burden of proof	213
		g. External financial support	213
I.	**CORRUPTION IN UNIONS—LANDRUM-GRIFFIN TITLES II, III, AND V**		**214**
	1.	Title II of the Landrum-Griffin Act—Reporting and Disclosure Provisions	214
		a. Basic union information	214
		b. Financial transactions by officials	214
		c. Reporting by employers	214
		d. Criminal penalties and civil remedies	214
	2.	Limitations on Union Officials—Title V	214
		a. Defraying legal costs of officers	214

3.	Disclosure of Information	215
4.	"Trusteeships"—Landrum-Griffin, Title III	215
	a. Background	215
	b. Requirements for trusteeships	216

TABLE OF CASES **217**

I. HISTORICAL BACKGROUND AND INTRODUCTION

A. HISTORICAL BACKGROUND

1. **Pre-Civil War Period.** It is important to understand the historical underpinnings of modern labor law because of the unique role that this history has played in shaping labor relations—constant reference is made in case law and legislative history to the early beginnings of labor law.

   a. **The beginnings.** Before 1800, little effort was made by workers to organize. There were numerous instances of workers (or "servants" as they were called at common law) temporarily joining together for united action against employers, or artisans combining together to maintain rates and keep competition from becoming too difficult. The early trade organizations were not called unions, but were generally referred to as societies. These societies existed in a quiescent state of trade unity and would come to life for particular occasions. The development of the large-scale factory system widened the distance between management and labor and increased the friction quotient.

   b. **Criminal conspiracy doctrine.** In 1794, the Philadelphia Cordwainers organized and became the first American labor union. It successfully struck against a cut in wages in 1799, and struck again in 1806, giving rise to the early doctrines of labor law. One of these early doctrines was that of "criminal conspiracy," which was later replaced with the "labor injunction."

2. **Civil War to World War I—The Growth of National Unions and Labor Unrest.**

   a. **The growth of unions.** Shortly before the Civil War and then after the war, a number of factors emerged that strongly influenced the development of labor unions:

      1) Large industrial empires were built by such figures as Harriman, Rockefeller, and Gould.

      2) The increase in population and the disappearance of the frontier created large cities, and urban dwellers became more dependent on their employee wages in order to exist.

      3) An increasing number of immigrants formed a growing pool of unskilled labor, stimulating the organization of skilled laborers.

      4) The nucleus of a strong trade union movement already existed in the form of societies of skilled craftsmen.

   b. **The 1880s—The Knights of Labor—confederations of local and national bodies into a larger unit.**

      1) **Origin.** Initially a secret society, the Knights were moralists and reformers. Their chief aim was to attack, through mass organization, what they perceived as the evils resulting from

industrialization. Their organization included almost all occupations, including capitalists and farmers, as well as laborers.

    2) Growth. From 1880 to 1886, the Knights' membership grew to 700,000, largely because of their advocacy of popular political reforms (such as tax reform) that were directed at equality for all.

    3) Decline. The Knights suffered a decline in membership that was as dramatic as their rapid growth, largely because the farmers and laborers in the organization sought conflicting goals. By 1890, the membership had dropped to 100,000, and by 1900, it had virtually disappeared.

c. 1880-1914—The American Federation of Labor—the growth of a national craft union.

    1) Origin. In 1886, the national craft unions, with a membership of 150,000, formed the American Federation of Labor ("AFL") and elected Samuel Gompers as its first president. Gompers's leadership of the AFL over the next 40 years had a major effect on the course of American unionism.

    2) The major tenets of the AFL philosophy.

        a) Political action took the form of nonpartisan lobbying aimed solely at improving economic conditions for its members. Other political involvement was rejected.

        b) Collective bargaining meant reliance on negotiations for settlement of disputes in order to achieve economic gains.

        c) Exclusive union jurisdiction of all workers in a single craft occupation was pursued in order to prevent competition between workers for jobs and to strengthen the union's bargaining position. The AFL advocated exclusive jurisdiction (*i.e.*, that each national or international union was to have its own sphere of jurisdiction into which no other union could trespass). The principle of exclusive jurisdiction has been difficult for the unions to apply, and caused a labor movement split in the 1930s, but it continues to be a basic tenet of labor today.

    3) Growth of the AFL and strong resistance. The early growth of the AFL was slow, reaching only 278,000 by 1898. The employers and the courts opposed the growth of unionism, the employers using self-help methods (including discharges, blacklists, and vigilante "goon squads") and the courts enjoining strikes and other concerted union activities. By 1914, membership had grown to more than 2,000,000.

3. Judicial Reaction to the Growth of Unionism—The "Labor Injunction."

    a. Introduction. During and after the decline of the "criminal conspiracy" doctrine, the courts turned to civil remedies that were mainly based on common law tort actions, and also to equitable relief in the form of injunctions.

1) **Permanent injunction--Vegelahn v. Guntner,** 44 N.E. 1077 (Mass. 1896).

    a) **Facts.** The employees (Ds) of Vegelahn's (P's) business established a picket line, or "patrol", of two men in front of the building and used persuasion and threats of violence to prevent other workers from crossing the picket line in order to attain their economic demands. P filed suit to enjoin any further picketing. The court, at a preliminary hearing, issued an injunction prohibiting the picketing workers from using threats or acts of violence, and from persuasion to break existing contracts. However, it allowed them to continue their patrol and other peaceful attempts to dissuade the other workers from entering the plant. P appeals in order to modify the preliminary injunction.

    b) **Issue.** May peaceful picketing be permanently enjoined?

    c) **Held.** Yes. Judgment for P. The preliminary injunction should be broadened to proscribe any further picketing by the workers.

        (1) A patrol, whether peaceful or accompanied by threats or acts of violence, interferes with the rights of the employer and the other employees. An employer may hire those who are willing to work for the wages offered, and such employees have the right to accept or reject such an offer without being subject to the intimidation inherent in a picket line.

        (2) A combination to commit acts that deprive others of their rights is an unlawful civil conspiracy and, since it results in a continuing injury to a business interest, it can be permanently enjoined.

    d) **Dissent** (Holmes, J.).

        (1) The injunction issued by the court is overbroad since there is no inherent coercion in a peaceful patrol.

        (2) Since the court has allowed free competition between businesses even when it has resulted in an economic loss for one of the businesses, the court should also extend an analogous right to engage in free competition through peaceful picketing to employees as well.

    e) **Comment.** This case applied the "ends—means" test for determining the propriety of concerted acts by employees: Even when the "ends" are lawful, if the "means" employed are unlawful the activity will be enjoined. Holmes's dissent explains the "free competition" doctrine later used to justify the right of employees to strike.

b. **The Restatement of Torts.** The Restatement (1939) adopted Holmes's arguments and sanctioned "fair persuasion." While peaceful picketing is authorized, any threat of physical harm to induce workers not to work for an employer, to strike, or to boycott the products of an employer is strictly unlawful.

Plant v. Woods

c. **The ends or purposes test--Plant v. Woods,** 176 Mass. 492 (1900).

1) **Facts.** Union A (P) broke away from union B (D). D talked to the employers, telling them to persuade P's members to rejoin D. D made no direct threats to the employers, but the idea was communicated that there would be trouble unless P's members rejoined. P sued in Massachusetts state court to enjoin D on the theory that D's conduct constituted an unlawful conspiracy.

2) **Issue.** Does urging employers to persuade their employees to join a particular union constitute an enjoinable conspiracy, where there are no direct threats of force or strikes?

3) **Held.** Yes. Injunction issued against D.

   a) Although workers may combine for some purposes, the facts here indicate a highly coercive situation in which employers were intimidated into persuading their employees to join a particular union.

   b) Such conduct limits the freedom of both employer and employee. It is not justified as "trade competition" and should therefore be enjoined.

4) **Dissent** (Holmes, J.). I am pleased that the majority has recognized that the organization of workers to obtain power in order to better their economic position is permissible as long as the end or purpose is good and the means used are lawful. The issue then is whether the purposes intended by D justify the means used. True, its immediate purpose was not to raise wages. But its ultimate purpose was to achieve enough strength to impose a higher wage scale. The activities that D employed in that context were therefore necessary and proper.

5) **Comment.** The following are other situations where the objectives were deemed unlawful: (i) striking and picketing for the purposes of bargaining while the company's employees were under one-year employment contracts; (ii) a customer boycott to induce the employer not to use labor-saving machinery; and (iii) a strike to force a contractor to allow members of a striking union to perform work already assigned to members of another union.

d. **Use of the Sherman Act against unions.**

1) **Introduction.** The Sherman Antitrust Act, although originally intended to guard against restraint of trade, also was used as a basis for federal judicial intervention in labor disputes. It was first applied in *United States v. Debs*, 64 F. 724 (N.D. Ill. 1894). In *Debs*, Pullman employees, who were members of the Railway Union organized by Debs, went on strike. The Union thereupon refused to handle Pullman cars on any railroads that they serviced. The United States Attorney General secured an injunction to prevent all persons from hindering or interfering with the business of the railroads or from encouraging others to do so. Debs disobeyed the injunction and was convicted of contempt. Although the United States Supreme

Court affirmed, it did not rely specifically on the injunction provisions of the Sherman Act to do so.

2) **Sherman Act applied--Loewe v. Lawlor,** 208 U.S. 274 (1908).

    a) **Facts.** Loewe (P), unorganized hat manufacturers, brought suit against Lawlor (D), United Hatters of North America, the union that represented employees at 70 out of 82 hat manufacturers in the country. The complaint alleged that D had combined and conspired to violate the federal antitrust laws by a combination of threats, strikes, and boycotts to allegedly interfere with P's interstate trade. The federal district court granted D's demurrer on the ground that union activities were not within the ambit of the Sherman Antitrust Act. P appeals.

    b) **Issue.** Does union concerted activity fall within the proscription of the federal antitrust laws?

    c) **Held.** Yes. Judgment reversed.

        (1) The provisions of the Sherman Antitrust Act are applicable to union activities, and, to the degree that unions combine or conspire to restrain interstate trade, they will be liable for treble damages under the antitrust laws.

    d) **Comment.** This case, although later abrogated by statute and case law, was a significant hurdle for the growth of national unionism.

3) **"Local" strikes.** In *Coronado Coal Co. v. United Mine Workers*, 268 U.S. 295 (1925), the United States Supreme Court took into account whether a strike had only a "local motive" or was one that had an interstate aspect. The mine owner (Coronado Coal) had closed down its already organized mines in Arkansas with the intention of reopening them on a nonunion basis. This effort provoked violent reactions that resulted in property damage, personal injuries, and two deaths. The Company sued the Union (United Mine Workers) under the Sherman Act and recovered $600,000 in treble damages. The Court said that if it "was in fact a local strike, local in its origin and motive, local in its waging, and local in its felonious and murderous ending," it fell outside the Sherman Act. On remand and retrial, evidence was produced that tended to show that the "intent" of the strike was to "restrain or control the supply (of coal) entering and moving in interstate commerce or the price." Thus, the Sherman Act applied and the divided verdict for the defendants was held erroneous.

4. **The Clayton Act.**

    a. **Introduction.** Agitation began after the Pullman dispute to affirm the right of workers to organize without interference and to require employers to recognize and deal with the unions. The Clayton Act of 1914 was intended primarily as an antitrust act. But two provisions favoring labor were included.

Loewe v. Lawlor

Labor Law - 5

1) **Objectives.** The normal objects of a labor organization are legitimate; "nothing in the antitrust acts shall be construed to forbid their members from lawfully carrying out their legitimate objectives" (section 6).

2) **Jurisdiction.** Jurisdiction was withdrawn from federal courts to issue injunctions in labor disputes (section 20).

b. **Ineffectual in practice.** Though initially hailed as "labor's charter of freedom," the Act proved ineffectual.

1) **Introduction.** Government policy, especially during World War I, began to recognize and to protect the right to organize, and as a result, union membership increased. Organizational efforts were directed to the large corporations in mass production industries. But in the 1920s, most court decisions were unfavorable to unions. Continued reliance was placed on the restrictive tests ("unlawful objectives" and "unlawful means") and the Clayton Act was rendered impotent by a series of Supreme Court decisions.

2) **Secondary boycotts may be enjoined--Duplex Printing Press Co. v. Deering,** 254 U.S. 443 (1921).

a) **Facts.** Duplex Printing Press Company (P) manufactured presses for interstate commerce; it undersold its organized closed shop competitors. The International Association of Machinists (D) wanted to impose a closed shop on P. D attempted to dissuade P's customers from dealing with P by threats aimed at preventing the transportation, installation, or maintenance of P's presses. P brought suit against D to enjoin the boycott of P's presses. The federal district court held that the injunction should issue unless prevented by the Clayton Act. P claims that its business is a property right requiring unrestrained access to interstate commerce; that D is a combination to hinder P's interstate commerce, an activity prevented by the Sherman Act; and that the limitation in section 6 of the Clayton Act is inapplicable since section 20, which regulates the issuance of injunctions, provides that unless the case at bar raises its primary issues "between employers and employees," the Clayton Act imposes no limitation on the granting of injunctions. The court of appeals affirmed. D appeals.

b) **Issue.** Are injunctions against secondary boycotts proscribed by the Clayton Act?

c) **Held.** No. Judgment affirmed.

(1) The term "employers and employees" in section 20 of the Clayton Act includes only those proximately and substantially concerned as parties to an actual dispute respecting the terms and conditions of their own employment.

  (2) Others are not within the limitations on injunctions and hence "secondary" boycotting activity is not protected from an injunction.

 d) **Dissent** (Brandeis, Holmes, Clarke, JJ.). The term "employees" should be broadly construed to include all engaged in labor. It is not confined to the legal relationship between a specific employer and its employees.

5. **The Norris-LaGuardia Act.**

 a. **Background.** Throughout the 1920s, injunctions were readily granted in labor disputes. A growing body of opinion, however, saw such actions by the courts as frustration of legislative policy. The Norris-LaGuardia Act, enacted in 1932, brought an end to the era of oppressive injunctions and restricted federal judicial intervention in labor disputes.

 b. **Reasons for the Norris-LaGuardia Act.**

  1) **Judicial problems.** The courts, as opposed to Congress, were found generally to be ill-equipped to handle substantive considerations of economic or social issues that existed in the relationship among employees and employers. Abstract references were made instead to a "means" test or "objectives" test. Even where a court sought to understand the merits of a dispute, it might decline to initiate a solution on the basis that it would thereby usurp legislative functions.

  2) **Yellow dog contracts.** These contracts provided that, before employment, an applicant must renounce any present union membership and promise not to join a union during his period of employment. Additionally, it was unlawful for a union to encourage any employee bound to such a contract to break its provisions. Hence, the unions were prevented from promoting the unionization of such an employee.

  3) **"Objectives" test.** This was criticized as a standard that permitted decisions according to the social and economic preferences of individual judges, often justifying a charge of court bias against union activity.

  4) **Vicarious liability.** Under a theory of conspiracy, labor cases held unions civilly and criminally liable for the violent acts of their members, or for persons having some sort of relation to the union, whether or not authorized to commit the act, even where the union had taken steps to prevent the violation in question.

  5) **Procedural objections.** Temporary restraining order hearings were ex parte proceedings in which the employer was heard first. Often, after restraining orders were given, delays arose to postpone a hearing on the merits, during which most strikes collapsed. The unions bore the brunt of this delay. There was also criticism that

Labor Law - 7

injunctions were difficult for the workers to interpret. Picketing might be allowed, but only up to a point. That point, however, was often not easily discernible. If a violation was claimed, the prosecution was for contempt of the court order, and it was tried before the same judge who had issued the injunction, without a jury. Unions attempted, often unsuccessfully, to ensure that such offenses would be tried as violations of the criminal law, before a different court.

c. **Provisions of the Act.**

1) **Employee rights.** Employees are granted freedom of association, organization, and designation of representatives.

2) **Agreements contrary to Act unenforceable.** Any undertaking between an employee and an employer contrary to the policy of the Act is not enforceable in federal court, specifically including any promise not to join a union (*i.e.*, yellow dog contracts).

3) **Limitation on injunctions.** No federal court can issue an injunction in a case arising out of a labor dispute, the effect of which is to prohibit persons "interested" in the dispute from:

   a) Ceasing to perform work or quitting employment;

   b) Becoming a member of a labor organization;

   c) Paying or withholding from persons participating in labor disputes, strikes, or unemployment any benefits, insurance, or other monies due;

   d) By lawful means aiding any person participating in the dispute who has been challenged in any court;

   e) Publicizing the dispute by advertising, speaking, or any other method not involving fraud or violence;

   f) Assembling peaceably to promote their interests in the dispute;

   g) Advising or urging others to do any of the acts herein mentioned; and

   h) Agreeing with others to do such acts.

4) **Findings required for injunction.**

   a) No injunction will issue in a labor dispute except after testimony of witnesses and cross-examination in support of and against such injunction, and except after findings that:

      (1) Unlawful acts have been threatened, or have happened—then it will be issued only against the person, persons, association, or organization making the threat or committing the unlawful act, or authorizing its committal;

        (2) Substantial, irreparable injury to complainant's property will follow in the absence of an injunction;

        (3) Greater injury will be inflicted by denial of relief to plaintiff than will be inflicted on defendant by granting relief;

        (4) There is no adequate remedy at law; and

        (5) Public officers charged with protection cannot or will not protect the property threatened.

    b) Under certain conditions, an injunction may issue without a hearing, but for only five days. Bond fixed by the court must be posted by the party seeking an injunction to cover loss to the defendant if the injunction is found (after a hearing) to have been improperly granted, or to cover the costs of defending an action where an injunction is sought and after a hearing is denied.

  5) Negotiation and mediation. Additional provisions of the Act deny injunctive relief to any party who has failed to make "every reasonable effort" to settle the dispute by negotiation or mediation, and impose procedural safeguards for defendants against whom contempt sanctions are sought.

6. Effect of the Antitrust Laws.

  a. Early law—*Danbury Hatters Case*. In an action for damages, the United States Supreme Court held that strikes at a manufacturer's factories and boycotts elsewhere were covered by the Sherman Act as combinations that constricted the free flow of interstate commerce. [Loewe v. Lawlor, *supra*]

  b. Clayton Act. After 1914, with passage of the Clayton Act, the remedy of injunctive relief against violations of the Sherman Act became available to employers, and many controversial labor injunctions were issued during this period.

  c. Limitations on the scope of the Sherman Act. In time, the usefulness of the Sherman Act was curtailed by decisions holding that strikes at manufacturing establishments did not have the necessary relationship to interstate commerce to be included under the Sherman Act. Actually, coverage depended on the strikers' purpose as courts went back to the "objectives" test.

    1) Sit-down strike not a "combination" in restraint of trade--Apex Hosiery Co. v. Leader, 310 U.S. 469 (1940).   *Apex Hosiery Co. v. Leader*

      a) **Facts.** Apex Hosiery Company (P) sued the union (D) for violating the Sherman Antitrust Act. D represented eight of P's 2,500 employees and called a strike and sit-in in order to convince P to sign a closed-shop agreement. D, aided by its members from other factories, seized the factory, changed the locks, and engaged in a sit-in for a month and a half. During this time, the members destroyed some expensive equipment and refused to allow P to remove completed merchandise valued at $800,000 for the purpose of filling orders. P brought this suit charging D with restraining interstate commerce. The trial judge awarded P $711,933. The court of appeals reversed on the grounds that the union's acts insubstantially affected interstate commerce since the company had only 3% of the market. P appeals.

b) **Issue.** Under the Sherman Act, is a union's refusal to allow an employer to ship goods a prohibited restraint on trade?

c) **Held.** No. Judgment affirmed.

(1) The words of the Sherman Act, which apply antitrust law to "every contract, combination . . . or conspiracy, in restraint of trade or commerce," do embrace, to some extent and in some circumstances, unions and their activities.

(2) However, the Sherman Act was not aimed at policing interstate transportation or movement of goods and property; rather, the Act's purpose is to prevent combinations which restrain free competition.

(3) The Act has never been applied to a labor case unless there was some form of restraint on commercial competition and unless the restrictions on shipment operated to restrain commercial competition in some way.

(4) Here, D's tortious acts had as their goal forcing P to accede to D's demands. An effect of D's acts was the prevention of the removal of goods for interstate shipment. Thus, D's actions are not violative of the Sherman Act.

(5) If we were to hold otherwise, practically every local strike would violate the Sherman Act, which result was certainly not intended.

d) **Comment.** The Court also noted that secondary boycotts violate the Sherman Act since such boycotts curtail a free market by suppressing competition of *nonunion*-made goods in the interstate market.

2) **Jurisdictional disputes—The Sherman and Norris-LaGuardia Acts--United States v. Hutcheson, 312 U.S. 219 (1941).**

a) **Facts.** Anheuser-Busch, a brewer, depended on interstate commerce to obtain materials and to sell finished products. When Anheuser contracted to build a new brewery, it gave the job of dismantling and erecting machinery to four of its employees who belonged to the International Association of Machinists. United Brotherhood of Carpenters and Joiners of

America (Ds), which represented Anheuser's carpenters, claimed that its members should have received the job. Anheuser had agreements with the unions to submit all disputes to arbitration, but Ds refused arbitration and called for a strike against Anheuser and a boycott of Anheuser products. Ds were indicted for a conspiracy and combination in restraint of trade in violation of section 1 of the Sherman Antitrust Act. The lower courts sustained demurrers denying that what was charged constituted a violation of the law. The United States appeals.

b) **Issue.** Does a strike and boycott of an employer's product by a union constitute a criminal conspiracy where the union's purpose is to secure work for its members?

c) **Held.** No. Judgment affirmed. The demurrers were properly sustained.

(1) The very meaning of the Clayton Act (section 20) and of the Norris-LaGuardia Act (section 4), which reiterated the Clayton Act, is the statement by Congress of its intent that all acts done within the specified guidelines are protected from attack as violations of the Sherman Act.

(2) Section 20 specifically denies a court the power to independently examine the quality of a union's "objectives" as a basis for testing whether an activity is lawful.

(3) Judicial discretion is very narrowly prescribed—a court may not simply proclaim an activity wise or unwise, right or wrong, selfish or unselfish and then according to its own wisdom decide its "lawfulness," if a union acts in its own self-interest and does not collide with any other guidelines provided (*e.g.*, nonviolence).

(4) Passage of Norris-LaGuardia showed Congress's disapproval of the narrow construction in *Duplex*, *supra*, of the Clayton Act and anticipates an era of greatly broadened union activity.

3) **Applicability of Norris-LaGuardia Act to secondary picketing--Burlington Northern Railroad Co. v. Brotherhood of Maintenance of Way Employees,** 481 U.S. 429 (1987).

a) **Facts.** The Brotherhood of Maintenance of Way Employees (D) had a primary dispute with a small local railroad. It extended a strike against all railroads owned by the parent corporation, and finally extended picketing to all railroads that interchanged traffic with the parent. Burlington Northern Railroad Company (P) petitioned to enjoin the picketing. The district court enjoined the extended picketing, applying the "substantial alignment" test. It ruled that sections 1 and 4 of the Norris Act were limited to employers having an ownership interest or providing essential services or facilities to the primary employer. The court of appeals reversed, finding that the district court had no jurisdiction to issue an injunction. Certiorari was granted because of division among the circuits.

Burlington Northern Railroad Co. v. Brotherhood of Maintenance of Way Employees

b) Issue. Is application of the Norris-LaGuardia Act limited only to secondary employers who are "substantially aligned" with the primary employer?

c) Held. No. Judgment affirmed.

(1) The Norris-LaGuardia Act establishes a basic policy against enjoining labor union activities. Section 20 of the Clayton Act contained provisions broad enough to protect secondary activities, but *Duplex, supra*, restricted that protection to primary situations. The Act was in direct response to *Duplex* and was intended to abolish the distinction between primary and secondary activities.

(2) There is no doubt that the Act extends to railroads.

(3) Section 13(c) contains such a broad definition of a "labor dispute" that the present secondary activities are ones "involving or growing out of" a labor dispute within the meaning of section 4. Narrowing the Act by the "substantial alignment test" would again commit the error that prompted Congress to pass the Act in the first place. Nothing in the Act distinguishes between permissible and impermissible secondary activity. There are neither usable standards nor administrative machinery to make such distinctions in the railway industry.

Thornhill v. Alabama

7. **Constitutional Protections--Thornhill v. Alabama,** 310 U.S. 88 (1940).

   a. **Facts.** Thornhill (D) was convicted of violating an Alabama statute that prohibited a person from picketing the premises or business of another. D had participated in a picket line at the plant of an employer and had informed workers that "we are on strike and do not want anybody to go there to work." D acted without anger or the use of threats or violence. D appeals, alleging that the state statute violated his First Amendment rights to free speech.

   b. **Issue.** Is a statute that forbids picketing to disseminate facts in a labor dispute a violation of the First Amendment?

   c. **Held.** Yes. Judgment reversed.

   1) The statute is unconstitutional on its face and as applied to D since it violates his First Amendment right of free speech. The statute has been applied to single individuals peacefully and passively carrying signs to be read by the public. D has a right to inform the public about the labor dispute. There was no threat of violence or breach of the peace here.

   d. **Comment.** This was a case of "primary" picketing (*i.e.*, picketing by workers of the employer at the site of employment). In this situation, the Supreme Court held that "the dissemination of information concerning the facts of a labor dispute must be regarded as within the area of free discussion guaranteed by the Constitution."

8. **The Wagner Act (NLRA) of 1935.**

   a. **Background—the era of encouragement for labor.**

      1) **Introduction.** Following the 1920s, union growth greatly accelerated as a result of the upheaval in the New Deal era. The collapse of the economy produced greater sympathy for the aims of organized labor, as did the new Keynesian theory of economics. In the legislative area, the federal wage-hour, child labor, and social security laws reflected this new social policy.

      2) **The Railway Labor Act (1926).**

         a) **Background.** As early as 1898, Congress sought to provide railroad unions with the machinery for settlement of disputes. During World War I, the interests of workers in collective bargaining received government protection, and after the war this policy was embodied in the Railway Labor Act, which was the product of agreement between the carriers and the railway unions.

            (1) The Act established adjustment boards to settle differences over the interpretation of union-employer contracts and to settle minor disputes over working conditions.

            (2) A mediation board, appointed by the President, was also established. In the event of a breakdown in negotiations the dispute could be carried to this board. If no settlement could be reached, the board was expected to help secure a commitment by both parties to submit to binding arbitration. If this failed, and the dispute "threatened interstate commerce," the President could appoint another board to investigate the matter for up to 30 days, during which time neither side could do anything. At the expiration of this time, however, the parties were free again to seek their own means to settle the dispute.

            (3) The Act provided that arbitrators on both sides could be chosen without coercion by the other. The right of union organization was reaffirmed.

         b) **1934 amendments to the Act.**

            (1) A provision made it unlawful for carriers to use their funds to assist company unions, or to induce employees to join such unions.

            (2) A method was established to ascertain the legitimacy of labor organizations. When employers challenged the authority of union representatives who claimed the right to

negotiate, the mediation board was directed to conduct an election among the employees to determine which union should prevail.

(3) To assure uniform interpretation of collective bargaining agreements among the various adjustment boards, a National Railroad Adjustment Board ("NRAB") was established with 18 representatives each from labor and management. Ties went to a neutral referee. Decisions of the board were enforceable in federal district courts.

c) **Air carriers.** The Act remains in effect with only minor changes and now covers air carriers as well. Presently, however, air carriers do not participate in the NRAB procedures to resolve their contract grievances. Instead, they utilize "system boards" and engage in more traditional industrial arbitration.

b. **Basic provisions of the Wagner Act.** The 1929 economic crash and the Depression that followed caused great changes in economic philosophy and in concepts about the proper role of government. Attitudes about organized labor became more sympathetic; political power shifted toward labor groups. Along with other legislative programs, the New Deal addressed the problem of labor, first as a part of the short-lived National Industrial Recovery Act ("NIRA") of 1934, which included wage and hour regulation and, more importantly for our purposes, assistance to organization and collective bargaining. In 1935, after the demise of the NIRA, the Wagner Act ("NLRA") was adopted. The Act established firmly the legally protected right of employees to organize and bargain collectively through representatives of their own choosing. The significant provisions of the Act are as follows:

1) **Sections 3 and 4.** The Act created a National Labor Relations Board ("NLRB") with jurisdiction over "unfair labor practices" and questions of union representation and with power to issue and prosecute complaints under section 10.

2) **Section 7.** The Act established that employees have the right to organize, form, join, or assist labor organizations, to bargain collectively through representatives of their own choosing, and to engage in concerted activities for the purpose of collective bargaining or other mutual aid or protection.

3) **Section 8(1) (changed to 8(a)(1) under the Taft-Hartley Act).** The Act made it an unfair labor practice for an employer to interfere with, restrain, or coerce employees in the exercise of rights guaranteed under section 7.

4) **Section 8(2) (changed to 8(a)(2) under the Taft-Hartley Act).** Employers are prohibited from unlawfully sponsoring or assisting a labor organization.

5) **Section 8(3) (changed to 8(a)(3) under the Taft-Hartley Act).** Employers are also prohibited from discriminating against an employee because of union activity.

- 6) **Section 8(5) (changed to 8(a)(5) under the Taft-Hartley Act).** The Act requires employers to bargain collectively with representatives designated by its employees.

- 7) **Section 9(a).** The Act also designates representatives selected for the purposes of collective bargaining by a majority of the employees in a unit appropriate for such purposes as the exclusive representatives of all employees.

- 8) **Sections 9(b) and 9(c).** Finally, the Act provides that the NLRB shall settle disputes with respect to what the appropriate unit for bargaining should be and other questions relating to election procedures.

c. **Constitutionality of the NLRA.** In *NLRB v. Jones & Laughlin Steel Corp.*, 301 U.S. 1 (1937), the Court upheld the NLRA, stating that the term "affecting" commerce means burdening or obstructing commerce or the free flow of commerce, or having led or tending to lead to a labor dispute burdening or obstructing commerce or the free flow of commerce. The Court found that labor strife at a steel plant could conceivably cripple the entire interstate operation of the company, and that the provisions of the Act were properly applied to the plant.

d. **Formation of the CIO.** The formation of the Congress of Industrial Organizations ("CIO") in the same year as the passage of the NLRA was a notable development in the field of labor relations. Certain leaders in the AFL desired to organize the large industries. In the face of great opposition, they left the AFL and organized the CIO, which was structured in a manner similar to the AFL, but with a different philosophy. The CIO embraced workers in entire industries or groups of industries, it included unskilled workers, and it took a greater interest in politics. The NLRA had not contemplated a division of labor into two competing national organizations. The AFL and CIO finally reunited in 1955.

9. **The Taft-Hartley Act (LMRA) of 1947.**

   a. **Background.** Following the passage of the Wagner Act in 1935, union membership increased tremendously. Aided by favorable legislation and government encouragement during World War II, the national unions became increasingly powerful. Immediately after the War a rash of strikes occurred in essential industries and many came to view the unions' new strength as a threat to the public welfare. Strong public pressure for reforms and increased governmental control over the unions culminated in the Labor-Management Relations Act of 1947 (Taft-Hartley Act), which amended the NLRA (the various provisions of the LMRA are discussed in detail below).

   b. **The effects of Taft-Hartley.**

   - 1) **Injunctions.** The Act revived the injunction as an option for dealing with labor disputes in certain specific instances. By adding section

8(b) of the NLRA, the following concerted activities become prohibited and enjoinable:

a) Secondary boycotts (a strike against Company B where B refuses to cease dealing with Company A, the union's real target);

b) Strikes to compel an employer to commit some unfair labor practice such as discharging an employee for belonging to a particular union; and

c) Jurisdictional strikes over work assignments.

2) **Restored governmental neutrality.** The Taft-Hartley Act upheld the fundamental rights to organize and bargain collectively, but provided a change in attitude. Section 7 was amended so as to place the right to refrain from these activities on equal footing with the rights originally guaranteed. Thus, Taft-Hartley changed national policy from one favoring union organization to one of neutrality, anticipating a competitive struggle between the employer and the union.

3) **Collective bargaining.** The Act extended government regulation in the negotiation of collective bargaining agreements to include both the subject matter and the conduct of bargaining. It imposed a duty on unions, as well as employers, to bargain collectively in good faith.

4) **Outlawed the "closed shop."**

5) **Federal court jurisdiction.** The Act provided for federal court jurisdiction in suits for violation of contracts against both labor unions and employers (section 301).

10. **The Landrum-Griffin Act (LMRDA) of 1959.**

   a. **Background.** During the 1950s, public sentiment for union reform was rekindled as a result of Senate investigations that disclosed widespread corruption and unethical behavior on the part of union leaders. The Labor-Management Reporting and Disclosure Act ("LMRDA"), more commonly known as the Landrum-Griffin Act, further amended the NLRA.

   b. **Basic provisions of the Act.**

   1) The LMRDA closed gaps in the ban on secondary boycotts, restricted the right of unions to picket in the process of organizational drives, and gave workers who were replaced in the course of a strike the right to vote in union elections (in order to prevent employers from provoking a strike in order to hire nonunion workers and oust the incumbent labor organization).

   2) Most importantly, internal union affairs were brought under regulation for the first time. Elections were required for local and national officers. Union members could nominate and comment on the qualifications of candidates.

B. **THE PRESENT SCOPE AND COVERAGE OF NATIONAL LABOR LEGISLATION**

1. **The Railway Labor Act.**

    a. **Jurisdiction.** Jurisdictional disputes arise that require the determination of which rail or air carriers and which employees are covered by the Act.

        1) **Air carriers.** With respect to air carriers, the National Mediation Board ("NMB") rules on questions of inclusion.

        2) **Rail carriers.** The Interstate Commerce Commission ("ICC") rules on this question for rail carriers.

        3) **Employee groups.** The NMB has assumed authority to rule on the inclusion of specific employee groups within the guidelines established by the ICC.

    b. **Coverage of employees.**

        1) **Factors considered.** The NMB distinctions between employees who are covered and those who are not covered have dealt with the following kinds of questions:

            a) Whether the employee is based outside United States territory.

            b) Whether the individual is an "official" or an "employee."

            c) Whether the employee's function is so remote from the company's carrier activity as to exclude the employee from coverage.

        2) **Employees not directly involved in transportation.** It should be noted that certain employees not directly involved in transportation have been included (*e.g.*, switchboard operators, bridge superintendents, missile workers).

    c. **Handling disputes.**

        1) **Section 6.** Notice must be given of desired changes in an existing agreement. The Act provides for compulsory interparty bargaining and the use of a government mediator to make proposals and attempts to help the parties reach agreement.

        2) **Section 10.** If a dispute is not settled, the President is empowered to appoint a board to investigate the facts and make recommendations where a threatened strike would significantly disrupt interstate commerce.

2. **The National Labor Relations Act (NLRA).**

a. **Jurisdiction.**

1) **Introduction.** The primary jurisdictional question for the NLRA is whether a labor dispute in the business involved would tend to affect or burden interstate commerce. Determination of those cases requires an examination of those sections of the Act that define the following key terms: labor dispute (section 2(9)); commerce (section 2(6)); and affecting commerce (section 2(7)).

2) **Labor dispute.** A labor dispute includes any controversy concerning terms or conditions of employment, or concerning the association or representation of persons in negotiating, fixing, maintaining, changing, or seeking to arrange terms or conditions of employment, regardless of whether the disputants stand in the proximate relation of employer and employee.

   a) The principal rule of interpretation found in the cases construing the defining provisions is one of broad inclusiveness.

3) **Commerce.** Commerce consists of trade, traffic, commerce, transportation, or communication among the several states, or between the District of Columbia or any territory of the United States and any state or other territory, or between any foreign country and any state, territory, or the District of Columbia, or within the District of Columbia or any territory, or between points in the same state but passing through another state, the District of Columbia, or any foreign country.

4) **Affecting commerce.** Finally, the term "affecting commerce" means "in commerce" or "burdening or obstructing commerce" or "the free flow of commerce," or having led or tending to lead to a labor dispute burdening or obstructing commerce or the free flow of commerce.

   a) Disputes "affecting" interstate commerce are much broader in scope than those disputes "in" interstate commerce.

   b) Thus, where an employer purchases her raw materials out of state and sells exclusively within the state, or conversely, buys her raw materials in state and sells out of state, she is covered on the theory that a labor dispute might have the effect of "obstructing the free flow" of commerce.

   c) In one case, an employer, whose interstate shipments constituted less than 1% of her total business output, urged that her case could not be tried by virtue of the principle of "de minimis non curat lex," but the Board nevertheless assumed jurisdiction.

5) **NLRB jurisdictional discretion.** While the scope of the Act covers small, local business when interstate commerce is affected, the NLRB may decline jurisdiction in instances where it finds the effect on interstate activities to be minute. In these situations, the NLRB refers the case to interested state and local agencies.

   a) **Basis for policy.** This policy of discretion is sanctioned in the Labor-Management Reporting and Disclosure Act of 1959, which specifies that the NLRB may broaden the scope of its coverage beyond those cases covered as of August 1, 1959, but may not decline to take any case it would have taken at that date.

- b) **Jurisdictional guidelines.** As a practical matter, the NLRB will follow "jurisdictional guidelines" set out for each industry or type of business. For example:

    (1) *Nonretail firms*—an annual direct or indirect outflow or inflow of goods in excess of $50,000.

    (2) *Retail concerns*—a gross annual volume of $500,000.

    (3) *Instrumentalities, links, and channels of interstate commerce*—$50,000 attributable to interstate commerce sources.

    (4) *Public utilities*—$250,000 in gross revenues (or meet the nonretail standard).

    (5) *Transit systems*—$250,000 in gross revenues (taxicabs are subject to the retail standard).

    (6) *Newspapers and communications*—$200,000 and $100,000 gross, respectively.

    (7) *National defense activities*—all forms having a substantial impact on national defense.

    (8) *Associations*—regarded as single entities.

    (9) *Private colleges and universities*—$1 million in gross revenues for operating expenses.

    (10) *Symphony orchestras*—$1 million in gross revenues.

    (11) *Hospitals*—$250,000 in gross annual revenues.

    (12) *Law firms and programs*—$250,000 in gross annual revenues.

b. **Coverage of employers and employees.**

  1) **Employers covered.** In addition to the above criteria, the determination of which employers are covered requires reference to section 2(2) of the Act.

    a) **Inclusions.** Included are all "persons" who act as employers or, directly or indirectly, as agents of employers.

    b) **Exceptions.** However, certain entities are specifically excluded from NLRA coverage—federal and state offices, Federal Reserve Banks, those subject to the RLA, and labor unions (when not acting as employers). Parochial schools are also not covered. Federal employees are covered by the Civil Service Reform Act of 1979.

2) **Employees covered.**

   a) **Inclusions.** The term "employee" is broadly construed and may be understood to include virtually any person within the meaning of that term as it is commonly used.

   b) **Exceptions.**

   (1) **Employees specifically excluded under section 2(3).** Agricultural workers, domestics, independent contractors, supervisors, and employees covered by the RLA are specifically excluded from NLRA coverage. Managerial employees are not covered. Employees transporting agricultural products or engaged in slaughtering, packing, processing, or refining agricultural products are subject to the NLRA.

   (2) **Independent contractors.** Many of the disputes as to whether an employee is covered involve situations where an employer has attempted to make it appear that the person is an "independent contractor." Normally the courts use the test of "management control over the performance of the work done." If control is present, the person is an employee.

C. **NATIONAL LABOR RELATIONS BOARD—ORGANIZATION AND PROCEDURE**

The NLRA is administered by the NLRB, the NLRB General Counsel, and numerous field agents of the NLRB and General Counsel. The NLRB is split into two separate and independent divisions. The Board itself is the adjudicatory body. The other division is the General Counsel's office, which handles election cases and litigates unfair labor practice cases.

1. **Organization of the Board.** The NLRB is composed of five members, each of whom is appointed by the President (with Senate approval) for a term of five years. Only the President may remove a Board member from office. Removal is permitted only for "malfeasance in office or neglect of duty" and must be preceded by a formal hearing.

   a. **Panel.** The Board may sit as a full panel of five or (in the interest of expediting cases) it may delegate its powers to a panel of three—any two members of which will constitute a majority for decision-making purposes.

   b. **Delegation of powers.** The Landrum-Griffin Act of 1959 authorized the Board to delegate its powers to the regional directors for cases involving union representation and deauthorization elections by the Board. In such cases, there may be limited review of the regional director's decisions.

   c. **The General Counsel.** Unfair labor practice charges may be filed at a regional office by any person against an employer or a union or a third party. The regional director has the discretion to issue a complaint. Refusals to issue are rarely reviewed by the General Counsel.

2. **Primary Functions of the Board.** The two major functions of the NLRB are (i) to determine employee representatives within industries under the jurisdiction of the NLRA, and (ii) to decide whether a particular challenged activity constitutes an unfair labor practice.

   a. **Representation cases.** In representation cases the Board has complete and final authority, although much of it is delegated to field personnel.

      1) Election petitions are filed in regional offices. Most are for permission to conduct an election to certify a collective bargaining agent. A smaller fraction are decertification elections. The authority to enter union security agreements may also be rescinded by an election. Petitions for a certification election may be filed by a union seeking to represent a unit or by an employer who has received a demand for recognition.

      2) The regional staff will make an investigation to determine jurisdictional coverage, appropriateness of the unit, voter eligibility, and whether there is a sufficient showing of interest (30% of the proposed unit).

      3) Consent election agreements are encouraged. These allow the Regional Director to conduct an election and resolve any disputes that may arise in connection with it. Contested matters will be the subject of a hearing before a regional hearing officer.

      4) In the proper case an election order will be made to conduct the election in approximately 30 days. Elections are conducted by secret ballot at the employer's premises during working hours under the supervision of a representative from the regional office. A labor organization will be certified as the exclusive bargaining representative if it receives a majority of the valid votes cast.

      5) Decisions of the regional director on any point are subject to limited review by the Board.

      6) Representational issues are not directly subject to judicial review. But they can be reviewed in connection with an unfair labor practice case arising out of the situation.

   b. **Unfair labor practice cases.** In unfair labor practice cases, NLRB authority is exercised somewhat more formally.

      1) After a complaint has been filed, a preliminary investigation will be made to determine whether to proceed to a hearing after the General Counsel (Regional Director) has issued a complaint. This decision will turn on whether continued prosecution would "effectuate the policies of the Act." At this point, the proceedings are conducted with all possible informality and with a view toward reaching a settlement.

2) A trial examiner then holds a hearing—at which the complaining party (generally the employer or union) may intervene—and issues an intermediate report with recommended findings and remedial measures.

3) If neither party files exceptions to the intermediate report within 20 days, the report ordinarily receives the same weight as a decision by the Board itself.

4) Where exceptions are filed, the Board assumes complete control over the case. After reviewing the record and the report, the Board may substitute its own findings and remedial order for those of the examiner—or it may simply adopt those of the trial examiner.

5) If either party takes exception to the Board's findings, that party may take the case to the appropriate federal court of appeals.

6) The court of appeals may set aside the Board's findings only if the court concludes that the Board's decision is not supported by "substantial evidence on the record considered as a whole," or if the Board has made errors of law. Appellate orders are enforced by contempt actions brought exclusively by the Board.

7) Note that the ordinary rules of evidence apply at every stage in the proceedings outlined above.

II. ESTABLISHMENT OF THE COLLECTIVE BARGAINING RELATIONSHIP

A. PROTECTING THE RIGHT TO SELF-ORGANIZATION

1. **Protection Against Employer Interference, Restraint, and Coercion.** The right of employees to band together to form unions, to bargain collectively, and to engage in other concerted activities is expressed in the NLRA section 7.

   The employees' organizational rights under section 7 are protected by sections 8(a)(1)-(5) and section 8(e) of the Act. Section 8(a)(1) makes it an unfair labor practice for an employer "to interfere with, restrain, or coerce employees in the exercise of the rights guaranteed in section 7."

   Note that the NLRA does not prohibit all employer activities that may tend to obstruct organizing efforts by employees. The Act recognizes that employers have certain rights, including freedom of speech on matters affecting the operation of their business. Accordingly, section 8(c) provides that the mere expression of views, argument, or opinion "shall not constitute an unfair labor practice . . . if such expression contains no threat of reprisal or force, or promise of benefit."

   a. **Restricting activities on company-owned property—solicitation and distribution rules.** The right to organize comes into conflict with an employer's property rights when organizing activity is conducted on company property. However, the United States Supreme Court has held that an employer must tolerate some inconvenience in this respect to safeguard his employees' section 7 rights. The courts and the Board permit certain nondiscriminatory restrictions by an employer upon solicitation and distribution of union organizing materials during working hours on company premises.

      1) **Solicitation by employees.** An employer may limit pro-union solicitation to an employee's free time (*i.e.*, before or after work, at breaks, or at mealtimes), and may impose these limitations even after the start of a union campaign.

         a) **Defined.** "Solicitation" refers generally to verbal communication, but also includes the handing out of union authorization cards.

         b) **Restrictive rules.** More stringent rules regarding where an employee may solicit during his free time may be imposed by certain employers, such as retail stores and hospitals, where there is considerable contact with the public or patients.

         c) **Off-duty employees.** A rule barring off-duty employees from union solicitation on company premises may be upheld, as long as the rule is nondiscriminatory (*i.e.*, designed to prevent access by such employees for any reason). [GTE Lenkurt, Inc., 204 N.L.R.B. 921 (1973)]

(1) Limitations. However, the NLRB has subsequently construed *GTE, supra,* narrowly to prevent undue interference with an employee's statutory right to communicate with those who work on different shifts. Thus, for example, an employer's rule denying off-duty employees entry to parking lots, gates, and other outside nonworking areas has been held invalid. [*See* Diamond Shamrock Co. v. NLRB, 443 F.2d 52 (3d Cir. 1971); Automotive Technologies, 313 N.L.R.B. 462 (1993)]

Republic Aviation Corp. v. NLRB

d) Employee solicitation--Republic Aviation Corp. v. NLRB, 324 U.S. 793 (1945).

(1) Facts. Republic Aviation Corporation (P) had a rule prohibiting union solicitation on company grounds. Several employees wore badges, including union steward badges, advertising the union. When asked to remove them, they refused and were discharged. One employee persisted in passing out application forms on his own time during lunch periods and was discharged for violation of the no-solicitation rule. P felt that wearing the union steward badges implied authority of the unions to represent employees. The NLRB (D) ruled that since there was no competing union, the steward badges did not imply union recognition. D held that P's broad no-solicitation rule presumptively violated section 8(1) of the NLRA, and that the discharge of the employees violated sections 8(1) and (3). The circuit court granted enforcement, and the United States Supreme Court granted certiorari.

(2) Issue. May an employer enforce a general nondiscriminatory no-solicitation rule to prevent solicitation of union support and membership during nonworking time and to prevent the wearing of union badges?

(3) Held. No. Judgment affirmed.

(a) It was not improper for the Board to adopt a general rule against overly broad restrictions on employee union solicitations. It could properly presume that such restrictions are "an unreasonable impediment to self-organization" without requiring proof of actual interference with organizational activities in each case.

(b) In balancing the employer's right to discipline and the employees' rights of organization, the Board, as an administrative agency, may make conclusions from evidential facts in an adversarial proceeding drawing upon its "appreciation of the complexities of the subject" entrusted to its administration.

(c) The Board adequately explained the theory upon which it based its conclusions and expressed the proof necessary to overcome the presumption applicable to rules restricting solicitation.

(d) The Board properly drew the line between permissible activity during nonworking time. No evidence was shown that the employer was somehow understood to be recognizing the union because of the steward's badges.

(e) The rule is justified even though there may be alternate means of communication.

(4) Comments.

(a) In *Beth Israel Hospital v. NLRB*, 437 U.S. 483 (1978), the hospital prohibited solicitation or distribution in "patient care and all other work areas" and "areas open to the public," such as "lobbies, cafeteria . . . corridors, elevators . . . etc." It disciplined employees for distributing the union newsletter in the cafeteria. The Board found that sections 8(2)(1) and (3) were violated, and ordered that the restriction not include the cafeteria and coffee shop. The United States Supreme Court, in a plurality opinion, affirmed the Board's action in the absence of proof that the solicitation distribution activities would disrupt patient care. It sustained the Board's judgment about the situation in the face of the hospital's claim that it was a medical judgment, and noted that there was no other adequate location for effective employee communication. Two concurring opinions considered the cafeteria as equivalent to an all-employee cafeteria.

(b) In *NLRB v. Magnavox Co.*, 415 U.S. 322 (1974), the company had for years prohibited employees from distributing literature at its plants and parking lots, even in nonworking areas during nonworking hours. The union, which represented the company's employees, had agreed to this ban. However, the union was allowed to post notices on company bulletin boards. The company rejected a union proposal to change the rule and the NLRB found a section 8(a)(1) violation. The court of appeals denied enforcement of the Board's order, stating that the union had waived the ban on on-premises distribution. The United States Supreme Court held that, in the absence of proof of exceptional circumstances, the union may not waive its members' rights to distribute literature during nonworking hours. The Court stated, "It is difficult to assume that an incumbent union has no self-interest of its own to serve by perpetuating itself as the bargaining representative." The Court indicated that the place of work is uniquely appropriate for dissemination of views concerning bargaining representation, and that dissemination of the various labor related viewpoints is something that courts will foster. The Court held that the use of a bulletin board is not an adequate substitute. In a separate opinion, Justice Stewart would narrow the rule to allow a waiver of a right by the union to restrict its own supporters to the bulletin boards.

2) **Solicitation or distribution by nonemployees.** An employer may prohibit solicitation or distribution on its premises by nonemployee organizers unless the employees do not have sufficient alternative means of obtaining information concerning organization advantages.

Lechmere, Inc. v. NLRB

a) **Distribution on employer premises by nonemployees--Lechmere, Inc. v. NLRB,** 502 U.S. 527 (1992).

(1) **Facts.** The union (P) was attempting to organize the employees of Lechmere's (D's) retail store, which was located in D's shopping plaza. Initially, P ran a full-page advertisement without much response. Then, it handbilled the automobiles parked in D's employee parking lot. D's manager immediately informed the organizers that D prohibited solicitation or handbilling of any kind on its property and asked them to leave. They did so. The organizers then focused activity for about seven months on a grassy public strip between the plaza and a four-lane public highway. They tried to distribute handbills to employee cars as they arrived to and departed from work. They recorded license numbers and obtained names and addresses of about 20% of D's workforce in the store. Phone calls, mailings, and visits were made, garnering only one authorization card. P filed unfair labor practices charges claiming that D had wrongfully excluded the organizers from its property. The NLRB, applying the *Jean Country,* 291 N.L.R.B. No. 4 (1988), rule, found a violation and ordered access and posting of notice that it would not prohibit distribution on the parking lot. The court of appeals enforced the Board's order, and the Supreme Court granted certiorari.

(2) **Issue.** Is the NLRB authorized to determine nonemployee access to an employer's property by balancing the degree of impairment to the employee's section 7 rights against the degree of impairment to the employer's private property rights and giving availability of alternate access special significance in the balancing?

(3) **Held.** No. Enforcement denied.

(a) The rule of *Jean Country*, which applies to all access cases, provides for a balancing of the degree of impairment of private property rights if access is allowed and the availability of reasonably effective alternative means of communication. This last is particularly significant in the balance. This approach is contrary to our rule in *NLRB v. Babcock & Wilcox Co.*, 351 U.S. 105 (1956), which established different rules for employee access cases and nonemployee access cases. This distinction has remained unchanged when considering constitutional and state preemption cases.

(b) While no restrictions may be placed upon the right of employees to discuss self-organization among themselves unless the employer can show restriction is necessary to maintain production or discipline, the NLRA confers rights only upon employees.

(c) *Babcock* held that no obligation exists to require access by nonemployee organizers unless the location of living quarters and the plant create a unique obstruction which places the employees beyond the reach of reasonable union efforts to communicate with them.

(d) The *Jean Country* rule is too broad and the facts of this case do not support the Board's conclusion that "no reasonable effective" alternative means were available to the union. Although the employees lived in a large metropolitan area, the union was able to contact a substantial percentage of the employees, and the union was able to use signs and picketing on the grassy access strip. Access—not success—is the crucial issue.

- (4) **Dissent** (White, Blackmun, JJ.).

    - (a) The majority states that the Board misapplied *Babcock*. The fact that *Babcock* held that inaccessibility to a logging camp would justify entry does not indicate that there would be no other circumstances which would warrant entry. Of course, the union must first show that "reasonable efforts" do not permit proper communication with employees.

    - (b) There is a difference between a secluded private parking lot and the one here which is open to the public without substantial limit. The mere notice of a campaign is not sufficient communication to sustain section 7 rights. Later cases have consistently declined to define *Babcock* as a general principal subject to narrow exceptions.

    - (c) Finally, and most fundamentally, *Babcock* is at odds with modern concepts of judicial deference. The Board's conclusion about reasonable alternatives was supported by evidence in the record. *Babcock* rests on questionable legal foundations, while *Jean Country* is both rational and consistent with the statute.

3) **The "captive audience" doctrine.** An employer on occasion will assemble employees during working hours and deliver noncoercive anti-union speeches despite the fact that it is otherwise enforcing a valid no-solicitation rule. In 1951, the Board decided in such circumstances that it was improper for the employer to deny the representative equal time. Only a short time later, the Board reversed this position in *Livingston Shirt Co.*, 107 N.L.R.B. 400 (1953). It concluded that section 8(c) did not allow burdening the employer's exercise of speech with an equal time requirement. Where a proper "broad" no-solicitation rule is in effect (such as in a department store), equal time would be allowed. The United States Supreme Court sustained this approach in *NLRB v. United Steelworkers (Nutone & Avondale)*, 357 U.S. 357 (1958), even where the employer's speech was coercive. The Court indicated that if the no-solicitation rule "truly diminished the ability of the labor organizations involved to carry their message to the employees" because of lack of reasonable alternatives, access would be required. In more recent years, the Board has included access in cases involving aggravated employer unfair labor practices (*e.g.*, election-eve speeches). The "*Peerless Plywood*" rule (107 N.L.R.B. 427 (1953)) prohibits captive audience speeches on company time within 24 hours of an election, whether made by an employer or a union. The Board's remedy may allow union access for solicitation or to address a "captive" audience.

4) **Duty to provide list of employee names and addresses.** When a union petitions for an election, the Board requires the employer to give the union a list of employee names and addresses. Failure to provide the list has not been held an unfair labor practice but may provide the basis for setting an election aside.

Excelsior Underwear Inc.

a) **Employee lists--Excelsior Underwear Inc.,** 156 N.L.R.B. 1236 (1966).

(1) **Facts.** The union lost a secret ballot to determine whether it would represent Excelsior Underwear Inc.'s (D's) employees by a vote of 206 to 35 (with five votes challenged). It challenged the election on the ground that D refused to give it a list of the names and addresses of D's employees. Thus, the union could not rebut a letter D mailed to its employees. (A case involving the same issue was consolidated with this case.) The NLRB agreed to hear oral arguments (which is rarely done).

(2) **Issue.** Must an employer accede to a union's request for the names and addresses of employees?

(3) **Held.** Yes.

   (a) For elections to be fair, not only must there be no interference, restraint, or coercion, but there must also be freedom of choice. This requires informed voters.

   (b) An employer has the opportunity to use the addresses of employees to inform all of them of its views. On the other hand, a union without those addresses is hindered in disseminating its views. This then inhibits the flow of information to the voting employees.

   (c) Therefore, within seven days after the Regional Director has approved a consent-election agreement or the Regional Director has directed an election, the employer must file with the Regional Director an election eligibility list containing the names and addresses of all the eligible voters. Heretofore, such lists have been required only shortly before the election.

   (d) The public interest in the disclosure of employee names and addresses greatly outweighs any legitimate secrecy interests the employer may have. Furthermore, this rule will reduce the number of challenges of voter eligibility that unions make since, in the past, many of these challenges have been based on the fact that the union had little information on "unknown" employees' identities. There is no need to consider the availability of alternate channels of communications (as in *Babcock-Wilcox, supra*).

(4) **Comments.**

   (a) In *NLRB v. Wyman-Gordon*, 394 U.S. 759 (1969), the Court considered the legality of the Board practice of announcing future rules of conduct in the context of decided cases. Justice Fortas, speaking for four justices, determined that the practice, as followed in *Excelsior Underwear*, was "rule-making and subject to the notice and hearing requirements of the Administrative Procedure Act ["APA"]." But the plurality opinion analyzed the Board's application of the *Excelsior* "rule" in the case and concluded that substantively the Board acted properly in requiring an election list to promote an informed electorate and balanced access, and that it could subpoena such evidence in a representation proceeding. Justice Black (and two others) agreed that the rule was invalidly promulgated under the

APA, but concluded that the order was a proper exercise of an adjudicative power in the disposition of the case. In dissenting opinions, Justice Douglas emphasized the need and value of the APA rulemaking procedures and Justice Harlan was concerned that the disposition of the case "completely trivialized" the APA requirements.

    (b)   In *NLRB v. Bell Aerospace Co.*, 416 U.S. 267 (1974), the Court reconsidered the Board's discretion to establish rules of conduct by adjudication. In this case, the Board had reversed prior decisions and found that buyers were "employees" under the Act. Finding that no penalties had been imposed on the employer due to its past activities and that there were no adverse consequences caused by possible reliance on the old rule, the Court concluded that "surely the Board has discretion to decide that the adjudicative procedure in this case may also produce the relevant information necessary to mature and fair consideration of the issues."

5) **Anti-union speech.** Although in the early years of the Wagner Act the NLRB felt that an employer should remain "neutral" with respect to unionism, that attitude had to be balanced against the employer's constitutional right of free speech. To clarify this area, section 8(c) of the Taft-Hartley Act was adopted, providing that the expression of views, etc., would not be evidence of an unfair labor practice unless it contained "threat of reprisal or force or promise of benefit." The legislative history of this provision indicates that its intent was to allow free speech by the employer, while protecting against economic reprisal or coercion.

    a)   **"Laboratory conditions" test for reelection orders.** In *General Shoe Corp.*, 77 N.L.R.B. 124 (1948), the Board, noting that the section 8(c) rule of evidence was applicable to unfair labor proceedings, announced that it did not limit its powers in election cases. It said that when conduct (including speech) "creates an atmosphere which renders improbable free choice," it may set aside an election and order a new one. The NLRB recognized that it was to "provide a laboratory in which an experiment may be conducted, under conditions as nearly as ideal as possible, to determine the uninhibited desires of the employees." Later, the Board allowed wider latitude for employer speeches by tolerating baleful expressions of "legal position," "opinion," or "prediction." More recently, the Board has moved again back toward the *General Shoe* "ideal" by scrutinizing election propaganda more closely. In *Dal-Tex Optical Co.*, 137 N.L.R.B. 1782 (1962), shortly before a rerun election (the previous one had been set aside for threats and promises), the employer made speeches to employees that emphasized risks (*e.g.,* strikes, replacements, etc.) that could occur if the union won, and the possible benefits that could be lost when it bargains on a "cold-blooded business basis." The Board found these speeches to be coercive and evidence of an unfair labor practice and clearly provided the basis for setting aside the election that was lost by the union. The NLRB announced that in the future it would look to the economic realities of the relationship and would set aside elections where the employer conduct had resulted in "substantial interference" with the election without regard to the form of the statement.

Labor Law - 29

b) **Board considerations.** The Board follows a case-by-case method of approaching such questions, where the same words in one context may not bring the same decision if uttered in another. The level of employment in the area, employer past dealings, etc., will be considered.

6) **Noncoercive speech cannot be used as evidence of other employer violations.** Statements that are protected under the free speech provisions of section 8(c) cannot be used as evidence of some other unfair labor practice by the employer (such as bad motives or anti-union bias). [Pittsburgh S.S. Co. v. NLRB, 180 F.2d 731 (6th Cir. 1950)]

7) **Coercive statements not protected.** There is no "free speech" protection for threats of reprisal or force against employees exercising their rights to self-organization, or promises of benefits to those who do not exercise those rights. Such statements, whether oral or written, are deemed "coercive" and are unfair labor practices per se. [Textile Workers Union v. Darlington Manufacturing Co., *infra*]

   a) **Employer's assertion of legal rights.** Coercion may be found whether the threats or promises are express or merely implied. But where the employer merely asserts how it legally intends to deal with the union, this has been held not to constitute coercion. [*See* NLRB v. Herman Wilson Lumber Co., 355 F.2d 426 (8th Cir. 1966)—"I intend to deal hard with the union" and "you may be replaced if you strike" held *not* impliedly coercive]

   b) **Employer's prediction of adverse consequences.** An employer's statements to his employees predicting adverse economic consequences from unionization may be held coercive if such predictions are based on factors over which the employer had control or will result of his own volition and for his own reasons. On the other hand, if his predictions of adverse consequences are reasonably based on objective factors over which the employer has no control, the statements will be protected as employer free speech. [NLRB v. Golub Corp., 388 F.2d 921 (2d Cir. (1967)]

   NLRB v. Gissel Packing Co.

   c) **Statements held coercive--NLRB v. Gissel Packing Co.,** 395 U.S. 575 (1969).

      (1) **Facts.** When the president of Gissel Packing Company (D) learned of a union organization campaign, he spoke with employees to dissuade them from joining the union. He emphasized that the company was on "thin ice" financially, and that a strike "could lead to closing the plant." He reminded them of a strike in 1952 that closed the plant for three months, and called their attention to other plants that had closed in the area. Immediately prior to the scheduled election, the president distributed pamphlets calling the union a strike-happy outfit, and listing local businesses that had closed because of union activity. The contentions were reiterated the day before the election, which the union lost 7-6. The NLRB found that the president's statements were threatening rather than mere predictions of "demonstrable economic consequences." The court of appeals sustained the Board and the case was taken to the Supreme Court.

30 - Labor Law

(2) Issue. May an employer disseminate his beliefs with respect to unionization independent of their economic or factual substantiation?

(3) Held. No. Finding sustained.

(a) The Board's order was properly enforced. An employer's right to free speech is limited to communications that do not contain threats of economic reprisal or promise of benefits.

(b) Employers may express their views about a particular union and make noncoercive economic predictions, but such predictions and views must be based on fact.

(c) Any balancing of employer and employee rights must take into account the economic dependency of the employees. An employer's statements of belief about the effects of unionization, however sincere, will be seen as threatening unless they are simply economic predictions based on demonstrable fact, about consequences beyond the employer's control.

d) **Nonfactual statements.** Under the standard in *Gissel*, the employer's statements charging that the union was dominated by "strike-happy hoodlums" who would make impossible demands on the company and force it out of business were held not based on objective facts and hence coercive.

e) **Predictions based on facts.** A prediction that the union would make certain demands on the employer that he would be forced to grant, at the cost of impairing existing employee benefits, has been held protected speech where shown to be based on previous dealings with other unions in the same plant and thus based on objective facts. [NLRB v. Lenkurt Electric, 438 F.2d 1102 (1971)]

f) **Predictions not based on facts.** In *Gissel, supra*, the Court stated that an employer's prediction, even though sincere, that unionization "will or may" result in closing the plant (*i.e.*, as a result of union demands) would by itself be coercive, unless the likelihood of closing was capable of objective proof.

g) **Employer can cease business.** At the time, the Court recognized that an employer has the absolute right to go out of business for any reason, including anti-union hostility. [Textile Workers Union v. Darlington Manufacturing Co., *infra*]

h) **Employer can cite history.** Moreover, the NLRB has held that recitation of a history of closing stores for "economic reasons" after successful union organizing was protected free speech. [J.J. Newberry Co., 1973 N.L.R.B. Decisions (CCH) ¶25,147]

8) **Misrepresentations.** Unlike political elections, union elections require "laboratory conditions" and both the employer and the union are constrained from communicating or doing anything that will have the effect of destroying that environment, including making factual misrepresentations.

a) **Board screening of electioneering.** In 1962, the Board announced that it would more closely screen factual misrepresentations made during a representation election campaign that would disrupt the "laboratory conditions." In *Hollywood Ceramics Co.*, 140 N.L.R.B. 221 (1962), the Board set aside an election in which the victorious union circulated shortly before the election a handbill that compared wage rates at the company with other companies in a misleading way by seriously understating the company's rates. It announced that it would overturn the results of an election in which there had been a "substantial departure from the truth" that "may reasonably be expected to have a significant impact on the election."

Despite criticism of that rule from some courts of appeals and some members of the Board, it continued to apply it until 1977, when in *Shopping Kart Food Market, Inc.*, 228 N.L.R.B. 1311 (1977), the Board, with changed membership, not only criticized the effects of the *Hollywood Ceramics* rule, but questioned the validity of its underlying assumptions. It was strongly influenced by the conclusions and recommendations of an empirical study of election influences. [*See* Getman, Goldberg, & Herman, Union Representation Elections: Law and Reality (1976)]

The turnaround was short lived. The Board came back to *Hollywood Ceramics* in 1978 in *General Knit of California, Inc.*, 239 N.L.R.B. 619 (1978), but subsequently reversed itself again in *Midland*, below.

Midland National Life Insurance Co. v. Local 304A, United Food & Commercial Workers

b) **Latest position--Midland National Life Insurance Co. v. Local 304A, United Food & Commercial Workers,** 263 N.L.R.B. 127 (1982).

(1) **Facts.** In a rerun election, the vote ended in a tie. On the day before the election, too late for effective response by the union, Midland National Life Insurance Company (D) distributed misleading campaign literature implying that the union caused one company to go out of business and that it had been ineffective in bargaining with other companies. It also disseminated portions of an LMRDA financial report that implied that the union had made no disbursements on behalf of its members. The union filed objections to the election, and the Hearing Officer found that material misrepresentations had been made and recommended that the election be set aside.

(2) **Issue.** Should material misrepresentations made in an organizational election campaign be the basis for overturning the election if the other party has no opportunity to reply?

(3) **Held.** No. The Hearing Officer's recommendations are rejected and different standards for the conduct of election campaigns are adopted.

(a) The *Hollywood Ceramics* standards, *supra,* applied by the Hearing Officer resisted every effort at clear formulation. We now revert back to the *Shopping Kart* standards, *supra,* which draw a clear line between the substance of a representation and the deceptive manner in which it is made.

32 - Labor Law

(b) As long as the material is what it purports to be—that is, propaganda of one of the contestants—the Board will leave it to the voters to evaluate its content.

(c) If forgery or deception prevents the communication from being recognized as partisan propaganda, the Board will intervene.

(d) The Board will continue to protect against other campaign misconduct, such as threats and promises, that interferes with employee free choice.

(4) **Dissent** (Fanning, Jenkins, Members). The majority is turning its back on the accumulated experience and wisdom of several generations of Board members. The majority is sacrificing the integrity of the campaign process for doubtful reduction of election campaign litigation. The misrepresentations in this campaign were serious, extreme, and material. They could have made a difference in the outcome of this vote.

(5) **Comments.**

(a) Note that the standards employed in testing the propriety of statements in the context of a union election are judged by different standards than those in a political contest, where only libel and slander are proscribed.

(b) The Board's new approach was approved in *NLRB v. Best Products*, 765 F.2d 903 (9th Cir. 1985).

9) **Inflammatory appeals.** In *Sewell Manufacturing Co.*, 138 N.L.R.B. 66 (1962), the union lost an election at two plants in two small Georgia towns by a vote of 985 to 331. For four months preceding the election, the company had circulated materials linking the union with blacks, racial integration, Communism, and anti-Christianity. During the campaign, it mailed to its employees a picture of an unidentified black man dancing with an unidentified white woman and an article recounting another representation election held four years previously in another state that referred to "race mixing." The Board overturned the election, saying "the law permits wide latitude in the way of propaganda—truth and untruth, promises, threats, appeals to prejudice." It indicated that "a deliberate appeal to such prejudice" would interfere with an employee's "reasoned, untrammeled choice."

a) **Interrogation--NLRB v. Lorben Corp.**, 345 F.2d 346 (2d Cir. 1965).

NLRB v. Lorben Corp.

(1) **Facts.** Suit by NLRB to enforce an order. The IBEW (Electrical Workers) began organizing Lorben's (D's) plants. Four of the 25 or 26 employees joined the union. One of the four lost his job. Since the union believed this was due to that employee's stance on unionization, it struck. D's president passed around a paper asking the question, "Do you wish (the IBEW) to represent you?" Employees

could sign either yes or no. All signed in the "no" column. The Board found that D's president had no legitimate purpose for the interrogation, and D appeals.

(2) Issue. May an employer interrogate employees as to whether they want a union to represent them if he does so without coercion?

(3) Held. Yes. Order reversed.

(a) Employer interrogation of employees as to their desire to be represented by a union is not coercive on its face.

(b) Thus, the courts have taken the position that such interrogation is not unlawful unless the circumstances taken as a whole indicate that the interrogation interferes with, restrains, and coerces employees.

(c) Here, there was no showing of any hostility or coercion. D's president had been asked if he wanted to talk to the union and he merely polled his employees. The Board's order is founded on too narrow a basis.

(4) Dissent (Friendly, J.). The Board's power to rule that particular types of conduct tend to restrain or interfere with protected rights has been sustained in the past and should also be sustained here.

(5) Comment. An important factor in such cases is the "coercive atmosphere" within which such interrogation takes place. Some have argued, like the dissent in the instant case, that the very nature of employer interrogation is coercive.

10) **Interrogation of employees.** An employer's questioning of his employees about union membership or activities, while not unlawful per se, is subject to very close scrutiny.

a) **Anti-union environment.** Absent an "anti-union" environment, one isolated instance of questioning might not constitute an unfair labor practice, and an employer may of course listen to anything his employees volunteer to him.

b. **Coercive atmosphere defined--Operating Engineers, Local 49 v. NLRB (Struksnes Construction Co.),** 353 F.2d 852 (D.C. Cir. 1965), *on remand*, 165 N.L.R.B. 1062 (1967).

1) **Facts.** Struksnes Construction Company (D), a highway construction company, took an open, signed poll of its employees at a job site when a union representative claimed he had the support of 20 of D's 26 employees at the site. There was no showing that D was hostile or biased against the union, nor did D interfere with the union's organizing efforts. The poll resulted

in nine voting for the union and 15 against it. The Board found that the poll did not violate section 8(a)(1).

2) **Issue.** Is it coercive for an employer to use a written poll to determine whether a union has majority support among its employees?

3) **Held.** Yes. Order reversed and case remanded.

   a) **Opinion of the court of appeals.**

      (1) The Board here simply ignored the fact that a signed permanent record of the vote of each employee was generated by D and its foremen.

      (2) Although most of the men were members of the union, they voted against a union contract. This raises the possibility of an inherent restraint resulting from such polls, which the Board ignored.

      (3) The Board should devise at least minimum standards to protect employees and recognize the rights of employers acting in good faith.

   b) **NLRB supplemental decision and order.**

      (1) An employer's poll of his employees raises fears in the employee's mind of reprisals. Because of this inherent coercion, such a poll is a per se violation of section 8(a)(1).

      (2) It is also clear that there are noncoercive methods for employers to verify a union's majority status (*e.g.*, requesting proof, filing a petition, etc.).

      (3) Thus, we adopt the following revision of the criteria set forth in *Blue Flash Express, Inc.*, 109 N.L.R.B. 591 (1954). Absent unusual circumstances, an employer's polling of employees will violate section 8(a)(1) of the Act unless the following safeguards are observed: (i) the purpose of the poll must be to determine the truth of a union's claim of majority; (ii) this purpose must be communicated to the employees; (iii) assurances against reprisals must be given; (iv) the employees must be polled by secret ballot; and (v) the employer must not engage in unfair labor practices or otherwise create a coercive atmosphere.

      (4) Such a rule recognizes the employer's legitimate interests and protects the employees.

      (5) Here, under the rule just enunciated, the poll would be improper. However, the poll was not coercive under the *Blue Flash* rule applicable at the time. Furthermore, the job at that site terminated more than three years ago. Thus, a remedial order is not appropriate in this case.

c. **Economic coercion and inducement.**

1) **Changing employee benefits to influence election.** During a union organizing campaign, the employer must conduct "business as usual" with respect to existing personnel policies and practices. Failure to do so is likely to be an unfair labor practice, especially where new steps are undertaken for the purpose of influencing the campaign.

NLRB v. Exchange Parts Co.

a) **Application--NLRB v. Exchange Parts Co.,** 375 U.S. 405 (1964).

   (1) **Facts.** Shortly after the NLRB ordered an election, Exchange Parts Company (D), the employer, held a dinner for its employees and announced a new "Floating Holiday" in addition to delivering the antiunion speech. Later, D sent the employees a letter announcing other new benefits, including new overtime and vacation policies. The NLRB found that the timing of the new benefits was designed to induce employees to vote against the union and thereby violated section 8(a)(1). The court of appeals declined to enforce the Board's order and held for D. The NLRB appeals.

   (2) **Issue.** Does the conferral of new employee benefits while a representation election is pending interfere with the employees' right to organize?

   (3) **Held.** Yes. Judgment reversed.

      (a) An employer may not confer economic benefits, such as additional paid holidays and vacation time or higher overtime pay, shortly before an election. Such conduct is an unfair labor practice in and of itself, despite the fact that such benefits may be "permanent and unconditional."

      (b) Benefits motivated by the threat of unionization were likely to be ephemeral and of little real value to employees, and would be interpreted by employees as a reminder that the employer controls the employees' economic purse strings—*i.e.*, the proverbial "fist in the velvet glove."

   (4) **Comments.**

      (a) The converse of the *Exchange Parts* rule is also true. An employer may not withhold a general wage increase customary at a specified time each year because his employees have elected to seek union representation. [Pacific Southwest Airlines, 201 N.L.R.B. No. 8 (1973)]

      (b) However, in *Singer Co.*, 198 N.L.R.B. 870 (1972), the NLRB held that the withholding of employee promotions during the period before a representation election was not coercive, even though such promotions "probably would have been granted" but for the union campaign. The Board distinguished this case on the ground that promotions by the employer had not previously been made on any regular or periodic basis and that the employer made no formal announcement concerning promotions.

2) **Union unfair practices.** The original Wagner Act did not provide for union misconduct, but the Taft-Hartley amendments reversed that and also created the right to refrain from exercising organizational activities. Thus, government was placed in a position of neutrality. Section 8(b)(1), the union equivalent to section 8(a)(1), left out the word "interfere." A union's stock-in-trade during an election campaign is the promise of improved economic and working conditions if it is elected (something an employer may not promise for a negative vote). Unions may also use social pressures to induce support. These kinds of tactics are not generally violations of 8(b)(1). But the grant of certain types of tangible benefits may be violations.

3) **Employee benefits.** Unions sometimes will offer prospective benefits to members of the prospective unit at or near the time of the election. It has been held improper for a union soliciting authorization cards to waive membership fees or fines for those who sign on while denying such waivers to employees who decline. The Supreme Court determined that allowing the union to buy endorsements creates a false impression about the real support of the union during the campaign. Employees who sign on under such circumstances may have a false sense of obligation to vote for the union, or they may sign under a sense of apprehension about repercussions that might follow if they do not sign and the union wins. [NLRB v. Savair Manufacturing Co., 414 U.S. 270 (1973)]

   a) **Representation election realities.** The study by Getman, Goldberg, and Herman, cited *supra,* which figured in the *Shopping Kart* and *General Knit* cases, *supra,* questioned the Board's basic assumptions about the characteristics of worker-voters and the influence of various campaign tactics on them. They concluded that worker-voters were fairly sophisticated about what went on in a campaign and most were not vitally influenced by the campaign itself, all but about 20% having already made a choice before the campaign. The authors recommended that the Board not be concerned with election tactics except for flagrant retaliatory acts. They also recommended extending equal opportunity to the union if the company uses its premises for campaigning.

2. **Employer Domination or Assistance.** NLRA section 8(a)(2) prohibits both employer domination or interference with the formation or administration of labor organizations and the contribution of financial or other support to such organizations. Determining whether an employer is guilty of "domination or undue interference or support" is a difficult task. Creating a company union; aiding the formation of a union; soliciting membership or financial assistance; and the use of company facilities, checkoffs, and/or coercion in aid of a particular union have all been found to violate section 8(a)(2).

   a. **Test.** When employer activity reaches a point where it is reasonable to infer that the union is not truly representing the employees in disputes arising between the employer and the employee, the employer has violated section 8(a)(2).

Electromation, Inc.

1) **Employer consultative committees--Electromation, Inc.,** 309 N.L.R.B. 990 (1992), *enf'd,* 35 F.3d 1148 (7th Cir. 1994).

   a) **Facts.** Electromation, Inc. (D) experienced financial difficulties in 1988 and curtailed expected wage increases and attendance bonuses. This prompted the employees to petition D for a meeting held with the president and several employees. Later, D, after consulting with supervisors, decided that a set of action committees would be useful in dealing with employee concerns. The employees reluctantly agreed and five action committees were devised by D, consisting of six employees and one or two supervisors. The committees were: (i) Absenteeism/Infractions, (ii) No Smoking Policy, (iii) Communications Network, (iv) Pay Progression for Premium Positions, and (v) Attendance Bonus Program. The employees were told that if the committees came up with "solutions" that D believed to be within the budget and generally acceptable to the employees, the solutions would be implemented. Employees were allowed to sign up for one committee of his or her choice. D drafted the policy goals for each committee. Committee members were announced by D and their names remained on the bulletin boards. The committees met beginning in January, with various supervisors participating. The Employee Benefits Manager, appointed by D to be the Coordinator of Action Committees, attended all meetings. The Union (P) made a demand for recognition in mid-February. D informed the committees that D could no longer participate, but the committees could continue if they wished. D continued to pay employees for time spent on committee work. The Pay Committee disbanded. The Absenteeism and Communication Committees voted to continue. The Attendance Bonus Committee decided to present a proposal and disband. An earlier proposal devised by this Committee had been rejected by D's Controller, who was then a member, because it was too costly. A second proposal was acceptable to him, but it was never presented to the company. In mid-March, D suspended the operation of the committees until after the election, scheduled for March 31. An unfair labor practice was filed. The ALJ held that the committees were "labor organizations" within the definition of section 2(a) and that D had dominated and assisted them in violation of section 8(b)(2).

   b) **Issues.**

      (1) Were the action committees labor organizations?

      (2) Did D dominate and impermissibly assist them?

   c) **Held.** (1) Yes. (2) Yes.

      (1) As Senator Wagner said, the "question is entirely one of fact and turns upon whether or not the employee organization is entirely the agency of the workers." The term "labor organization" covers a broad range of employee groups; a group is one if the employees participate in the organization; if it exists, at least in part, to deal with an employer and the dealings concern conditions of work or other statutory subjects (*e.g.*, grievances, labor disputes, rates of pay or hours); and finally, if its purpose is to represent employees. The action committees met these conditions. There need be no formal organization or by-laws. "Dealing with" is broader than just collective

bargaining.

- (2) There can be no doubt that D's conduct amounted to domination of the committees. It was D's idea to organize the committees. The employees were not immediately receptive to the idea, and D drafted the written purposes and goals, determined how many members would be on the committees, and appointed the supervisors to be on each committee. D paid the employees while they participated in this structure of its own making.

d) Concurrence (Oviatt, Member).

- (1) I write separately to identify the broad range of lawful activities that may be carried on which do not involve grievances, labor disputes, or conditions of employment.

- (2) Not caught up in the principles of this case would be "quality circles," which use employee expertise to address operational problems of efficiency, waste improvement, and communications. Also not covered are "quality-of-work-life" programs where management draws upon the creativity of employees in making decisions which affect their work lives. Such organizations may compliment an existing union, but they cannot usurp the union's traditional functions.

- (3) The employer's good faith will not validate domination or impermissible assistance.

e) Concurrence (Raudabaugh, Member).

- (1) Section 8(a)(2) should be reinterpreted. Cooperative programs are seen "as a necessary response to competition in a global economy." Most employee participation programs ("EPPs") amount to labor organizations under the Act.

- (2) Section 8(a)(2) does not contemplate only the "adversarial model" of labor relations. The following factors should be considered: (i) the extent of the employer's involvement in the structure and operation, (ii) whether the employees reasonably perceive the EPP as a substitute for full collective bargaining, (iii) whether employees have been assured their section 7 rights to choose a union and to conduct bargaining, and (iv) the employer's motives for establishing the EPP.

f) Comments.

- (1) In *Hertzka & Knowles v. NLRB*, 503 F.2d 625 (9th Cir. 1974), the court of appeals refused to accept the Board's conclusion that employer membership on committees set up at employee instigation to discuss compensation and working conditions amounted to unlawful interference. The court noted that the Act does not outlaw cooperative efforts freely chosen by the employees.

- (2) The collective bargaining model proceeds on the assumption that each side will form self-controlled and self-directed organizations and will bargain at arm's length. A conflict of interests is presumed and economic pressure has a legitimate and appropriate role in the process. Various integrative models contemplate employer-employee joint participation in the determination of working conditions and acceptance of management's goals. The hope is that conflict can be avoided or at least minimized. [*See* Kohler, Models of Worker Participation: The Uncertain Significance of Section 8(a)(2), 27 B.C. L. Rev. (1986)] But, without a union, the ultimate power is with the employer.

2) **Negotiation with a union prior to formal recognition proscribed--International Ladies' Garment Workers v. NLRB (Bernhard-Altmann Texas Corp.),** 366 U.S. 731 (1961).

International Ladies' Garment Workers v. NLRB (Bernhard-Altmann Texas Corp.)

a) **Facts.** The union (D) began an organizational drive. Among the Bernhard-Altmann employees were employees who were not represented by any union. During the drive, an independent group of employees went on strike protesting wage cuts. D claimed to represent a majority of the employees and negotiated a strike settlement with employer; five weeks later both sides signed a collective bargaining agreement. The NLRB brought charges against both, alleging that D represented only a minority of employees when the strike settlement was negotiated. The court of appeals affirmed, and the Supreme Court granted certiorari.

b) **Issue.** Is it an unfair labor practice if an employer and union negotiate when both in good faith believe that the union represents a majority of employees, when in fact it represents only a minority?

c) **Held.** Yes. Judgment affirmed.

(1) By granting exclusive bargaining rights to a minority union, an employer violates NLRA section 7.

(2) Employees have the right "to bargain collectively through representatives of their own choosing." [NLRA §7] Employers are required by NLRA section 8(a)(1) to refrain from interfering with employees' section 7 rights.

(3) When a minority union is given exclusive bargaining rights, an employer infringes on the section 7 rights of its employees and impermissibly supports the union.

d) **Comment.** Of course, not all intervention by an employer is improper. Section 8(a)(2) specifically provides that an employer "shall not be prohibited from permitting employees to confer with him during working hours without loss of time or pay." This means that an employer may pay the employee or his representative for time spent discussing grievances or other matters, without violating the statute.

b. **Methods of determining unlawful domination or support.** A wide variety of conduct has been held to constitute illegal "domination" or "support" of a union by an employer. The following are the major areas of activity likely to violate section 8(a)(2).

1) **Solicitation of membership.** An employer may not actively solicit union members (*e.g.*, for a union favored by the employer, as opposed to another union). However, the employer can establish rules permitting employees to solicit for a union, provided such rules are not discriminatorily applied to prohibit anti-union arguments or solicitation by rival unions.

   a) Thus, an employer violated section 8(a)(2) by allowing one union to solicit on company time and property while prohibiting solicitation by a rival union.

2) **Undue assistance.** If an employer takes active part in the establishment of a union or its affairs, the employer may be guilty of unlawful "domination or assistance."

   a) The employer need not take part personally, since a supervisor or other party may be considered an agent acting for the employer.

   b) A violation of the Act has been found where the employer merely aided in drafting the charter and by-laws that started the union.

   c) An employer's anti-union campaign against one union, resulting in the formation of a company union, was found to be unlawful assistance.

   d) It is unlawful for a company to recognize a union before a substantial proportion of employees have been hired. [*See* Deklewa v. IABW, 282 N.L.R.B. 1375 (1987), *enf'd*, 843 F.2d 770 (3d Cir. 1988)]

3) **Use of company facilities.** Supplying company facilities (*e.g.*, legal services, office space, secretarial services, and printing or other equipment) to one union, while denying them to another, would be unlawful employer support under section 8(a)(2).

   a) For example, an employer violated the Act by granting one union the use of company premises, time to hold committee elections, and a motel room to be used as a meeting place by the union, while refusing to consider the claim of a rival union for recognition.

   b) But where the employer merely introduced an employee to a union agent, allowed the agent to contact employees in nonpublic areas of the employer's premises during working hours, and then promptly recognized the union, the NLRB concluded that there was not enough evidence to support a finding of unlawful "assistance." [Mace Food Stores, Inc., 167 N.L.R.B. 441] The Board in *Mace* found that the employer had permitted access to the premises by rival unions, had not solicited members for the union, and had not recognized the union in question before it represented a majority of the employees or after another union had filed a representation claim.

   c) In another case, a court of appeals held that an incidental benefit—in the form of receipts totaling $120 a year from a coffee machine operation on company premises—granted to one union over another but not used to gain concessions from that union during bargaining sessions, did not constitute domination or assistance. [NLRB v. Post Publishing Co., 311 F.2d 565 (7th Cir. 1963)] The court in *Post Publishing* drew a line between "support" and "cooperation." The court held that mere "cooperation" would not be unlawful absent evidence that it had been calculated to (or did) coerce employees.

4) **Domination through union by-laws or constitutional provisions.** Provisions in a union constitution or by-laws that evidence employer control will violate section 8(a)(2). Moreover, the absence of any constitution, by-laws, or membership requirements other than employment at the employer's plant is considered evidence of employer domination.

   a) A by-law provision that gives the employer equal representation on a "committee" governing the employee organization, plus the power to determine which employees would sit on the committee, violates the Act.

   b) However, the employer may be represented on employee committees if the employees so desire, and if such representation was not thrust upon them and does not inhibit them from voicing their demands.

5) **Employer choice between rival unions--Abraham Grossman d/b/a Bruckner Nursing Home,** 262 N.L.R.B. 955 (1982).

   a) **Facts.** Both Local 144 and Local 1115 (P) began organization campaigns at Bruckner Nursing Home (D). After several months, Local 144 notified D that it had a majority of signed authorization cards and arrangements were made for a neutral card count. Shortly afterwards, P notified D that it was organizing D's employees and that it should not recognize any other union. It filed section 8(a)(1) charges against D and section 8(b)(1) (A) charges against Local 144. The card count revealed that Local 144 had a significant majority. After the unfair labor practice charges had been dismissed, D and Local 144 began negotiations and executed an agreement. P filed new charges against D. The Administrative Law Judge found that in September, Local 144 had an 80% to 90% majority and that P had two cards. The Judge found that P had a "colorable claim" of representation and that D had violated section 8(a)(2) by giving unlawful assistance to Local 144 when it recognized and negotiated with it. D was directed to cease giving effect to the agreement and to withdraw its recognition.

   b) **Issue.** Is it a violation of section 8(a)(2) for an employer to recognize and negotiate with a labor organization that has a clear authorization card majority when another organization has some support and neither organization has petitioned for an election?

   c) **Held.** No. The complaint is dismissed.

      (1) The *Midwest Piping* "colorable claim" to representation doctrine (63 N.L.R.B. 1060 (1945)) has proved to be ineffective in reconciling the various interests at stake in this type of case.

      (2) The Board will no longer find an 8(a)(2) violation in rival union, initial organization situations when the employer recognizes a union that represents an uncoerced, unassisted majority, provided that a petition for an election has not been filed.

(3) Once a valid election petition has been filed, the employer must refrain from recognizing any of the rival unions.

(4) Basing the rule on a valid petition will establish a clearly defined course of conduct and will encourage employee free choice and industrial stability.

d) Comment. Where there is no question with respect to the union that enjoys majority status, an employer does not violate the Act by negotiating with the majority representative. [NLRB v. Air Master Corp., 339 F.2d 553 (3d Cir. 1964)]

3. Employer Discrimination on the Basis of Union Membership. NLRA section 8(a)(3) makes it unlawful for an employer to discourage or encourage membership in any labor organization by discrimination in regard to hiring or tenure of employment, or with respect to any term or condition of employment.

a. Proving discrimination. In order to prove that an employer has unlawfully discriminated against an employee, it must be shown that the employee's union activity—or lack of same—was the motivating force behind the employer conduct in question.

1) Degree of proof required. The procedures and rules adopted and followed by the NLRB greatly influence this determination.

a) Before 1947, the Board was not required to base its findings upon a preponderance of the evidence. In other words, a Board decision would be upheld by the court of appeals if it was merely "supported by the evidence."

b) The Taft-Hartley Act of 1947, however, established more stringent standards for both NLRB findings of fact and judicial review of Board decisions. Section 10(c) now specifically provides that Board findings must be based on a "preponderance" of the evidence. Sections 10(e) and (f) provide that in reviewing Board decisions, courts must uphold findings of fact if they are supported by "substantial evidence contained in the record as a whole." [*See* Universal Camera Corp. v. NLRB, 340 U.S. 474 (1951)] The Federal Rules of Evidence apply.

c) Of course, findings of law by the NLRB may be reviewed *ab initio* on appeal.

2) Examples of employer discrimination.

a) **Discrimination in hiring or firing.** An employer may not hire or fire an employee on the basis of the employee's membership or lack of membership in a union. [Phelps Dodge Corp. v. NLRB, *infra*]

b) **Discrimination in tenure, terms, or conditions of employment.** It is also an unfair labor practice under section 8(a)(3) for an employer "by discrimination in regard to tenure or employment or any term or condition of employment, to encourage or discourage membership in any labor organization." This means that an employer may not discharge, lay off, demote, transfer, etc., where the decision to do so is based on union considerations, or where the employer's action would have the practical effect of encouraging or discouraging membership in any labor organization.

b. **Union security agreements.** Agreements that permit an employer (at the request of the union) to discharge an employee for nonpayment of dues or initiation fees are allowed. [§8(a)(3), 1st proviso]

c. **Discriminatory discharge.** An employer may not discharge an employee where the motivation for the discharge is to encourage or discourage union membership.

  1) **Examples.** Violations of section 8(a)(3) were found where (i) an employer discharged a nonunion employee solely because he had attended a union organizational meeting and (ii) an employer discharged an employee who refused to join a company-dominated union. Note that the employer in the latter case also violated section 8(a)(2).

d. **Discriminatory lay-offs.** Similarly, an employer may not lay off or suspend an employee because of his union activity.

Edward G. Budd Manufacturing Co. v. NLRB

e. **Other justifications irrelevant--Edward G. Budd Manufacturing Co. v. NLRB,** 138 F.2d 86 (3d Cir. 1943).

  1) **Facts.** In 1933, Edward G. Budd Manufacturing Company's (D's) employees formed an association designed and suggested by D. This association represented the employees, and D cooperated with the association. In 1941, the UAW failed in an attempt to organize D's employees. The UAW then filed charges that D illegally fired two employees for supporting the UAW. The Board found for the union on both counts. The portion of the opinion relative to the firing of an employee, Walter Weigand, who was a representative of the association, is considered here. The Board found that Weigand was discharged for his union activities and ordered him reinstated.

  2) **Issue.** May an employee be discharged for his support of a union?

  3) **Held.** No. Order enforced.

   a) Weigand sometimes came to work drunk, and came and left as he pleased; if any employee deserved summary discharge, it was he. His discharge was requested many times.

   b) Furthermore, an employer can discharge an employee "for a good reason, a poor reason, or no reason at all so long as the provisions of the NLRA are not violated."

   c) Here, however, it appears from the facts that Weigand was discharged for his support of the union and not for his terrible work record. This violates the NLRA. Thus, the Board's order will be enforced.

f. **Scope of review of NLRA cases.** At the time of the Taft-Hartley amendments, Congress registered dissatisfaction with what was considered too tolerant judicial review of NLRB decisions by some courts. Section 10 of the Act was amended to confine the Board to legal evidence and to consider the whole record of evidence. In *Universal Camera Corp. v. NLRB, supra,* the United States Supreme Court indicated that the appellate courts must now assume primary responsibility for the "reasonableness and fairness" of the Board's decisions. The courts should not interfere with decisions based on the Board's expertise when the choice is between two "fairly conflicting views" or when findings of fact are supported by substantial evidence when considering the whole record. The Supreme Court's role is to be limited. The Court also indicated that the Board should give due weight to an ALJ's findings.

1) **"Substantial evidence" standard in a "mixed motive" case--Mueller Brass Co. v. NLRB,** 544 F.2d 815 (5th Cir. 1977).

    a) **Facts.** Mueller Brass Company (D) was in the midst of its third organizational campaign. In an earlier case it had been found to have committed unfair labor practices (sections 8(a)(1) and (3)). D was concededly "anti-union." Employee Stone had received a verbal and a written warning for absenteeism and was reminded that he could face termination. He was known to be sympathetic to the union. Shortly afterwards, Stone was hospitalized and did not report to work until 10 days after release. He had not notified D during that time. D received a doctor's note that Stone was able to return to work two days after his hospital stay. D terminated Stone as a "voluntary quit" under a plant rule. Stone was not permitted to return to his job and D refused to reconsider even after he presented a doctor's note that voided his earlier ones. Employee Rogers had been a long time union activist and D knew of his involvement. He worked the night shift and on two nights running he embarrassed female employees by displaying sexual paraphernalia to one female employee and propositioning another. After extensive investigation, D interviewed Rogers and he admitted being the offender. He was fired under a plant rule for immoral or indecent conduct. The ALJ felt that Stone's discharge was for overstaying his excused absence and not because of his union sympathies. On the other hand, he felt that Rogers was fired because of his union sympathies and the reason cited by D was a pretext. The Board found that both employees had been fired because of their union identifications.

    b) **Issue.** Are the Board's determinations supported by "substantial evidence on the record considered as a whole?"

    c) **Held.** No. Enforcement denied.

        (1) The mere fact that an employee breaks a company rule and becomes a union supporter is not sufficient to destroy just cause

for the discharge. There must be improper motive and there must be disparate treatment of like cases because of the anti-union animus.

    (2) The Board overstepped its bounds in reversing the ALJ's conclusion regarding Stone. The Board must not second guess management. However unreasonable the company's failure to notify Stone before he reported back to work or its refusal to credit the final note from the doctor might have been, there is no substantial evidence that his discharge was discriminatory.

    (3) The court is shocked by the Board's conclusion about Rogers, whose conduct and statements were vulgar and offensive by any standard of decency. If the conduct is so flagrant that the employee would almost certainly be fired anyway, there is no room for discrimination to play a part. The Board is reversed in both instances.

    d) **Dissent** (Godbold, J.). The court has overstepped its proper role. It has proceeded to retry Stone's case. D was hostile to the union, it had been before the Board already, there was no effort to contact Stone before his return and D gave him no notice of termination. D also admitted it had no reason to doubt the last note from the doctor. There was substantial evidence to support the Board's findings and conclusion. In the case of Rogers, he had already been targeted by D and his conduct was not out of keeping with the general level of conduct at the plant. No other employee had been fired under the plant rule applied against him. The Board was entitled to infer that Rogers would not have been fired in the absence of an anti-union bias.

2) **Proof in "mixed motive" or "pretext" cases.** In these kinds of cases the Board has ruled that a prima facie case must be established by the General Counsel's showing that an impermissible reason was a motivating factor for the employer's action. Then it is up to the employer to prove that its action would have been the same even in the absence of the impermissible factor. [*See* Wright Line, 251 N.L.R.B. 1083 (1980)] This allocation of burdens was approved by the Supreme Court in *NLRB v. Transportation Management Corp.*, 462 U.S. 393 (1983).

3) **Compare—section 8(a)(1).** Section 8(a)(1) cases should be contrasted in regard to "motive". An employer in good faith fired an employee on the basis of a report, which was false, that the employee had threatened to use dynamite. The discharge was a violation of section 8(a)(1). [NLRB v. Burnip & Simms, 379 U.S. 21 (1964)]

4) **The "runaway" shop.** When an employer relocates its plant because of anti-union animus, there is little doubt that a section 8(a)(3) violation may be found. Some courts of appeals have been more willing than the Board to allow relocations based on economic considerations where the organizational effort has resulted in higher wage costs.

NLRB v. Adkins Transfer Co.

5) **Closing down a department--NLRB v. Adkins Transfer Co.**, 226 F.2d 324 (6th Cir. 1995).

a) **Facts.** Suit was brought by the NLRB to enforce its order against Adkins Transfer Company (D), a small truck line, for allegedly violating sections 8(a)(1) and (3) of the Act. D hired a mechanic and a mechanic's helper to repair and service its trucks. The two new employees joined the same union as all of D's other employees. The union presented two contracts to D, calling for D to increase the mechanic's wage by 50 cents per hour and the helper's wage by 50-65 cents per hour. Evidence indicated that if D did not comply with the proposed contract, there would be a strike shutting down D's operations. D, rather than sign the contract, discontinued repairing and servicing its own vehicles and discharged both the mechanic and the helper. D was charged with violating the sections of the Act noted above. The trial examiner found for D. The Board reversed, holding that a prima facie case of unfair labor practices had been established. D appeals.

b) **Issue.** May an employer in good faith close down a department and discharge employees in the department rather than sign a union contract covering the department's employees?

c) **Held.** Yes. Judgment reversed.

(1) The Act applies only to discrimination that encourages or discourages membership in a labor organization.

(2) Thus, employers are free to discontinue departments and discharge employees, with or without cause, as long as said activity is not for the illegal purpose of encouraging or discouraging union membership.

(3) The fact that the two employees were members of a union was incidental to the real reason for their discharge. Evidence here shows that D had no feelings against the unions; rather, it was shown that the union pay scales were too high for D to continue to operate the department in question profitably.

g. **Discriminatory demotions and transfers.** Changes in employment conditions based on legitimate economic considerations are, of course, permissible. However, any change in the employment conditions of an employee where the motivation for the change is to "encourage or discourage" union activity violates section 8(a)(3).

1) Thus, it is an unfair labor practice for an employer to reduce the seniority standing of an employee because the employee failed to pay union dues.

2) An employer violates the Act if it gives the union the sole right to fix the seniority levels of employees, since this enables the union to discriminate in favor of its own members.

3) However, it is not a violation of the Act for contract terms to provide that seniority will be determined by a joint employer-union committee.

Textile Workers Union v. Darlington Manufacturing Co.

h. **Shutting down operations--Textile Workers Union v. Darlington Manufacturing Co., 380 U.S. 263 (1965).**

1) **Facts.** Darlington Manufacturing Company (D) operated one textile mill that was part of a conglomerate dominated by the Millikin family, which operated a number of other mills. On September 6, 1956, the Textile Workers Union (P) won a representational election. On September 12, the board of directors of the company that controlled D voted to close D down and liquidate its assets, and did so. P filed sections 8(a)(1), (3), and (5) charges. The Board ruled that D's action was the product of an anti-union animus and found a section 8(a)(3) violation. It ordered D's employees to be paid back pay until they had received equivalent jobs, that they be placed on a preferential hiring list at other Millikin mills, and that the company bargain with the union over compliance. The court of appeals denied enforcement, taking the position that as a single employer, D had an absolute right to close part or all of its business regardless of its motive. The Supreme Court granted certiorari.

2) **Issue.** Does an employer have an absolute right to go out of business if its motive is to frustrate the section 7 rights of its employees?

3) **Held.** No. Judgment reversed and case remanded.

   a) The Board properly treated this as a violation of section 8(a)(3) rather than of section 8(a)(1), which is concerned with effects rather than motives. Certain decisions are "so peculiarly matters of management prerogative" that they would be a violation only upon a discriminatory motive. A sole business person has the right to elect to go completely out of business without regard for any discriminatory anti-union animus. Such a drastic and complete action would yield no future benefits. This would be more than a runaway shop or shutdown of a department, which could be reversed if the employees denounce their rights. Though D was the sole employer for operation of its mill, its actions may have repercussions on the remaining businesses.

   b) We remand for the Board to determine what impact the decision to close D's mill may have had on other employees of the conglomerate. We do not suggest that organizational integration of plants or corporations is necessary. If the person in control closes a plant with anti-union animus and (i) has a sufficient interest in another business as to enjoy a benefit of discouraging organization of that business; (ii) acts to close the plant with the purpose of producing such a result; and (iii) occupies a relationship to the other businesses that makes it realistically foreseeable that the employees of the other businesses will fear similar treatment if they persist in organizational activities, a violation has been made out.

4) **Remand.** On remand, the Board found that the plant had been closed down for the purpose of deterring organization at other establishments in which the family had a dominant interest.

i. **Status of supervisors under the Act.** Under the original Act, the Board ultimately recognized the rights of supervisors to organize and bargain in units separate from rank and file employees. The Taft-Hartley amendments excepted supervisors from the section 2(3) definition of "employee." The Board since has responded to cases where treatment of supervisors has had the effect of frustrating the exercise of employee statutory rights. Thus, a supervisor should not be disciplined for testifying at a Board hearing, for processing a grievance, or for refusing to commit an unfair labor practice. It would be improper for an employer to discipline a supervisor in a way that "directly interferes with a section 7 right." In this sense, supervisors may receive derivative protection to the extent necessary to promote the purposes of the Act. [*See* Parker-Robb Chevrolet, Inc., 262 N.L.R.B. 402 (1983)]

4. **Remedies for Violation of the Right to Organize.** Where judicial relief is sought by the Board for refusal to abide by an NLRB order concerning violations of employee rights under section 7, the order generally takes the form of cease and desist orders and/or orders requiring affirmative action (*e.g.*, reinstatement with back pay, preferential hiring). The scope of remedy imposed must be determined by the circumstances of each case.

   a. **Cease and desist orders.** Such orders are usually directed against specific conduct. Where a long history of violations or anti-union sentiment exists, however, a blanket order may be imposed directing the employer to "cease and desist in any manner" from interfering with employees' organizational rights.

   b. **Orders for affirmative action.** In appropriate situations, the Board may order an employer to take affirmative action in order to correct the effects of past unfair labor practices. For example, in *J.P. Stevens & Co. v. NLRB*, 380 F.2d 292 (2d Cir. 1967), the court upheld a Board order directing reinstatement in order to offset an employer's "major campaign of illegal anti-union activity spearheaded by retaliatory discharges."

      1) The NLRB could also require that a notice of reinstatement be posted in all of the employer's plants and a copy of the notice be mailed to all employees. However, the Board could not require the employer to read the notice to his employees on company time.

      2) Moreover, the facts did not justify requiring the employer to make company bulletin boards available to the union for the posting of a notice of reinstatement.

   c. **Discrimination in the hiring of employees--Phelps Dodge Corp. v. NLRB,** 313 U.S. 177 (1941).

      Phelps Dodge Corp. v. NLRB

      1) **Facts.** Phelps Dodge Corporation (D) denied employment to two employees who had voluntarily quit before a strike and to certain strikers because of their union affiliations. The Board ordered all of them to be reemployed without loss of pay. The court of appeals enforced the reinstatement of the strikers, but refused to enforce the

order concerning the two applicants for rehire. The Supreme Court granted certiorari.

2) **Issue.** May an employer discriminate in hiring, rehiring, or reinstating employees because of their union affiliations?

3) **Held.** No. All employees in question are ordered reinstated.

   a) Section 8(a)(3) prohibits an employer from discriminating in both hiring and dismissal based upon union membership or activities.

   b) Those who quit were former employees of D who had been discriminated against by D's refusal to rehire them based on their union membership. Even if they had never been employed by D, the Board could compel D to hire them if they had been refused employment because they were union members. Section 8(a)(3) proscribes such discrimination as an unfair labor practice, and the Board's remedies include ordering reinstatement even where the employees have found comparable alternative employment. Back pay should be calculated on the basis of lost pay minus any amount actually earned while discharged and, in appropriate circumstances, what the employees could have earned.

4) **Comment.** This holding broadens the scope of sections 2(3) and 8(a), *supra*, by including those who have never before been employed by the company, since the protection of the Act might be read as applying only to cases where people have been former employees and have been discriminated against by reason of union activity during the course of their employment. The Court directs the Board to take "such affirmative action, including reinstatement of 'employees' with or without back pay, as will effectuate the policies of the Act." Commentators and the Board have recognized that mitigated back pay may appear cheaper to employers than the costs of organization. Efforts to add "punitive" double-back pay without mitigation have been unsuccessful.

d. **Temporary injunctions.** NLRA section 10(j) authorizes the Board in "emergency" situations to seek a temporary injunction in federal district court restraining the employer or union unfair labor practices, even before a hearing on the charges.

e. **Prerequisites for injunctive relief.** In order to obtain a section 19(j) injunction, the NLRB must file a petition in federal court that alleges all of the following:

   (i)   The filing of an unfair labor practice charge;

   (ii) The issuance of a complaint on the charge;

   (iii) Facts supporting the charge; and

   (iv) A likelihood that the unfair practice will continue unless restrained.

Where these pleading requirements are met, and where the facts presented at the show-cause hearing indicate that the Board had reasonable cause to believe the unfair practice had been committed, a proper case exists for injunctive relief.

f. Range of NLRB remedies. J.P. Stevens & Company, a multi-plant textile complex, steadfastly resisted organizational efforts and was found on numerous occasions by the Board to have violated the protected rights of its employees. Among the remedies ordered by the Board were posting notices (both in the plant where the offense occurred and also in the company's other plants); mailing notices to all employees in the other plants; requiring company officials to read the notices on company time; giving the union use of bulletin boards for one year; giving organizers access to parking lots and nonworking areas; giving union organizers equal time on the shop floor whenever the company made anti-union speeches; providing the union employee lists; and reimbursing the NLRB for its litigation expenses. The company and some of its supervisors were found to be in civil contempt. [J.P. Stevens & Co. v. NLRB, *supra*]

g. Ordering recognition of union. When a company has committed such unfair practices that dissipate a union's majority support to the extent that it is doubtful that a fair and free election could be conducted, the Board has ordered the company to recognize and bargain with the union. [*See* NLRB v. Gissel Packing Co., *supra*]

h. Runaway shop remedies. The runaway shop presents perplexing remedy problems. In *Local 57 Ladies Garment Workers v. NLRB (Garwin Corp.)*, 374 F.2d 295 (D.C. Cir. 1969), the Board had ordered recognition and bargaining with the union at the new plant location. The court of appeals overturned the bargaining order, emphasizing that the order nullified the rights of the new employees at the new plant to make their own choice. On remand, the Board ordered the company to provide the union a list of the employees at the new plant, to allow the union access to bulletin boards for one year and access to parking lots, and also to bargain upon proof that a majority of the new employees has designated the union as their representative.

i. Coercion and discrimination cases—back pay. Serious weaknesses have been identified in the Board's remedies for coercion and discrimination cases. Back pay awards in practice tend to be delayed and relatively small, and thus may have little deterrent effect. Reinstatements to the job are not always effective because employees may choose not to return, or if they do their tenure may be short-lived. Bargaining orders often prove to be exercises in futility. Long delays between the wrongful action and the corrective order also minimize remedial effectiveness.

B. SELECTION OF THE BARGAINING REPRESENTATIVE

1. Introduction.

a. Employer refusal to bargain—section 8(a)(5). It is an unfair labor practice for an employer to "refuse to bargain collectively with the representatives of his employees," subject to section 9(a), which stipulates that representatives selected by a majority of the employees of the appropriate unit will be the exclusive representatives for collective bargaining.

1) **Immediate duty to bargain.** Once a representative has been designated by a majority of employees, the employer is under an immediate duty to bargain collectively. To hold an employer for an unfair labor practice, the Board must find that: (i) the unit claimed is the correct one; (ii) a majority of the employees were in favor of the union at the time of the employer's refusal to bargain; and (iii) the employer improperly refused to bargain. This is a difficult question since the employer can refuse to bargain where there are honest doubts as to whether a majority of the employees want the union, or about the propriety of the unit. Then the question must go to the Board for decision and/or an election. (*See* discussion of *Gissel Packing*, *supra*, and *Linden Lumber*, *infra*.)

2) **Uncertain cases.** In cases where there is uncertainty, the Board must balance the need for dealing firmly with unfair labor practices with the need or desirability of obtaining a more accurate reflection of the employees' wishes made possible by an election.

b. **Election proceedings.** Section 9 proceedings are commenced by a union petition for an election. The employer may also file whenever two or more unions present conflicting representation claims, and the Taft-Hartley Act now allows the employer to file whenever a union puts in a claim for recognition.

c. **Decertification.** The Taft-Hartley Act added section 9(c)(1)(A), which states that any employee can file a petition alleging that a majority of the employees in the unit do *not* wish to be represented by the current union. If the Board finds such a question to exist, it may then order a decertification election.

d. **Restrictions of section 9 rights.**

1) **Substantial interest requirement.** The Board will investigate only when there is a "question concerning representation" and a substantial showing of interest by the union (normally, authorization cards signed by at least 30% of the proposed bargaining unit).

2) **Grounds for denying an election.**

a) **Unremedied unfair labor practices.** For years, the Board has followed a rule not to hold an election while unfair labor practices are outstanding, unless the union waives its rights to pursue the unfair labor practices charge.

b) **Election bar.** Before 1947, whenever a union would appear and make an adequate showing, the Board would hold another election. Since 1947, by statute, there has been a one-year election bar. The rationale is that employees have shown their preference for no union, and this preference should be given the same credence that a union preference decision would receive (*i.e.*, a one-year ban on elections).

c) **Certification bar.** After an earlier election, if union A is certified on November 1, 1978, when is the earliest date that union B can secure an election?

- (1) The earliest is one year after union A's certification. This is the certification bar.

- (2) This bar is meant to stabilize employer-employee relationships. Union A should have a reasonable period in which to succeed after its status has been certified. The certification bar is Board-developed and is therefore discretionary. The election bar, on the other hand, is statutory.

- (3) Note that there is a one-year bar to decertification petitions as well.

e. **Contract bar—effect of a valid collective bargaining agreement.** If union A is certified in November of 1994, and signed a four-year contract with the employer in April of 1995 (to run until April 1999), when is the earliest time union B can ask for an election?

1) The rule here has been changed often. This is called the contract bar.

2) The idea is to balance freedom of employee choice with the need for employer-union stability. The current rule is three years (April 1998). An agreement with no expiration date is no bar at all.

3) An obvious and logical alternative would provide a bar for whatever period the parties have contracted.

4) *Suppose* that the contract with union A was for three years (to April 1998), and that union B in early 1997 wants an election. When should union B file?

   a) Section 8(d)(1) deals with renegotiation of contracts. It provides a cooling off period of 60 days for negotiating at the end of the CBA. So the last date that B could file would be for the 30 days preceding that period, *i.e.*, in February 1998. After this date, the Board would not entertain the petition, and union A and the employer could sign another contract that would act as a further contract bar. If no new contract is entered, then a petition may be filed upon expiration of the old one. The periods for health care institutions are 90 and 120 days.

   b) These time periods apply to anyone filing a petition—for example, an employer who might think the union no longer represents a majority, another union, etc.

f. **Removal of the contract bar.**

1) **Introduction.** Numerous things will remove the contract bar, including (i) if the union becomes "defunct"; (ii) if the unit for bargaining is involved in a "schism"; and (iii) if there are "changes in circumstances," such as a large expansion, a merger, etc., or a change in job classifications. Also, the Board has ruled that if a contract discriminates between employees on racial grounds, it will not act as a bar.

2) **Invalid provisions.** In many cases, contracts are held no bar because of invalid provisions in the contracts themselves (*e.g.*, if the contract contained provisions for a "closed shop").

3) **Premature extension.** Suppose the contract is to expire in April 1998. Union A and the employer make an agreement in April 1997 to extend their contract until April 1999. Union B may ask for an election at the end of the first three-year period; the prematurely extended contract would not act as a bar.

4) **Defeating purposes of NLRA.** Although generally an existing agreement is a bar, where such an agreement defeats the purposes of the NLRA, it is subject to modification by the NLRB.

   a) **Example—new bargaining agent.** In *American Seating Co.*, 106 N.L.R.B. 250 (1953), a different bargaining agent had been elected to represent a portion of employees during the term of a collective agreement. The Board ruled that the agreement would not be a bar to bargaining with the new agent for the new unit. It said the occurrence of strikes would be lessened if the new representative could bargain for its employees.

2. **Determining the Appropriate Bargaining Unit.**

   a. **Introduction.** Appropriate units for bargaining and elections are determined on the basis of precedent, custom, and in some cases by employer consent to union claims. Where a voluntary agreement cannot be reached, hearings are held by the Regional Director, and determinations are subject to limited review by the Board. Job classifications are the building blocks for unit composition, not particular employees.

   b. **Board discretion.** In establishing the bargaining unit, the Board has broad discretion. Employees in a single plant might be grouped as one unit, or divided according to a craft or a department, or into larger classifications. If a single company has several plants, they may constitute one unit or several units. Bargaining also can take place in multi-employer units on a citywide, regional, or even industry-wide basis. [*See* §§9(b), (c)(5)]

   c. **Multi-employer bargaining.** The Board generally finds multi-unit unions appropriate where there is such a controlling bargaining history.

      1) **Joint negotiations required.** Whether the employees are included in a multi-employer unit depends primarily on whether the separate employers intend to be bound or are in fact bound by joint negotiations.

      2) **Separate employer units.** An employer or a union that has bargained in a multi-employer unit has a right, if exercised at an appropriate time and in an unequivocal fashion, to insist on conducting negotiations as a separate employer unit.

d. **"Community of interest."** Section 9(b) indicates that an appropriate unit should "assure to employees the fullest freedoms in exercising the rights guaranteed by this act." A unit that is too large might interfere with effective communication of the collective bargaining agent or among employees, diverse interests may be lost or ignored in the mass, and conflicting interests may interfere with bargaining the contract and administering it. On the other hand, a unit that is too small could fragment groups of employees who overall have a community of interest or lead to multi-union jurisdictional disputes. To ascertain a "community of interest," the Board considers: (i) scale and way of determining earnings; (ii) similarity of benefits, hours, and working conditions; (iii) similarity of jobs; (iv) similarity of skills and training; (v) contact and interchange among employees; (vi) geographic proximity; (vii) integration of production process; (viii) common supervision and labor-relations policy making; (ix) history of bargaining; (x) desires of employees; and (xi) extent of organization.

e. **Single-plant vs. multi-plant units.** The early cases showed the Board's tendency to favor small bargaining units, because this tended to make the union's organizing job easier. Section 9(c)(5) has precluded reliance exclusively on what unit has been organized in the past: "In determining whether a unit is appropriate for the purposes specified in subsection (b), the extent to which the employees have organized shall not be controlling."

   1) **Early history.** The AFL took the attitude that it had jurisdiction over particular trades and crafts. At the time the NLRA was enacted, the AFL was dominant. Congress did not have to consider the issue of determining which unit the workers desired. With the coming of the CIO, however, the question arose of deciding between industrial and craft units.

   2) **Considerations.** These considerations should enter into deciding between larger or smaller units:

      a) The principle of self-determination;

      b) Industrial stability;

      c) Efficiency of production;

      d) Industrial organization; and

      e) Status as an "effective" bargaining unit.

   3) **Rule of discretion.** In making unit determinations, the Board contends that section 9(c)(5) does not prevent it from certifying a unit smaller than a more comprehensive unit that would also be appropriate. The courts would probably uphold this rule.

      a) **Application—Single versus multi-location unit--NLRB v. Chicago Health & Tennis Clubs, Inc.,** 567 F.2d 331 (7th Cir. 1977), *cert. denied*, 437 U.S. 904 (1978).

NLRB v. Chicago Health & Tennis Clubs, Inc.

(1) Facts. The NLRB (P) petitions for enforcement of bargaining orders in two cases (*Saxon Paint* and *Chicago Health*) that present identical legal issues. Chicago Health & Tennis Clubs, Inc. (D) operates 16 exercise and weight loss clubs in the Chicago metropolitan area, all within a 28-mile radius of its central office. Saxon Paint & Home Care (D) operates 21 paint and wall paper stores in the Chicago metropolitan area, all within a 30-mile radius. In each case, the Regional Director determined a single club/store as the appropriate unit. The Board denied review. The Union won in both elections. The companies refused to bargain, claiming each unit was inappropriate.

(2) Issue. Did the Board abuse its discretion in certifying a single retail location in a chain of commonly owned locations in the metropolitan area?

(3) Held. No abuse in *Chicago Health & Tennis*. Abuse of discretion in *Saxon Paint*.

    (a) Board determinations are subject to limited judicial review, but the court is not to be a rubber stamp. The Board considers a number of criteria; in these two cases, the geographic considerations are the same so we should consider the other factors. The Board now seems to follow a rule that a single store is "presumptively an appropriate unit."

    (b) *Saxon Paint*. All stores are alike physically and operationally. Operations and labor relations are centralized. Individual store managers have little discretion in personnel and labor relations matters. Hiring and training are centralized. Interstore transfers are not uncommon. Bargaining history has been on a larger than local store basis. Because of the integration and centralization shown, the Board's determination is not supported by substantial evidence.

    (c) *Chicago Health & Tennis*. While very similar to *Saxon* in many ways, there are distinctions. There is no prior bargaining history. Clubs differ in type of operations and facilities. Operations are not particularly centralized and club managers have marked control over personnel and labor relations matters. Most employees are hired and fired by the managers, who exercise disciplinary discretion. Because of the autonomy of club managers, the Board's unit determination of a single club is not improper.

4) Hospital unit standards by rule. Private nonprofit hospitals were excluded from coverage of the Act until 1974. Proceeding on a case-by-case basis, the Board had difficulties in applying the "community of interests" principle and in accommodating the various disparate interests found in a hospital and at the same time avoiding the proliferation of units.

    a) Finally, in 1989, the Board adopted final administrative rules for hospital unit determination. Except under extraordinary circumstances, it will consider the following units appropriate: (i) all registered nurses; (ii) all physicians; (iii) all other professionals; (iv) all technical employees; (v) all skilled maintenance workers; (vi) all business office clerical workers; (vii) all guards; and (viii) all remaining employees. A unit of less than five employees would be an extraordinary circumstance. A combination might be appropriate.

5) **Rule valid--American Hospital Association v. NLRB,** 499 U.S. 606 (1991).

    a) **Facts.** The NLRB (D) announced a substantive rule defining bargaining units appropriate for acute care hospitals (29 C.F.R. Pt. 105). The rule provides for eight units: (i) all registered nurses, (ii) all physicians, (iii) all other professionals, (iv) all technicians, (v) all skilled maintenance workers, (vi) all business office clericals, (vii) all guards, and (viii) all other nonprofessionals. Exceptions may be made in three circumstances: (i) extraordinary circumstance (automatically, if application of the rules produce a unit of five or fewer members), (ii) where nonconforming units exist already, and (iii) where a labor organization seeks to combine two or more of the specified units. The Hospital Association (P) challenges the validity of the rule, claiming that NLRA section 9(b) requires that D make a separate unit determination in each case, that the rule violates the congressional requirement that it avoid undue proliferation of units in the health care industry, and finally, that the rule is arbitrary and capricious.

    b) **Issues.**

        (1) Does D's health-care unit rule violate the NLRA?

        (2) Is the rule arbitrary and capricious?

    c) **Held.** (1) No. (2) No.

        (1) Sections 3, 4, and 5 of the NLRA confer rulemaking powers on D broad enough to cover this case. The language "decides each case" in section 9(b) is not a limitation of this rulemaking power. It comes into operation only when there is a particular dispute about the appropriateness of a particular unit. We would defer to D's reasonable interpretation if there were any ambiguity.

        (2) We do not take the congressional committee statements about "proliferation" as a binding authoritative statement to the Board. In any event, in devising the rule, D gave due consideration to that kind of problem. If this is incorrect, Congress can fashion an appropriate enactment.

        (3) The rule is not arbitrary or capricious. It drew upon D's 13 years' experience in dealing with health care industry unit issues. There was extensive notice and comment rulemaking here, D gave careful consideration of comments, and it provided a well reasoned justification for the rule. There was reasoned analysis based on an extensive record.

American Hospital Association v. NLRB

f. Multi-employer bargaining. A number of employers within a single area or industry may agree to band together as a group to bargain with a single union representing their employees. These associations must initially have the consent of the union. The Board will also determine whether the proposed grouping is an appropriate unit, giving primary consideration to the desires of the parties and their prior bargaining history.

1) **Withdrawal from a multi-employer unit--Charles D. Bonanno Linen Service, Inc. v. NLRB,** 454 U.S. 404 (1982).

   a) **Facts.** For several years, Charles D. Bonanno Linen Service, Inc. (D) had been a member of a multi-employer bargaining unit. Negotiations for a new labor agreement had commenced and after months of bargaining, an impasse was reached. The union called a selective strike against D. Most other members locked out their drivers. D hired permanent replacements and notified the employer association that it was withdrawing from it because of the impasse. Shortly afterwards, negotiations began again, without D's participation, and months later a contract was agreed to. In the meantime, the union had filed section 8(a)(1) and (5) charges against D. The Board found that D had no justification for withdrawing from the bargaining group and ordered D to sign and implement the contract retroactively. The court of appeals enforced the Board's order. The Supreme Court granted certiorari to resolve conflict among the circuits.

   b) **Issue.** Does a bargaining impasse justify withdrawal from an employers' bargaining unit?

   c) **Held.** No. Judgment affirmed.

   (1) The scope of review of the Board's decision in this case is a limited one.

   (2) Multi-employer bargaining is the preferred way in many industries. The Board's guidelines have been that once negotiations have begun, an employer may not unilaterally withdraw absent unusual circumstances, such as extreme financial pressures or fragmentation of the unit.

   (3) We agree with the Board that an impasse, which is a recurring feature of bargaining and is usually short-lived, is not such a rupture of the bargaining relationship as to justify unilateral withdrawal. Allowing withdrawal at impasse would undermine the utility of multi-employer bargaining.

   (4) We also agree with the Board that the execution of a temporary interim agreement during impasse is not such an unusual circumstance that would justify withdrawal. Such agreements, which will be subject to the final multi-employer agreement, do not fragment the unit or significantly weaken it.

(5) The Board's reasons are surely adequate to survive judicial review.

g. **"Coalition" bargaining.**

1) **Introduction.** Where one large employer deals with several unions, one way of strengthening a union's bargaining position is to coordinate its bargaining efforts with the other unions.

2) **Employer must bargain--General Electric Co. v. NLRB,** 412 F.2d 512 (2d Cir. 1969).

    General Electric Co. v. NLRB

    a) **Facts.** General Electric Company (D) refused to bargain with the International Union of Electrical, Radio and Machine Workers because seven out of eight members of its bargaining committee were members of other unions who also bargained with D. The purpose of the group was to formulate national goals. The NLRB found no bad faith, conspiracy, or joint bargaining and held that D's refusal to bargain with the committee constituted a violation of sections 8(a)(1) and (5). P appeals.

    b) **Issue.** Can an employer refuse to bargain with a committee comprised of members of other unions?

    c) **Held.** No. Judgment affirmed.

    (1) Section 7 allows employees to choose whomever they want to represent them in negotiations. The fact that the committee had members of other unions, standing alone, did not justify D's refusal to bargain.

    (2) Absent evidence of a conspiracy to ignore bargaining unit lines or other ulterior or improper motives, unions can coordinate their efforts to increase their strength.

    d) **Comment.** Multi-union bargaining committees can strengthen a union's position by confronting an employer with a united front similar to the multi-employer units discussed *supra*.

3. **Representation Elections.**

    a. **Introduction.** Regional Directors have been delegated the authority to decide whether a question of representation exists, to determine the appropriate bargaining unit, and to rule on objections and challenges after an election.

    b. **Review.** The Regional Director's decision will be reviewed by the Board on the following grounds:

    (i) For alleged departures from official Board precedents;

    (ii) To reconsider important rules or policies; and

(iii) To hear a claim of prejudicial error in determining the facts.

Review will not stay the Regional Director's action unless specifically ordered. The Supreme Court held in *Magnesium Casting v. NLRB*, 401 U.S. 137 (1971), that the Board is *not* required to give "plenary review" to a Regional Director's determination concerning the scope of an appropriate bargaining unit; the delegation of this authority by the Board to its Regional Directors was proper.

c. **Meaning of a "majority."** A majority is relative to the number of those voting, *not* to all employees in the unit. When more than two unions are on the ballot and none receives a majority, a runoff election between the two highest is held (in which one selection may be "no union").

d. **Eligibility to vote: economic strikers.**

1) **Early NLRB view.** Strikers, in economic strikes, were allowed to vote. The idea was that the employees preserved their status during the strike. Later, the Board took the position that both strikers and their replacements should be able to vote.

2) **Taft-Hartley Act.** The Taft-Hartley Act states that employees on strike who are not entitled to reinstatement shall not be eligible to vote. Legally, permanently replaced economic strikers are not entitled to reinstatement. This means that not all strikers can vote.

a) The Taft-Hartley Act had little adverse effect on union activity from 1947 to 1959, since employment was very high from 1947 to 1959 and employers could not readily replace strikers.

b) In 1959, the statute was amended. Employees not entitled to reinstatement could vote (under rules set up by the Board) when the election was conducted within 12 months of the beginning of the strike. [*See* §9(c)(3)] The idea was that all of these workers have an interest in the outcome of the election. (In fact, whether the strikers go back to work or the replacements stay on after the strike would depend on the outcome of the union-employer strike settlement.)

e. **Unfair labor practice strikers.** All of such strikers are eligible to vote.

4. **Review of Representation Proceedings.**

a. **Introduction.** NLRA section 9(d) provides that judicial review of Board rulings on certification and decertification shall occur only when such review is incidental to an unfair labor practice charge (such as a refusal to bargain). Section 10 provides that only a "person aggrieved by a final order" may obtain review of such rulings.

The result is that NLRB rulings in this area are subject to judicial review only after (i) a party to the election files an unfair labor practice charge with respect to the election, and (ii) the Board issues a "final order" with respect to that charge. An employer may refuse to bargain in order to provide the basis for reviewing a representation order.

b. **Effect.** If the Board refuses to hear the unfair labor practice charges, any direct review of a Board determination on certification under the NLRA is foreclosed.

c. **Relief in equity.** However, apart from the judicial review authorized by the NLRA, federal district courts have original jurisdiction (under 28 U.S.C. section 1337) to hear any claim "arising under the laws of the United States." Pursuant thereto, a federal district court may grant equitable relief with respect to NLRB determinations in representation cases (*i.e.*, compelling or restraining an election) upon a showing that the Board's action was contrary to the NLRA (a "law of the United States") and has caused or threatens to cause an irreparable injury or deprivation of a right.

d. **Application of jurisdiction--Leedom v. Kyne,** 358 U.S. 184 (1958). — Leedom v. Kyne

   1) **Facts.** An association representing 233 professional employees sought certification. Another union representing technical employees intervened and asked that the professional unit be expanded to include some of its members. Although the NLRB found that the employees of the intervening union were not professional employees, the Board allowed nine of them to be included in the new unit without allowing the professional employees to vote on their inclusion. Section 9(b)(1) prohibits certification of a unit that includes both professional and nonprofessional employees without a vote by the professionals. The association representing the professionals (P) filed suit in federal district court against the NLRB (D) to set aside the determination. The lower court held for P, and the court of appeals affirmed. D appeals.

   2) **Issue.** May a federal district court set aside an NLRB certification order in direct conflict with section 9(b)(1)?

   3) **Held.** Yes. Judgment affirmed.

       a) Even though an NLRB order under section 9 certification is not a final order and hence is nonreviewable, the district court has jurisdiction to strike down a certification order made in excess of the Board's jurisdiction.

       b) The district court, under the circumstances of this case, has jurisdiction to protect the employees' rights guaranteed by the NLRA by invalidating any NLRB order clearly contrary to the NLRA and therefore in excess of its jurisdiction.

   4) **Dissent** (Brennan, Frankfurter, JJ.). The legislative history shows a considered congressional intent to restrict judicial review of representational certifications. Although the issue was debated during the Taft-Hartley amendments, only indirect access to judicial review was retained. Today's decision opens a gaping hole in the congressional wall against direct resort to the courts.

   5) **Comment.** When an order involves an alleged abuse of discretion by the Board, no judicial review is possible. Such review is appropriate only where the order in question is in excess of the Board's powers. [*See* Boire v. Greyhound Corp., 376 U.S. 473 (1964)]

5. **Alternates to Board-Conducted Elections.**

   a. **Introduction.** Aside from a Board-conducted representation election, other modes of attaining representation status include: (i) voluntary recognition of a union having majority support in an appropriate unit, and (ii) a bargaining order mandated by the Board to remedy an unfair labor practice of the sort that would make a fair election appear unlikely.

   NLRB v. Gissel Packing Co.

   1) **Fair election unlikely--NLRB v. Gissel Packing Co.,** 395 U.S. 575 (1969).

      a) **Facts.** Several cases were consolidated here for review. In three cases, employers refused to bargain with unions having authorization cards from a majority of the employees. The employers then waged anti-union campaigns and committed numerous alleged unfair labor practices. In each case, the Board found that the employers' doubt as to the union's majority status was not based on "good faith" and therefore ordered the employers to bargain despite the absence of an election in two cases and the employer's victory in an election in the third case. The Fourth Circuit Court of Appeals refused to enforce the Board's orders. In another case, the company declined a union's request for representative status on the basis that the authorization cards were inherently unreliable. An election was called. Before this and prior to the election, which the union lost, the employer waged a vigorous anti-union campaign that violated section 8(a)(1). The Board set the election aside and ordered the company to bargain. The First Circuit Court of Appeals sustained the Board's order. The Supreme Court granted certiorari to resolve the conflict between the two circuits.

      b) **Issues.**

         (1) May a bargaining obligation be established by means other than an election?

         (2) May authorization cards be used to indicate employees' desires regarding representation?

         (3) Is a bargaining order a proper remedy for employer refusals to bargain where independent unfair labor practices have made the holding of a fair election unlikely or have undermined a union's majority?

      c) **Held.** Yes as to all three issues.

         (1) Both the original and the amended acts indicate that a representative may be "designated or selected" by a majority.

            (a) Almost from the beginning, it has been recognized that a union does not have to be certified by the Board to invoke a bargaining obligation. Majority status may be established by other means such as participation in a strike or strike vote or by authorization cards.

      (b) While section 9(c) may permit an employer to test good faith doubts by petitioning for an election, it was not intended to relieve the employer of its obligation to bargain with a majority representative.

  (2) While cards are inferior to the election process, they can adequately reflect employee sentiments even though the employer has not had the opportunity to present its side and even though cards may on occasion be obtained by misrepresentation.

  (3) This Court has recognized the Board's authority to issue a bargaining order where a union has lost its majority status due to substantial pervasive and outrageous misconduct on the part of the employer.

      (a) Our holding today approves use of a bargaining order in less extraordinary circumstances that nevertheless still have a tendency to undermine majority strength and impede the election process.

      (b) There is still a third category of less extensive or minor misconduct that will not support a bargaining order.

  d) **Comment.** On remand, the NLRB held that in each case, the employer's conduct had constituted such an unfair labor practice that a fair election was impossible. Each employer was ordered to bargain.

2) *Cumberland Shoe* **doctrine.** In *Cumberland Shoe Corp.*, 144 N.L.R.B. 1268 (1964), the Board considered some problems concerning the solicitation of authorization cards. If the card is itself unambiguous (*i.e.*, it states on its face that the signer authorizes the union to represent the employee for bargaining purposes and not merely to seek an election), it will be counted in determining whether the union had majority status. However, if it is proven that the employee was told that the card would be used solely for the purpose of obtaining an election, it will not be counted in determining whether the union had majority status. In other words, the language of the card will control unless the solicitor makes representations calculated to make the signer disregard the language on the card.

3) **Criteria for bargaining orders.** In *NLRB v. General Stencils, Inc.*, 438 F.2d 894 (2d Cir. 1971), the court of appeals criticized the Board for a persistent failure to establish criteria by which to determine whether employer misconduct was serious enough to warrant a bargaining order, either by way of a rulemaking procedure or a pronouncement of a general rule in a case or greater explanation in each case. The Board failed to develop a general rule on remand, although Chairman Miller, in dissent, attempted to do so. Miller recognized two circumstances that would justify a bargaining order: (i) grant of significant benefits, and (ii) persistent violations of section 8(a)(3). The Second Circuit Court of Appeals and other circuits continue to criticize the Board's approach.

4) **Union never had majority.** In *Gourmet Foods, Inc. v. Warehouse Employees of St. Paul*, 270 N.L.R.B. 578 (1984), the Board ruled that it has no authority

to issue a bargaining order under any circumstances if the union has not had a majority support at some time in the past. A dissenting member asserted that a nonmajority order would be justified in circumstances so coercive that a majority support could never develop.

Linden Lumber Division, Summer & Co. v. NLRB

5) **Bargaining order not warranted--Linden Lumber Division, Summer & Co. v. NLRB,** 419 U.S. 301 (1974).

   a) **Facts.** The union secured signatures of 12 employees, claimed a bargaining unit of 12, and sought recognition from the employer (D). D claimed that two employees were "supervisors" and suggested that the union seek an election. The union eventually went on strike. Upon termination of the strike, D refused to rehire one "supervisor" (claiming that he had quit) and one other striker (for violence). The union filed a section 8(a)(5) action for refusal to recognize and bargain. The Board ruled that no violation of section 8(a)(5) was shown, and the union appeals.

   b) **Issue.** Did the employer violate section 8(a)(5) by either refusing to rehire the two employees or refusing to bargain prior to an election?

   c) **Held.** No. A section 8(a)(5) action will not lie.

      (1) D's violations (such as not rehiring the two employees) did not have such an effect that a fair election could not be held.

      (2) Mere refusal to bargain on the basis of a card showing is not enough for a section 8(a)(5) violation.

         (a) It is not wise for a court to try and determine the extent of employer knowledge and its intent at the time it refuses to accede to a union demand for recognition.

         (b) The union and the employer never decided on a mutually acceptable means (other than an election) to determine majority status.

      (3) The union has two choices: (i) it can file a petition for an election, which can be held in a matter of months; or (ii) it can file an unfair labor practice charge, which may take years to complete.

      (4) There is no indication that the statutory option given to employers to petition for an election was designed to place upon the employer the burden of getting a secret election.

   d) **Dissent** (Stewart, White, Marshall, Powell, JJ.). The language of the Act seems purposefully designed to impose a duty on an employer to bargain when presented with convincing evidence of majority support. In such circumstances, the employer should voluntarily recognize and deal with the union or file an election petition, or run the risk of a section 8(a)(5) violation.

Brooks v. NLRB

6) **Duration of the representative's authority--Brooks v. NLRB,** 348 U.S. 96 (1954).

a) **Facts.** The union won the election, and a week later, a majority of the employees wrote the employer saying that they no longer wished to be represented by the union. Brooks (D), the employer, then refused to bargain with the union. The NLRB found that D had committed an unfair labor practice by refusing to bargain. The court of appeals enforced the order to bargain, and D appeals.

b) **Issue.** Is an employer required to bargain with a union that loses a majority of employees shortly after being certified?

c) **Held.** Yes. Judgment affirmed.

   (1) The Board-established rule that, once a union is certified, it must be honored as the bargaining representative for a "reasonable period" is justified. Once this period is up, the employer can question the union's majority by refusing to bargain. The "reasonable period" is appropriate for the following reasons:

   (a) The binding effect of the election promotes a sense of responsibility in the electorate;

   (b) Union revocation should be as solemn a procedure as is union affirmation;

   (c) The union should have a chance to carry out its program without pressure to get immediate results; and

   (d) It promotes good faith bargaining by the employer who knows that attempts to undermine union support will be useless.

   (2) Even if there were no "reasonable period" requirement and a majority of the employees disavowed the union as representative, the recourse would be to the Board and not to self-help.

d) **Comments.**

   (1) Other decisions have held that the reasonable period of one year means an actual bargaining period. If the employer delays and refuses to bargain, it cannot run out the period and ask for another election; the bargaining period will be extended.

   (2) There is a prima facie presumption of continued majority status following the expiration of a "certification year" or a labor agreement. This is designed to promote stability in the bargaining relationship. It can be rebutted by showing either that the union in fact no longer enjoys majority status or that the employer's refusal was based on a good faith and reasonably grounded doubt of continued majority status. [See Bartenders Association, 213 N.L.R.B. 651 (1974)] In contract expiration cases, the presumption applies whether the union's

bargaining status was certified by the Board or was established by other ways. The employer also must demonstrate a good faith doubt in order to initiate an election petition.

b. **Where successor acquires business other than by merger or purchase of assets.** An employer may occasionally replace another employer without a formal merger or sale of assets, and yet the new employer will properly be considered a "successor" in terms of continuity of the business.

1) **Unfair labor practice proceedings.** In the leading case in this area (below), an unfair labor practice charge was filed against the new bidder for security guard services for refusing to bargain with the union representing the former bidder's employees and for not honoring the existing contract. The Supreme Court held that the union could *not* enforce arbitration provisions in the contract despite a substantial continuity in business operations and work force between the prior employer and its successor.

2) **Presumption concerning preferences of strike replacements--NLRB v. Curtin Matheson Scientific, Inc.,** 494 U.S. 775 (1990).

   a) **Facts.** In 1970, Teamsters Local 968 (P) was certified as the bargaining agent for Curtin Matheson Scientific, Inc.'s (D's) employees. Negotiations for the 1979 agreement broke down and D locked out the 27 employees of the bargaining unit. P began an economic strike. Five employees crossed the picket line and within two weeks, 29 employees had been hired as permanent striker replacements. Shortly afterwards, D withdrew its last offer and notified P that it was withdrawing recognition of P, saying that it doubted P's majority status. P filed a charge and the Board found that D had insufficient objective basis to doubt P's continued majority support. The Board refused to adopt any presumption in respect to the wishes of strike replacements, deciding rather to consider each case on its own facts. The Board noted that D had relied on the expressed sentiment of only one employee replacement and found sections 8(a)(1) and (5) violations. The court of appeals refused to enforce, adopting a presumption that strike replacements generally can be assumed not to support the incumbent union. The Supreme Court granted certiorari.

   b) **Issue.** Was it an abuse of discretion for the Board to refuse to adopt a presumption of striker replacement opposition to the union in cases concerned with the continuation of majority support?

   c) **Held.** No. Judgment reversed.

      (1) Upon certification, a union enjoys an irrebuttable presumption of continuing majority support for a year. After that period, an employer may refuse to bargain with the union by showing that the union has in fact lost its majority status or by showing a sufficient objective basis for doubting the union's majority status.

      (2) The question in this case is whether D presented sufficient evidence to show a good faith doubt. The Board's approach to

this problem has changed from time to time. In 1987, it decided that a presumption one way or the other was not justified. The Board has primary responsibility for developing and applying labor policy, and we will grant it considerable deference.

(3) The no-presumption rule has a rational basis. D's arguments that the striker replacements' and the union's interests are invariably opposed is unpersuasive. The Board's approach is also consistent with the policies of the Act—attaining industrial peace. An anti-union presumption would encourage an employer to hire sufficient replacements to eliminate a union. It would permit the strike to be used as a union breaking device, thereby chilling the use of the strike.

d) **Concurrence** (Rehnquist, C.J.). This case pushes deference to the Board to its outer limits.

e) **Dissent** (Scalia, O'Connor, Kennedy, JJ.). The Board sharply limits the employer's ability to satisfy its doubts by questioning employees. The Board's presumption should be treated as an inference of fact, and there is not enough evidence in this case to support it.

III. COLLECTIVE BARGAINING

A. NEGOTIATING THE COLLECTIVE BARGAINING AGREEMENT

Once the bargaining unit and the bargaining representative have been determined, the process of bargaining itself must begin. The give and take of collective bargaining between the employer and the union is relied upon to achieve economic stability and growth. Through contract, therefore, American labor law is designed to implement and compel this process wherever possible.

1. **Scope of Union Negotiating Authority.** Once a union has been selected by a majority of employees in the bargaining unit, it has exclusive authority to represent all employees in the unit on matters that are properly the subject of collective bargaining. [NLRA §9(a)]

   a. **Individual contracts superseded on matters covered by collective agreement.** The employer may not negotiate individual contracts with employees, nor may it use the existence of individual contracts before certification as grounds for refusing to bargain with the union.

   b. **No exceptions.** Not even "exceptional circumstances" will justify negotiating with individuals where a certified representative and a collective agreement exist.

      1) **Example.** In *Order of Railroad Telegraphers v. Railway Express Agency*, 321 U.S. 342 (1944), the defendant-employer took over another company and assumed that company's obligations under a collective bargaining agreement. When the defendant instituted certain changes in freight handling, a few uniquely situated employees became entitled to huge salary increases under the existing agreement—a situation clearly not envisioned when that agreement was entered into. The employer proceeded to negotiate new individual contracts with the employees affected without consulting the union. These individual contracts were held invalid. The Court reasoned that the "exceptional circumstances" affecting the individual employee might well have permitted the union to obtain concessions on other matters of concern to all employees. Note that while the *Telegraphers* case was decided under the Railway Labor Act, the result would be the same for areas governed by the NLRA.

2. **Individual Contracts Permitted Where Not in Conflict with Collective Agreement.** In *Telegraphers, supra*, the Supreme Court recognized that individual contracts between employers and employees might be valid in certain limited situations.

J.I. Case Co. v. NLRB

   a. **No justification for refusal to bargain--J.I. Case Co. v. NLRB,** 321 U.S. 332 (1944).

      1) **Facts.** For many years, J.I. Case Company (P) offered each employee a uniform contract for employment. P claimed these individual contracts as a bar to representation proceedings when

a CIO union petitioned for certification as the exclusive bargaining representative. The NLRB (D), however, directed an election, which was won by the union. P still refused to bargain until contracts expired, declaring that it could not deal with the union while the individual contracts were in effect, except for specific matters not affecting items covered by the contracts. D declared that P had refused to bargain collectively in violation of section 8(5) of the NLRA.

2) **Issue.** Does an employer commit an unfair labor practice under section 8(5) if it refuses to bargain until individual contracts made prior to unionization expire?

3) **Held.** Yes. Judgment affirmed.

   a) The individual contracts cannot be effective as waivers of any benefit to which the employee would be entitled under a trade agreement.

   b) The very purpose of provision by statute for collective agreements is to supersede the terms of separate agreements of employees with terms that reflect the strength and bargaining power and serve the welfare of the group.

   c) Individual contracts may embody matters that are not necessarily included within the scope of collective bargaining, such as stock purchase or medical attention, but employers must not diminish their own obligations or increase the employees' obligations in matters covered by collective bargaining.

4) **Comments.**

   a) Individual agreements are, of course, valid and enforceable where collective bargaining does not exist (*i.e.*, where no representative has been recognized as the exclusive bargaining agent for employees). Even where a collective agreement exists, individual contracts on matters not covered by and/or not inconsistent with the agreement are permitted. For example, the collective agreement might set minimum wage rates and permit individual negotiation for better terms by employees with special skills.

   b) At all times, the collective agreement is paramount. The employer may not, by negotiations with individual employees, reduce its own obligations under the agreement, increase the obligations of the employees, or otherwise take away concessions obtained by the union.

3. **Section 9(a) Supersedes Section 7 Rights of Individual Employees.** Moreover, where a union has exclusive authority under section 9(a) to represent all employees in the unit, individual employees who engage in concerted activities without union approval are not protected from discipline (including discharge) by section 7.

Emporium Capwell Co. v. Western Addition Community Organization

a. **No individual bargaining of discrimination claim--Emporium Capwell Co. v. Western Addition Community Organization,** 420 U.S. 50 (1975).

1) **Facts.** Emporium Capwell Company (D), a department store, and the union entered a collective bargaining agreement that prohibited employment discrimination on the basis of race and contained a no-strike clause and a grievance system for handling and arbitrating violations of the antidiscrimination provision. When a group of D's black employees submitted a list of grievances against D for racial discrimination in making assignments and promotions, the union agreed to press charges and notified Emporium that arbitration over this matter was needed. However, the black employees attempted to negotiate directly with D, objecting to the philosophy of correcting inequities on an individual level of the bargaining agreement, but D refused to negotiate. Two of the black employees picketed the store, urging consumer boycott, and were fired when they ignored D's warning that they would be fired unless they discontinued picketing. Western Addition Community Organization (P), a civil rights association of which the two fired employees were members, filed against D. The Board held that the employees' activity leading to their discharge was not protected by section 7 and the discharge did not violate section 8(a). The court of appeals reversed, in reliance on the national antidiscrimination labor policy as reflected in the NLRA and Title VII of the Civil Rights Act of 1964. D appeals.

2) **Issue.** May minority employees charging employer racial discrimination circumvent their union and negotiate this matter directly with the employer?

3) **Held.** No. Judgment reversed.

   a) Minority interests in union affairs sometimes become subordinated to the interests of the majority rule to heighten the union's collective strength and bargaining power.

   b) However, the minority was not intended to be tyrannized. Unions must be based on common interests; unions are democratic institutions in which minority interests can be heard and the elected bargaining representative has the duty to give fair representation to the minority voices of its unit.

   c) The bargaining contract involved in this case prohibited employer racial discrimination and provided for grievance and arbitration procedures to remedy any such violations. Section 7 does not require fragmentation of the bargaining unit along racial lines in order to be consistent with national labor policy against discrimination.

   d) It is unreasonable to assume that the processing of discrimination grievances is limited only to individual cases. It is unlikely that an employer continually confronted with arbitration decisions against him would indefinitely continue a discriminatory practice.

   e) If there is evidence that the two fired employees were discharged on discriminatory grounds. they can file for relief under Title VII with the Equal Employment Opportunity Commission.

4) **Dissent** (Douglas, J.). These were "concerted activities" protected by section 7. The employees are made prisoners of the union. They should be able to protect their jobs if it is shown that the union is not prosecuting their complaints fully and expeditiously.

5) **Comment.** Where employer discipline in such cases violates Title VII of the Civil Rights Act, the employees may seek relief under the provisions of that Act, but the employer cannot be charged with an unfair labor practice under NLRA section 8(a)(1).

4. **Limitations on Union Authority and Majority Rule.** Recognizing that the power resulting from the union's exclusive bargaining authority may invite abuse, however, the law also provides certain safeguards against unfair treatment by the union of individuals or groups within the bargaining unit.

   a. **Exclusion of employees.** In determining an appropriate unit, the Board will exclude employees not having a community of interest or having conflicting interests.

   b. **Duty to employees.** Note that the union has broad discretion but it also has a duty to bargain fairly on behalf of all employees, including nonmembers, and that its failure to do so may be an unfair labor practice.

   c. **Decertification.** A union may be ousted by a decertification election.

   d. **Landrum-Griffin Act.** The Landrum-Griffin Act provides protective standards and procedures to assure proper conduct of union internal affairs.

   e. **Membership.** Unit members will not automatically become members of the union. A *unit* member must become a *union* member only if the employer and the union negotiate a proper collective bargaining provision making membership a condition of continued employment.

   f. **Nonmandatory subjects.** Nonmandatory subjects may be adjusted by individual or minority "bargaining."

   g. **Additional safeguards.** An additional safeguard is provided by NLRA section 9(a), which permits employees to present and adjust grievances directly with the employer, as long as (i) the adjustment is not inconsistent with the collective agreement, and (ii) the union is given the opportunity to be present at the adjustment. It is not clear, however, whether an employee may seek assistance from a rival union in pressing her grievance.

   h. **Racial discrimination by union.** The union's duty to represent fairly all members of the bargaining unit was first recognized in cases where the union itself was involved in racial discrimination.

      1) **Duty owed to all employees in unit--Steele v. Louisville & Nashville Railroad Co.,** 323 U.S. 192 (1944).

         a) **Facts.** The Brotherhood was elected to be the exclusive bargaining agent for railroad firemen. By requiring railroad companies to negotiate with the bargaining agent elected by a

Steele v. Louisville & Nashville Railroad Co.

craft majority, the Railway Labor Act bars other unions from representing the craft, but does not stipulate in what manner the bargaining agent should conduct itself in carrying out its role. The black firemen (Ps), bound by the Act to uphold the Brotherhood as their agent, at the same time were not allowed membership in the union. When the carriers (Ds) and the Brotherhood agreed to the phasing out of all black firemen from the craft, Ps attempted to get an injunction against the Brotherhood for a declaratory judgment and damages as long as the Brotherhood's discriminatory practices continued, and an injunction against enforcement of the union-railroad agreement. The Alabama trial court issued a demurrer to their suit and Ps appeal.

b) **Issue.** Is the collective bargaining agent of a craft required by the Railway Labor Act to carry out its duties without discrimination for all of those it represents?

c) **Held.** Yes. Judgment reversed.

(1) As the Railway Labor Act stipulates that a bargaining representative represents the entire craft and not just the majority that elected it, that representative is obliged to not discriminate against nonunion members in agreements in which it is their representative.

(2) Unions under the Act are not prevented from entering agreements which might not have positive effects for all craft members, but the line is not drawn on the basis of race, but on employee issues such as seniority, competence, skill, etc.

d) **Comments.**

(1) The same result has also been reached under NLRA section 9(a) in *Wallace Corp. v. NLRB*, 323 U.S. 248 (1944). And in *Brotherhood of Railroad Trainmen v. Howard*, 343 U.S. 768 (1952), the Court applied the same doctrine where the union had pressured the employer to discharge black workers who were not union members, but who held jobs in the bargaining unit that the union purported to represent. The Court stressed the fact that the union's duty of fair representation extended not only to union members, but to ***all*** members of the bargaining unit—specifically including nonunion members.

(2) A union has the discretion to negotiate in a way that makes reasonable distinctions among the interests and circumstances of categories of employees within the unit. Thus an agreement may affect individuals and groups of employees differently. A wide range of reasonableness must be allowed the union in serving the unit. It may make distinctions which are "within the reasonable bounds of relevancy" in respect to wages and working conditions.

5. **The Duty to Bargain in Good Faith.** NLRA section 8(d) requires the employer and the union to meet and confer at reasonable times, and also to bargain "in good faith." This applies both to the employer and the union.

a. **Statutory policy behind the "good faith" requirement.** Unless the employer was forced to bargain meaningfully with the union, the employer could simply "talk a weak union to death," thereby frustrating the goals of mutual negotiation and industrial peace. The same reasoning is applied to relatively strong unions.

b. **The "good faith" standard.** Each party must make a sincere effort to reach agreement, and must participate in negotiations to that end by meeting at reasonable times.

c. **Deadlocked negotiations.** Good faith means more than merely going through the motions of bargaining. When it appears that there is a deadlock and further discussion would be fruitless, an "impasse" has been reached, and further meetings may be broken off until circumstances change sufficiently to break the deadlock.

d. **Present intent to agree.** "Good faith" contemplates an active participation in deliberations evincing a present intention to find a basis for agreement and a sincere effort to find a common ground. But section 8(d) does not compel either party to accept a proposal or make a concession.

e. **Subjective intent.** Good faith is a subjective intent and usually depends on external manifestations.

f. **"Bad faith."** "Bad faith" may be demonstrated by the substantive nature of proposals made by a party or by the tactics and conduct employed.

g. **Look to conduct of the parties.** The approach in each case is to consider the total course of conduct of the party, rather than isolated actions. Thus, a violation of section 8(d) may result from the "sum" of several incidents that, looked at separately, might not establish bad faith.

h. **Inferences of "bad faith."** While each case must be judged on its own facts, the Board and the courts will infer bad faith in certain situations. In these situations, the actual motives of the party are irrelevant.

   1) **Content of proposals.** The NLRB may look at the reasonableness of the proposal in determining whether the proposal was adopted for the purpose of frustrating negotiations and preventing agreement.

      a) **Employer retains full authority.** An employer proposal that offers terms that no responsible employee representative could accept raises an inference of bad faith. In *Alba-Waldensian, Inc.*, 167 N.L.R.B. No. 101 (1967), the employer proposed to retain absolute authority over wages while depriving the union of any effective weapon to protest grievances. Bad faith was found.

      b) **Employees lose benefits.** Likewise, a proposal that would result in employees receiving *less* at the end of the year following certification than they had received before the union became their bargaining agent demonstrates a refusal to bargain in good faith.

   2) **Conduct or tactics in negotiations.** A variety of negotiating tactics by employers may constitute "bad faith" bargaining.

a) **Dilatory tactics.** Where an employer uses dilatory tactics, simply shifting position whenever an agreement seemed to have been reached, he may be found guilty of "bad faith" bargaining. However, an employer's withdrawing earlier offers does not in itself indicate bad faith, where none of his earlier proposals had been unconditionally accepted by the union.

b) **Demands that union drop pending charges.** In *NLRB v. Southwestern Porcelain Steel Corp.*, 317 F.2d 527 (10th Cir. 1963), the court found that an employer was not bargaining in good faith when it made no effort to conclude an agreement and threatened to postpone negotiations until the union withdrew certain unfair labor practice charges it had lodged against the employer.

c) **"Take it or leave it" proposals.** An employer who maintains a "take it or leave it" attitude in negotiations may have engaged in bad faith bargaining. Such proposals were the basis for the trilogy of cases involving the General Electric Co., which have established much of the law in the area of "bad faith" bargaining.

3) **Inference of bad faith from subject matter--NLRB v. A-1 King Size Sandwiches, Inc.**, 732 F.2d 872 (11th Cir. 1984), *cert. denied,* 469 U.S. 1035 (1984).

a) **Facts.** Local 737 (P) was the certified bargaining agent for A-1 King Size Sandwiches, Inc. (D) employees. The certification was unsuccessfully challenged. After 18 bargaining sessions over 11 months, no agreement had been reached, though some terms had been agreed upon, such as union access, union stewards, bulletin boards, days off, and grievance and arbitration. D's bargaining position was to retain unilateral control of the more important terms and conditions of employment. P filed charges, claiming that D had engaged in surface bargaining. The ALJ found D in violation of sections 8(a)(1) and (5). The Board agreed, and D appeals.

b) **Issue.** Can the content of an employer's bargaining proposals together with the positions it has taken be sufficient to demonstrate it has no real intent to reach an agreement?

c) **Held.** Yes. Judgment affirmed.

(1) The question before us is a narrow one, and we defer to the Board to make the initial determination; we review to determine if there is substantial evidence to support its findings. P met at reasonable times and places, and there is no evidence that D engaged in any other conduct to show that it did not intend to reach an agreement. The Act does not require either party to reach an agreement and the Board cannot compel them to do so or to make any concession. However, the duty to bargain in good faith requires more than engagement in sterile discussion, and the board may consider the substance of proposals that the parties have made.

(2) D proposed to retain its old way of total control over pay and merit increases, giving P only consultative rights. P could not grieve or strike over wage matters or even discuss them because of the proposed zipper clause.

(3) The management rights clause would give D the absolute right to subcontract work or to assign work to supervisors. D could abolish jobs, transfer, discontinue, or assign its operations and P would waive its statutory right to bargain about or discuss these decisions.

(4) The grievance and arbitration clauses were illusory since they were limited only to the few express rights that are conferred by the proposed contract. Discharge and discipline decisions would not be grievable. The zipper clause would prevent further bargaining for the life of the agreement. The no-strike clause would prohibit all strikes, including unfair labor practice strikes. Lay-offs and recalls would be solely at D's discretion.

(5) It is clear that after months of bargaining, D insisted on unilateral control over virtually all significant terms and conditions of employment. D crossed the line of good faith bargaining into a position of obstructionist intransigence. D would deny P any voice over mandatory subjects. When P objected to the breadth of the initial management rights clause, D countered with an even broader one. Bad faith was properly inferred from D's insistence upon unusually harsh, unreasonable and unworkable terms. P and the employees would have had substantially fewer rights than if they had merely relied on P's certification.

d) **Comment.** Some courts of appeals have reversed the Board's finding of bad faith, emphasizing that the Act does not compel agreement or require concessions, or have recognized that a particular position was "genuinely and sincerely" held. Hard bargaining from a position of economic strength has not been accepted as proof of bad faith.

i. **Duty to disclose information.** In *NLRB v. Truitt Manufacturing Co.*, 351 U.S. 149 (1956), the Supreme Court ruled that when an employer refuses a wage demand by raising a claim of economic inability during bargaining, good faith requires the employer to allow the union to examine the employer's confidential books and records if the union requests. The Court said that if such an argument is important enough to assert, it is important enough to produce proof of its accuracy. The Court indicated that each case must be considered on its own facts. This duty to share information carries over into the administration of the contract, including grievance processing, once it is entered. [*See* NLRB v. Acme Industrial Co., 385 U.S. 432 (1967)]

j. **Balancing against the interests of others--Detroit Edison Co. v. NLRB,** 440 U.S. 301 (1979).

> Detroit Edison Co. v. NLRB

1) **Facts.** In preparing for the arbitration of a grievance over promotions, the union requested information about employee aptitude tests. Detroit Edison (P) supplied the information except for: (i) actual test questions, (ii) actual employee answer sheets, and (iii) scores of employees by name without a waiver by each employee. An unfair labor practice charge was filed. The NLRB (D), which determined that the items were relevant and useful to processing the grievance, ordered that the information be given to the

union. The court of appeals enforced the order, and P appeals.

2) **Issue.** Does D have remedial discretionary powers to order that the test and answer sheets and the employees' actual scores be given to the union?

3) **Held.** No. Judgment reversed.

   a) With regard to the test and answer sheets, the "remedy selected by [D] does not adequately protect the security of the tests." P had spent considerable time and money to validate the tests and answer sheets and the security of the results is necessary to assure their reliability.

   b) The restrictions imposed to protect secrecy are not likely to be effective, because the union was not a party to the enforcement proceedings and would be beyond the reach of the court of appeals. D abused its discretion when it provided such scant protection.

   c) With respect to the individual scores, even though they may be relevant, it was improper for D to require disclosure of the scores without the consent of the individual employees.

   d) It was not improper for P to unilaterally promise confidentiality. The sensitivity of such information can readily be noticed and the slight burden on the union to obtain consents from the employees does not outweigh the need for security of the information.

4) **Dissent** (White, Brennan, Marshall, JJ.). The Board did not abuse its remedial discretion.

   a) D had sound grounds for concluding that the union would respect the restrictions about releasing the tests and answer sheets to employees, and the majority minimizes the usefulness of the tests and answer sheets to the union in the administration of the bargaining agreement.

   b) In respect to test scores, there was no evidence that employee sensitivities would be abused by disclosure. The burden for justifying nondisclosure should be on the company.

   c) D should balance the considerations of confidentiality with the union's representational obligations and the enforcement of the agreement.

k. **Work slowdown not bad faith--NLRB v. Insurance Agents' International Union,** 361 U.S. 477 (1960).

1) **Facts.** Collective negotiations themselves were carried on in good faith between an employer and a union for six months. However, during the course of negotiations, the union members (Ds) engaged in a work slow-

down. The employer filed a complaint under section 8(b)(3)—refusal to bargain collectively. The NLRB (P) issued a cease and desist order holding that irrespective of Ds' good faith in conferring with the employer at the bargaining table, its tactics were a per se violation of section 8(b)(3). The court of appeals refused to enforce P's order, and P appeals.

2) **Issue.** May the NLRB order a union to cease and desist from applying economic pressure to employers?

3) **Held.** No. Judgment affirmed.

   a) There is no inconsistency between the application of economic pressure and good faith collective bargaining; it is part of that process.

   b) Therefore, P exceeded its power by inferring a lack of good faith, not from deficiencies in the union's performance at the bargaining table, but solely because of the tactics used to exert economic pressure, even if they involved unprotected activity.

4) **Comment.** Each case must be judged on its own facts. However, in certain situations, the Board and the courts can and will infer that certain conduct constitutes "bad faith."

l. **Unilateral change in employment conditions--NLRB v. Katz,** 369 U.S. 736 (1962).

NLRB v. Katz

1) **Facts.** During negotiations, Katz (D) unilaterally made three changes in employment conditions: (i) the number of sick leave days given per year was reduced, but the number allowed to be carried over was increased; (ii) a new wage increase system was implemented, substantially more generous than the one proposed to and rejected by the union during negotiations; and (iii) a merit increase for 40% of the employees was granted. The Board (P), although not finding any bad faith in the negotiations, held that D's conduct had violated the section 8(a)(5) duty to bargain in good faith. The court of appeals reversed, and D appeals.

2) **Issue.** Did D violate the section 8(a)(5) duty to bargain in good faith by unilaterally instituting changes in some of the terms and conditions of employment during negotiations?

3) **Held.** Yes. Judgment reversed.

   a) Even absent bad faith, unilateral action by an employer affecting mandatory subjects of negotiations can be a violation of the section 8(a)(5) duty to bargain in good faith. Such action tends to create uncertainty and factions among the employees, thereby interfering with the union's ability to carry on useful discussion with the employer.

   b) Such action by an employer amounts to a refusal to negotiate those conditions changed and rarely has any economic or business justifica-

Labor Law - 77

tion. While an employer need not lead with its best offer, even after an impasse, the employer cannot in good faith offer wage increases greater than the last offer.

      c) All of the changes involved herein related to "wages, hours . . . or terms and conditions of employment," which section 8(d) makes mandatory subjects of a section 8(a)(5) bargaining.

    4) Comment. Such unilateral actions can be offered if negotiations have broken down to an impasse and if the changes are essentially those offered to the union.

  m. "Boulwarism." It may be an unfair labor practice for an employer to present a carefully researched benefit package and then assume a "take-it-or-leave-it" bargaining position, while at the same time undertaking an extensive publicity campaign directed at both the public and its employees about the merits of the package and indicating that it will not horsetrade or give in to a strike.

  n. Remedies in the event of failure to bargain in good faith. Where the employer *or* the union refuses to bargain in good faith, the NLRB may take "such action as will effectuate the policies of the Act." [NLRA §10(c)] This may consist of a cease-and-desist order to the offending party, or it may entail affirmative steps to remedy the situation.

    1) Board-ordered bargaining. The Board may order the recalcitrant party to bargain in good faith on a specific subject and enforce its order in the courts through the contempt procedure.

    2) Compensatory relief. Similarly, where the refusal to bargain is "clear and flagrant," the NLRB may order limited compensatory relief.

    3) Refusal unfair but not flagrant. However, compensatory relief is not appropriate where the refusal to bargain is less than brazen or flagrant—although still an unfair labor practice.

    4) No forced agreements. However, the Board may not impose or force a party to accept any particular agreement. Thus, the NLRB is not "effectuating NLRA policies" under section 10(c) when it orders an employer to accept a checkoff provision on which the parties could not independently agree.

B. SUBJECTS OF COLLECTIVE BARGAINING

  1. Permissive, Compulsory, and Illegal Subjects of Bargaining. The possible subjects of collective bargaining fall into three categories: (i) those over which bargaining is required by statute (compulsory); (ii) those over which the parties may bargain if they choose (permissive); and (iii) those over which the parties may not bargain under any condition (illegal).

2. **Compulsory Subjects.** NLRA section 8(d) requires employers and unions to bargain collectively on "wages, hours, and other terms and conditions of employment, or the negotiation of an agreement, or any question arising thereunder." Since the Act does not define "wages, hours, and other terms and conditions of employment," the NLRB and the courts must determine what subjects are within the statutory requirement. Examples follow.

   a. **Retirement plan benefits.** Such benefits fall within the meaning of "wages, rate of pay, hours of employment, or other conditions of employment," and therefore are compulsory bargaining subjects for active employees.

      1) **Manner of payment.** However, the manner in which retiree health benefits are paid by the employer (*i.e.*, whether through a union-negotiated insurance plan or a supplemental Medicare premium initiated unilaterally by the employer) is not a mandatory subject for bargaining, since it does not "vitally affect" the terms and conditions for active employees. [Allied Chemical & Alkali Workers v. Pittsburgh Plate Glass Co., *infra*]

   b. **Work assignments.** An employer's refusal to bargain over reclassification and transfer of employees and work assignments violates section 8(d), since a "condition of employment" is involved.

   c. **Grievances.** The area of grievances normally concerns work conditions and is therefore a mandatory subject of bargaining, but the Act permits the settlement of individual grievances without collective bargaining. [NLRA §9(a)]

   d. **Safety rules and practices.** The phrase "other terms and conditions of employment" includes safety rules and practices, and this area is a mandatory subject of bargaining.

      1) **Early practice.** As a practical matter, however, very few substantive protections were incorporated in bargaining agreements prior to 1970. In most contracts, a "management rights" clause gave the employer unilateral control over safety and health; employees were obliged to seek relief "after the fact" through workers' compensation programs for injuries incurred on the job.

      2) **Occupational Safety and Health Act.** In 1970, Congress passed the Occupational Safety and Health Act ("OSHA") in response to increasing industrial accidents and health hazards. Basically, the Act empowers the Secretary of Labor to establish health and safety standards, to investigate complaints of employees and issue citations to employers for violation of such standards, and to seek penalties for uncorrected violations from the OSHA Review Commission. Commission rulings in turn are subject to judicial review by United States courts of appeals.

         a) **Incorporating OSHA standards.** As a result of OSHA, it is not uncommon for collective bargaining agreements to incorporate OSHA (and related state) standards by reference—thereby creating the possibility of grievance arbitration for violations thereof.

NLRB v. American National Insurance Co.

e. **Management functions clause--NLRB v. American National Insurance Co.,** 343 U.S. 395 (1952).

1) **Facts.** Negotiations between the union and American National Insurance Company (D) failed to produce an agreement. The union proposed unlimited arbitration for all contract disputes, but D, objecting to this, counterproposed a "management functions clause," which excluded promotions, discipline, and work schedules from arbitration. The NLRB (P) filed a complaint that D had refused to bargain as required by the NLRA, and that D was guilty of (i) interfering with the rights of employees (section 7) and (ii) unfair labor practices under sections 8(a)(1) and (a)(5). Negotiations continued, however, with management's clause as an obstacle to settlement. Finally, an agreement was reached containing a management functions clause that rendered nonarbitrable matters of discipline and work schedules. Meanwhile, P found that D had not bargained in good faith and had prohibited D from bargaining for any management functions clause affecting a condition of employment. The court of appeals reversed.

2) **Issue.** Is it lawful for an employer to bargain for a management functions clause in an employment agreement?

3) **Held.** Yes. Judgment affirmed.

   a) The Board cannot directly or indirectly compel concessions from either party to bargaining.

   b) The NLRA requires only that parties bargain in good faith. Bargaining for a management clause is common and therefore the employer was not in bad faith in negotiating about it. It is not improper for an employer to insist upon having some flexible control over certain conditions of employment.

4) **Dissent** (Minton, Black, Douglas, JJ.). Not all management function clauses are per se valid. Where an employer will agree to bargain over wages only if the employees are willing to agree not to bargain over other working conditions, the employer has refused to bargain.

5) **Comment.** This case illustrates the difficult line that must be drawn between those conditions of employment that must be left to management and those that should properly be bargained for.

3. **Permissive Subjects.** If a subject is "bargainable" in the sense that it is not an outlawed or a compulsory subject, the employer and the union may bargain collectively about the subject only if both elect to do so.

   a. **Examples.** Areas such as corporate organization, size and composition of the supervisory force, general business practices, and location of plants are generally considered to be management prerogatives. But they may become subjects for bargaining at the option of the employer.

b. **Cannot be prerequisite to mandatory subjects.** A party may not require an agreement to bargain about voluntary subjects as a precondition to collective bargaining on mandatory subjects.

c. **Cannot be condition for overall agreement--NLRB v. Wooster Division of Borg-Warner Corp.,** 356 U.S. 342 (1958).

    1) **Facts.** During negotiations with the union, Wooster Division of Borg-Warner (D) insisted that the contract contain (i) an advisory pre-strike vote of all union and nonunion employees as to D's last offer (a "ballot" clause), and (ii) a clause excluding the certified international union as a party to the contract and substituting the noncertified local in its stead. Although it bargained with respect to other issues, it held firm to its request for the two clauses. The union filed a charge with the Board alleging refusal to bargain. The Board held that the insistence on the two clauses, which were not a part of "wages, hours, and other terms and conditions of employment," was a refusal to bargain.

    2) **Issue.** Is insistence upon terms which are not mandatory subjects of bargaining a refusal to bargain in good faith?

    3) **Held.** Yes. Judgment affirmed.

        a) Although other areas may be subjects of collective bargaining insistence upon the adoption of voluntary terms as a condition of any agreement, only mandatory subjects of bargaining can be conditions for the overall agreement. The duty to bargain is limited to mandatory subjects.

    4) **Concurrence in part** (Frankfurter, J.). The ballot clause was within the range of reasonable industrial bargaining and should not be proscribed because it is not within the vague scope of the mandatory provisions.

    5) **Concurrence and dissent** (Harlan, Clark, Whittaker, JJ.). The NLRB should not determine what should be bargained by the parties, only that they should bargain.

    6) **Comment.** The mere fact that the parties have bargained upon a permissive subject matter and have included it in their collective bargaining agreement does not change the nature of the subject from "permissive" to "mandatory." Thus, an employer is not guilty of an unfair labor practice if she thereafter unilaterally changes or modifies the agreement without consulting the union. The union's remedy is a breach of contract action or a grievance. In *Allied Chemical & Alkali Workers v. Pittsburgh Plate Glass Co., infra*, the employer and the union had agreed on the manner of paying retirement benefits, but the employer unilaterally changed this. The Court held that it was not an unfair labor practice because the subject matter was only permissive.

d. **No duty to bargain on policy objectives.** A union demand that the employer contribute to a fund used exclusively to promote the industry is not a compulsory bargaining subject.

1) **Rationale.** To hold that a party must bargain over any matter which might conceivably enhance prospects for the industry would turn collective bargaining into a debate on policy objectives.

e. **Management prerogative and union participation.** Most managerial prerogatives—such as expansion of company facilities, production decisions, and the like—are considered permissive subjects of bargaining. Under certain circumstances, however, an area generally considered to be the prerogative of management may become a mandatory subject.

1) **Unit work by supervisors.** The performance of production work by a supervisor has been held a compulsory bargaining subject (not a management prerogative) where the union contends that the supervisor is depriving union employees of overtime pay.

2) **In-plant food service.** Company-provided (or subcontracted) food services are subject to mandatory bargaining. Prices, availability, and conditions under which they are to be consumed are examples. The company must bargain about changes or proposed changes when requested to do so by the union.

f. **Other topics.**

1) **Subcontracting--Fiberboard Paper Products Corp. v. NLRB,** 379 U.S. 203 (1964).

a) **Facts.** The Steelworkers Union (P) had long represented Fiberboard Paper Product's (D's) employees. At a bargaining meeting four days prior to the expiration of the current agreement, D announced that on the basis of cost saving it had decided to contract out its maintenance work. On the day before expiration, D entered a contract with a maintenance service and terminated its own maintenance employees the next day. P picketed and filed sections 8(a)(1), (3), and (5) charges. The Board found an 8(a)(5) violation and ordered reinstatement of the maintenance employees with back pay. The court of appeals enforced the order, and the Supreme Court granted certiorari.

b) **Issue.** Is an employer required to bargain collectively over a decision to contract out work formerly done by unit employees?

c) **Held.** Yes, in this case. Judgment affirmed.

(1) The subject matter is well within the literal meaning of "terms and conditions of employment," and it is frequently the subject of bargaining in industry.

(2) The facts here indicate the propriety of bargaining: (i) the same work is still to be performed in the plant, and (ii) no capital investment is contemplated.

(3) To require the employer to bargain about the matter will not significantly abridge its freedom to manage its business.

(4) Labor cost reduction matters are peculiarly suitable for bargaining. The Board's order is a proper remedy.

d) **Concurrence** (Stewart, Douglas, Harlan, JJ.). This case stirs large issues, broader than the facts before us. Many management decisions affect job security of employees, including advertising and product design. Yet they need not be bargained about. As a general matter, subcontracting is not a condition of employment. However, in this case, the employer in effect merely substituted one set of employees to do the same job in the same plant. This sort of subcontracting falls short of the larger type of entrepreneurial question.

e) **Comments.**

(1) In a Railway Labor Act case, the Supreme Court held that the Norris-LaGuardia Act applied to a strike following negotiations over the elimination of small stations (and consequent loss of jobs), and rejected the court of appeals characterization as an attempt to "usurp legitimate managerial prerogative." The Court said the action was a "controversy concerning terms or conditions of employment" under section 17(c). [Order of Railroad Telegraphers v. Chicago & Northwestern Railway, 362 U.S. 330 (1960)]

(2) Even though a particular subcontracting may be a "term or condition of employment," it may not be necessary to bargain to impasse before implementation. If done during the existence of a collective bargaining agreement, there may be a contractual basis for an action. There may have been a "waiver" to bargaining due to a "past practice" of subcontracting (which was not the case in *Fiberboard*), especially if the impact on job security is minimal. [*See* Westinghouse Electric Corp., 150 N.L.R.B. 1574 (1965)] The Board has indicated that the sale of a business is "at the core of entrepreneurial control" and requires no bargaining. [*See* UAW v. NLRB (General Motors Corp.), 470 F.2d 422 (D.C. Cir. 1972)—denying the union's request for review]

2) **Decision to terminate business--First National Maintenance Corp. v. NLRB,** 452 U.S. 666 (1981).

First National Maintenance Corp. v. NLRB

a) **Facts.** First National Maintenance (D) provided maintenance services to various clients under contract. In its contract with Greenpark Nursing, relations had not gone well. D had reduced its monthly service fee for Greenpark in 1976. District 1199 (P) became the certified representative of D's employees in March 1977. P initiated bargaining on July 12. D had already requested Greenpark to pay its full fee, and on July 6 it informed Greenpark that it would cease operations there on August 1 if the fee was not restored. It terminated the contract on July 28 and terminated its employees working at Greenpark on July 29 without bargaining with P. It refused P's request to bargain about the decision. P filed unfair labor charges and the Board found D guilty of section 8(a)(1) and (5) violations. The court of appeals enforced, ruling such a decision was presumptively bargainable in the absence of any showing that bargaining over the decision would not further the purposes of the Act.

b) **Issue.** Must a company subject to the Act negotiate about a decision to close part of its business?

c) **Held.** No. Judgment reversed.

(1) Some management decisions, such as advertising policy and product design, have such an attenuated impact on the employment relation as to not require bargaining. Others, such as lay-offs and plant rules, have direct impact and must be bargained.

(2) This case involves a third type of decision that has direct impact, but has focus only on the company's profitability for a specific part of its operation. Management must be free of constraints of bargaining to the extent essential for the running of a profitable business and must have some degree of certainty about whether its conduct would be an unfair labor practice. The union's interests are sufficiently protected without bargaining. The company has recognized its clear duty to bargain about the "effects" of its decision, and in this bargaining the union may gain valuable concessions.

(3) Finally, section 8(a)(3) protects against a decision that is motivated by anti-union animus. When management's interests are much more complex, there may be a practical and legal need for speed and secrecy connected to the decision and bargaining may be futile. Mandatory bargaining could thwart management intentions and a presumption in that direction injects uncertainty as to whether and when there might be a duty to bargain.

d) **Dissent** (Brennan, Marshall, JJ.). The majority balancing test favors management interests and interferes with the NLRB's proper judgment. In any event, the Court improperly applied the test in this case.

e) **Comment.** The Board has struggled to find a rationale for applying the *First National Maintenance* principles. In one case concerning the shutdown of a facility, some members emphasized that such a change in the nature of the business is a matter within the core of entrepreneurial control. One member focused on whether the matter was amenable to bargaining and, if so, would inquire whether the benefits of bargaining outweigh the burdens that it would impose on management. Another member inquired whether bargaining could reasonably be expected to make a difference. [*See* Otis Elevator Co. (United Technologies), 269 N.L.R.B. 891 (1984)]

3) **Transfer of operation--UFCW, Local 150-A v. NLRB (Dubuque Packing Co.),** 1 F.3d 24 (D.C. Cir. 1993), *cert. denied*, 114 S. Ct. 2157 (1994).

a) **Facts.** Dubuque Packing Company (D) had been losing money at its Dubuque, Iowa home plant since 1977. It had won various concessions from the union over the years. Finally, in March of 1981, D gave six-months' notice that it intended to close its hog kill and cut unit and reduce operations at Dubuque. The union rejected a wage freeze and in June, D announced that it was considering relocating hog kill and cut operations to another plant, relocating 900 jobs. The union requested financial information which D refused to supply. The wage freeze was resubmitted and rejected by the union until D opened its books, and by the employees at an election. Three days later, D announced that its decision to relocate was irrevocable. The parties negotiated over the proposed relocation. On October 1, D opened up a hog kill and cut operation in a newly acquired plant in Illinois and eliminated over 500 jobs at Dubuque. Unfair labor practice charges had been filed against D for refusal to bargain. In 1985, the ALJ found that D had refused to bargain in good faith, but found no violation of section 8(a)(5) since D was under no duty to bargain over the relocation. The Board adopted the ALJ's finding and opinion. In review of the case, the court of appeals remanded, finding that the Board's opinion was inadequately explained. On remand, the Board adopted a new test for relocation cases and found D guilty of unfair labor practice for failure to bargain.

b) **Issue.** Was D's relocation of its hog kill operations a mandatory subject for bargaining?

c) **Held.** Yes. Order enforced.

   (1) If the plant relocation here was a "term" or "condition" of employment under section 8(d), D has a duty to bargain about it under section 8(b)(5). The two controlling cases are *First National* and *Fibreboard, supra*. We should respect the Board's policy choices if its interpretation of the Act's requirements is reasonable in light of the purposes of the Act and controlling precedent of the Supreme Court.

   (2) The Board's rule places on the General Counsel the initial burden to show that the employer's decision involved relocation of unit work without a basic change in the nature of its operation. If the General Counsel makes out a prima facie case, the employer must produce evidence in rebuttal showing that the work in the new location varies significantly or that the move involved a change in the scope and direction of the enterprise. In the alternative, the employer may show that labor costs were a factor and that the union could not have offered concessions that would have changed the decision to relocate.

   (3) The Board's test involves three distinct layers of analysis. The first is the entrepreneurial level recognized by *Fibreboard*—change in the nature of the employer's operation or scope and direction of the enterprise. The second layer concerns a subjective one—whether the motive was related to labor costs. And the third layer concerns "futility" considerations in which negotiations could make no difference because the union could not or would not make concessions where negotiations would frustrate legitimate business objectives of the employer.

   (4) The Board's rule sufficiently protects the employer's right to run the business and it is in accord with Supreme Court precedent. The fact that the topic of relocation may involve expenditure of capital does not invalidate the rule; many mandatory subjects do so. As long as managerial rights are adequately protected, this alone is not enough.

   (5) Finally, the Board's test is not so imprecise that an employer is denied adequate certainty and guidance.

(6) The Board properly applied the rule in this case. Shifting to the new location was not a change in operations or in the scope and direction of the enterprise. There is no indication that the union could not or would not make concessions which could have made a difference. The union's rejection of a wage freeze was related to D's refusal to provide information—it was not a categorical rejection of any movement at all. There was no retroactive application of a new rule in this case, but an application of a new rule, an adjudication that clarified the contours of established doctrine.

d) **Comment.** The Worker Adjustment and Retraining Notification Act ("WARN Act") became effective in 1988. An employer must give 60 days' notice to unorganized employees or their union, if organized, in the event of a permanent or temporary plant closing affecting 50 or more employees or of a mass lay-off affecting 50 employees or 33% of the workforce. Notice need not be given if to do so would preclude the employer from obtaining the capital needed to avoid the releases. The Act also excludes strikes, lockouts, and permanent replacement of economic strikers. [*See* 20 C.F.R. §§639.1-639.10]

4) **Modification of retirees' benefits--Allied Chemical & Alkali Workers v. Pittsburgh Plate Glass Co.**, 404 U.S. 157 (1971).

a) **Facts.** Pittsburgh Plate Glass Company (D) paid $4.00 per month per person for health insurance for retired employees. The contract with the union (P) gave the company the right to reduce the expenditure to $2.00 per month if a national health insurance plan became law. Subsequently, Medicare became law. D desired to reclaim the $2.00 per month, cancel the program for retirees, and substitute in its stead supplemental Medicare coverage. P agreed that D could reduce its monthly contribution to $2.00 but did not agree to the other two points. D contended that the union did not represent retired employees and circulated its proposal among the retired employees. P filed charges of unfair labor practices. The Board held for P. The court of appeals refused to enforce the Board's cease and desist order, and P appeals.

b) **Issue.** May an employer unilaterally modify benefits already given to retired employees by a labor contract?

c) **Held.** Yes. Judgment affirmed.

(1) The NLRA applies to "employees" and "workers"—not "retirees." It was designed to help the working person.

(2) Furthermore, in this case, pensioners are not employees within the meaning of the collective bargaining obligations of the Act. Here, the Board determined that the bargaining unit was D's "employees," "working" or "who work" at hourly rates of pay. This obviously excludes retirees.

(3) The Board found that bargaining over pensioners' rights was an industry practice. Even if that is so, that still does not alter the fact that pensioners are not "employees" or members of the bargaining unit.

(4) Pensioners' benefits are a mandatory subject of collective bargaining. However, once benefits are bargained-for, "active workers are not forever thereafter bound to that view or obliged to negotiate in behalf of retirees."

(5) Section 8(d) requires that "a party proposing a modification continue in full force and effect . . . all the terms and conditions of the existing contract until its expiration." Section 8(d) applies to *mandatory* bargaining topics, not *permissive*. This case involves a permissive topic, so section 8(d) does not apply.

(6) P's remedy lies in a suit for breach of contract, not one for unfair labor practices.

C. OTHER ISSUES INVOLVING COLLECTIVE BARGAINING

1. **Bargaining, the Strike, and Impasse Resolution.**

   a. **Statutory provisions.** Peaceful strikes are protected by section 7 and section 13 of the Act. Congress has also provided devices to reduce their potential or to postpone them. Section 8(d) provides for notification to state and federal mediation agencies during contract renegotiations of a cooling-off period prior to a strike or lockout. Section 8(g) provides for strike notice and mediation in the health care industry. Sections 206 through 210 provide for delay and fact-finding by a presidential board in cases of "national emergency" strikes or lockouts.

   b. **Strike threat overcoming impasse.** Strikes are usually called in the context of a bargaining impasse over economic issues. Negotiations tend to bring the parties close to the point of agreement, but the strike or the threat of a strike seems to be the catalyst that brings them to bridge the final gap.

2. **The Effect of Strike on Duty to Bargain.**

   a. **Introduction.** Board and judicial decisions have recognized that a peaceful work stoppage, even if not protected, does not amount to a breach of the duty to bargain in good faith and does not relieve the other party of its duty to continue bargaining. In the face of a strike, the employer may hire replacements or take other measures in an effort to counter the effects of the strike. Such conduct must not be unjustifiably inconsistent with its bargaining stance and offers already made in negotiations.

   b. **Subcontracting to maintain operations—Land Air Delivery, Inc. v. NLRB,** 862 F.2d 354 (D.C. Cir. 1988)

   Land Air Delivery, Inc. v. NLRB

   1) **Facts.** Teamsters Local 41 (P) was the collective bargaining agent for Land Air Delivery, Inc. (D) delivery employees. Independent contractors who transported freight for D were not in the unit. P called a strike in support of an arbitration award

and pending grievances. To continue in operation in Kansas City, D used a mix of employees from other locations, contract drivers, newly hired temporary employees, and supervisors. D continued using 12 contractors after the strike and all unit positions were eliminated. Unit employees made unconditional offers to return to work. After none were taken back, P filed charges. The Board found D guilty of section 8(a)(3) and (5) violations. D appeals.

2) **Issue.** Can an employer permanently replace unit employees by subcontractors during a strike without bargaining about it?

3) **Held.** No. Order enforced.

   a) The Board takes the position that an employer is never permitted to replace employees permanently without bargaining the decision. It has long been settled that an employer must bargain before deciding to subcontract. There is a legal difference between making permanent replacements which may lead to a decertification and unilaterally dissolving a unit by subcontracting.

   b) With replacement, the duty to bargain continues and decertification is not inevitable. The Board was within its authority to treat subcontracting differently under section 8(a)(5). A employer might not be required to bargain about the defensive use of permanent subcontractors to remain in operation as a matter of business necessity. However, it is clear in this case that D was not motivated by business necessity. It subcontracted three months after the strike began and had successfully operated with a mixture of other types of employees.

3. **Bargaining Remedies.**

   a. **Party cannot be compelled to accept mandatory contract provision-- H.K. Porter Co. v. NLRB,** 397 U.S. 99 (1970).

   1) **Facts.** During negotiations, the union proposed that H.K. Porter Company (D) deduct union dues from employee wages (dues checkoff). D refused on the grounds that it would "aid and comfort the union." The NLRB found that D had refused to bargain in good faith, and issued a cease and desist order with respect to the dues checkoff provision, then issued a new opinion directing the company to grant the union a dues checkoff clause. Section 8(d) provides that the duty to bargain collectively does "not compel either party to agree to a proposal or require the making of a concession." Section 10(c) allows the Board to take "such actions as will effectuate the policies of the Act" when there is a failure to bargain in good faith.

   2) **Issue.** Can the Board require a company to grant the union a dues checkoff clause in the contract?

   3) **Held.** No. Judgment reversed.

        a)   The NLRB has no authority to compel a party to accept a specific contractual provision. Although parties can be required to bargain, the Board cannot create or mandate contracts for parties.

    4)   **Dissent** (Douglas, Stewart, JJ.). In the case of flagrant refusals to bargain such as this, I see no answer but to recognize the Board's power to impose such a remedy.

b.   **Board cannot write contract for parties--Ex-Cell-O Corp.,** 185 N.L.R.B. 107 (1970).   *Ex-Cell-O Corp.*

    1)   **Facts.** Ex-Cell-O Corporation (D) refused to bargain with the union (P) for two years while it challenged the union's certification. The union charged that such a refusal to bargain violated section 8(a)(5), and the trial examiner recommended compensation for its members for the period during which company had so refused, based on the contract to which D would have agreed had the contract negotiations occurred. Section 10(c) allows the Board to take affirmative action, "including reinstatement of employees with or without back pay," to effectuate the Act's purposes.

    2)   **Issue.** May the NLRB require an employer to compensate employees for a contract that he might have adopted if he had bargained in good faith?

    3)   **Held.** No.

        a)   Such an order would simply punish the company for exercising its rights to have the question of certification determined through the appellate processes. Imposing such a sanction would also have the effect of writing a contract for the parties, which the Board is clearly not empowered to do.

    4)   **Dissent** (McCulloch, Brown, Members). The compensation remedy would not write a contract for the parties since it does not deal with future contract provisions; it solely remedies past failures to bargain by giving the employees the benefit of the contract they would have had.

    5)   **Comment.** The NLRB has ruled that it does not have statutory authority to issue a "make whole" order in refusal to bargain cases. (Such an order would make wage and other benefits ultimately obtained by the union retroactive to the date of the employer's refusal to bargain.)

IV. STRIKES, BOYCOTTS, AND PICKETING

A. INTRODUCTION

This section is concerned with the scope of affirmative protection afforded employees in the conduct of strikes, boycotts, and picketing, and the judicial restraints imposed on these activities. The Taft-Hartley Act of 1947, which introduced the regulation of employee activity, and the Landrum-Griffin Act of 1959, which imposed a greater regulation on picketing and other concerted conduct, have shaped the current balance of "countervailing powers" in this area. The problems that have emerged from this legislation will be considered under three headings.

1. **Interference with Concerted Activities.** What are the limitations on the employer's right to discipline, discharge, or otherwise interfere with employees who engage in concerted activities?

2. **Constitutional Limitations.** What are the limitations on the power of government to regulate strikes, picketing, and boycotts?

3. **The National Labor Relations Act.** How does the Act affect and regulate these activities?

B. EMPLOYEE CONCERTED ACTIONS UNDER THE NLRA

1. **Protected Activity.** Section 7 of the NLRA includes, in addition to the right to form, join, and assist labor organization and to bargain, the "right to engage in *other concerted activities* for the purpose of collective bargaining or *other mutual aid or protection*." This part will explore the kinds of activities that are protected or unprotected.

    a. **Employer responses to "concerted" activities.** This section will also explore whether employer responses to concerted action that hinder or discourage employee protected activities may be unfair labor practices under sections 8(a)(1) and 8(a)(3).

    b. **Unorganized and single employee activities may be "concerted."** Employee collective activities are deemed "concerted" under the Act even though no union has been selected as a collective bargaining agent. An example is a spontaneous walkout in protest against an uncomfortable or dangerous working environment. After an agent has been selected and an agreement signed, even a protest by a single employee may be "concerted action" within the meaning of the Act.

    c. **Collective bargaining claims as concerted action--NLRB v. City Disposal Systems, Inc.,** 465 U.S. 822 (1984).

    NLRB v. City Disposal Systems, Inc.

    1) **Facts.** Brown (P) was fired by City Disposal Systems, Inc. (D) after refusing to drive a truck because he had genuine doubts about the reliability of the truck's brakes. He made no reference to the provisions of the labor agreement, which contained a safety clause. He filed a grievance, but the union declined to process it. P then filed an unfair labor practice charge. The NLRB found a section 8(a)(1) violation, concluding that P had

Labor Law - 91

engaged in concerted activity since his protest was to enforce the interests of all employees covered by the agreement. The court of appeals refused to enforce the Board's order, and the Supreme Court granted certiorari.

2) **Issue.** Is the individual assertion of a right grounded in a collective agreement "concerted action" within the meaning of NLRA section 7?

3) **Held.** Yes. Judgment reversed.

   a) A decision on an issue involving the Board's expertise is entitled to considerable deference. The Board's construction here is a reasonable one.

   b) The invocation of a right rooted in a collective agreement is part of a complete process, which begins with organization and extends through the enforcement of the agreement.

   c) It would make no sense to negotiate a collective agreement if an employee could not invoke the rights created by it.

   d) The processing of a grievance is clearly concerted activity. There is no bright line between an incipient grievance and an individual complaint to the employer.

   e) The employee must act on a reasonable and honest belief and cannot do so in an abusive manner.

   f) *Interborough Contractors, Inc.*, 157 N.L.R.B. 1295 (1966), does not undermine the arbitration process. When faced with a parallel unfair labor practice charge, it can always defer to arbitration under *Collyer Insulated Wire*, 192 N.L.R.B. 837 (1971).

   g) It was not necessary for P to expressly invoke the provisions of the agreement at the time of his refusal.

4) **Dissent** (O'Connor, Powell, Rehnquist, JJ., Burger, C.J.). This case converts every contract claim into an unfair labor practice. Congress has refused to confer on the Board general jurisdiction over contract claims.

5) **Comment.** "Concerted activities . . . for mutual aid or protection" has been given a broad interpretation. In *NLRB v. J. Weingarten, Inc.*, 420 U.S. 251 (1975), the Supreme Court found that a request for union assistance by an employee in an interview with the employer that could lead to discipline was protected concerted activity. Assistance by a union representative to an employee in such an interview is likewise protected. [*See* ILGWU v. Quality Manufacturing Co., 420 U.S. 276 (1975)]

Eastex, Inc. v. NLRB

d. **Political appeals as concerted activity--Eastex, Inc. v. NLRB,** 437 U.S. 556 (1978).

   1) **Facts.** Employees requested the company to allow them to distribute a union newsletter in nonworking areas during nonworking time. The newsletter urged employees to support the union, to oppose the inclusion of a right-to-work provision in the state constitution, and to register, and

after referring to a presidential veto of an increase in the minimum wage law, it urged voting for political candidates sympathetic to labor. The company (D) refused and the union filed an unfair labor practice. The Board found a violation of section 8(a)(1), ruling that the newsletter was for the "mutual aid and protection" of the employees. The court of appeals enforced the Board's order, and D appeals.

2) **Issue.** Is the distribution on an employer's premises of literature containing appeals for "political" actions to improve the conditions of employees in general "concerted action" within the protection of section 7?

3) **Held.** Yes. Judgment affirmed.

   a) Efforts to improve the terms and conditions of employment are within the protection of the Act even though they are through channels outside the immediate employee-employer relationship. Appeals to executive and judicial branches are protected, as are appeals for legislative assistance.

   b) The Board did not err in recognizing that the "right-to-work" appeal was protected activity, because union security is a central union concept of strength.

   c) Concerns about the federal minimum wage laws are likewise protected.

   d) Finally, it was proper to distribute the materials on the company premises under the *Republic Aviation* rule, *supra*. D has shown no prejudice to managerial rights or any meaningful intrusion on its property rights.

2. **Discharge and Reinstatement of Strikers.** Whether strikers are entitled to reinstatement in jobs which the employer has filled with replacements during a strike is a key factor, from the union's standpoint, in determining whether a strike can be successful. Workers are understandably more reluctant to strike if they know (or believe) that they may lose their jobs as a result. At the same time, the employer has a legitimate interest in being able to continue operation of his plant during the strike. The courts have attempted to balance these competing interests in dealing with the problem of reinstatement.

   a. **Reinstatement depends on category of strikers.** Strikers generally fall into one of two basic categories: (i) "unfair labor practice" strikers (those striking because of an employer unfair labor practice, such as the discriminatory firing of employees), or (ii) economic strikers (all others, but most commonly those striking for an increase in benefits).

   b. **Economic strikers.** Those going out on strike for increased benefits or other nonunfair labor practice issues receive little protection as to reinstatement. The employer *is not* compelled to discharge persons hired as permanent replacements during the strike or otherwise to create jobs for economic strikers. Such strikers are entitled only to nondiscriminatory review and disposition of their job applications for rehiring.

1) **Abolishment of jobs.** Whether the employer has hired a replacement or not, the economic striker may not be entitled to reinstatement if, *due to changed economic or business conditions*, the employer has abolished the job; *i.e.*, the employer need not create a new job or revive the old one for an economic striker.

2) **Degree of activity.** However, the employer may not use the "degree" of activity by a striker during the strike to determine whether or not to reinstate the striker. [*See* NLRB v. Mackay Radio & Telegraph Co., *infra*—employer's refusal to reinstate those most active in forming strike held discriminatory and thus an unfair labor practice in violation of sections 8(a)(1) and (3)]

3) **Filling vacancies.** The employer's failure to consider outstanding applications of former strikers for reinstatement when vacancies do occur is discriminatory and an unfair labor practice. [Laidlaw Corp. v. NLRB, 414 F.2d 99 (7th Cir. 1969)] In this situation, the hiring of someone other than a striker-applicant is presumptively a violation of the Act, unless the employer can show a "legitimate and substantial business reason" therefor.

c. **Unfair labor practice strikers.** If employees strike because of employer unfair labor practices and the strike is not itself unlawful, the strikers are *entitled to reinstatement* during or after the strike even if it is necessary to discharge replacements hired during the strike. [*See* NLRB v. Mackay Radio & Telegraph Co., *infra*] However, the strikers are required to make an unconditional application for reinstatement before the employer is obligated to rehire them.

1) An employer who discharges an economic striker before hiring a permanent replacement may be found to have committed an unfair labor practice; *i.e.*, discriminating against employees for lawful union activity. The result is that the discharge converts the economic striker into an unfair labor practice striker, so that the discharged employee is unconditionally entitled to reinstatement (a right she would not have had as an economic striker).

d. **Limitation on reinstatement rights.** Both economic strikers and unfair labor practice strikers will lose their protected status if the strike is conducted in an unlawful manner, or is conducted for any illegal additional purpose. As to both categories of strikers, NLRA section 10(c) (added by Taft-Hartley) provides that the Board may not order reinstatement or back pay for striking employees who were suspended or discharged "for cause."

e. **Tactic.** As a practical matter, where there is a danger that strikers may lose their jobs, the union will usually bargain for a reinstatement agreement from the employer—thereby removing any need to resort to the rules just discussed

3. **Unprotected Employee Conduct.**

a. **Disciplining employees.** Even when employees are engaged in concerted activity for mutual aid or protection, they still may be subject to discipline or discharge if their conduct exceeds permissible limits. The Act provides no guidelines and the Board cases indicate that otherwise protected activity will fall outside the pale if the conduct is a violation of law or contrary to the essential duties of the employment relationship. Industrial sabotage, "disloyal" conduct, and efforts to squelch union dissenters have been held "unprotected," thereby permitting the employer to take disciplinary action against perpetrators.

b. **Employee discharge for disloyalty--NLRB v. Local 1229, IBEW (Jefferson Standard Broadcasting Co.),** 346 U.S. 464 (1953).

NLRB v. Local 1229, IBEW (Jefferson Standard Broadcasting Co.)

1) **Facts.** Jefferson Standard Broadcasting Company (D) owned a radio and TV broadcasting station. In 1949, after the labor contract expired, WBTV's technicians began picketing WBTV, although they did not strike. The picketing was peaceful. On August 24, 1949, certain of the technicians began to distribute handbills to the public and businesspersons denouncing WBTV for providing inferior service to its local audience. The handbill, entitled "Is Charlotte a Second-Class City?", was signed "WBT Technicians" and did not mention anything about a labor dispute or picketing. D fired 10 technicians whom it charged with sponsoring the handbill. The union (P) charged D with unfair labor practices. The trial examiner recommended that all the employees be reinstated with back pay. The Board found that one of the employees had not sponsored the bill and ordered him reinstated, and found that the other nine were discharged for cause. The court of appeals found that the Board failed to make findings as to the unlawfulness of the 10 employees' conduct, which findings it deemed essential, and remanded the case. The Supreme Court granted certiorari.

2) **Issue.** Under section 10(c), may employees be discharged for cause if they are disloyal to their employer?

3) **Held.** Yes. Order set aside and case remanded.

   a) Section 10(c) states that the Board shall not order the reinstatement of an employee who has been discharged for cause. "There is no more elemental cause for discharge of an employee than disloyalty to his employer."

   b) The difficulty in this case is determining whether the employees were discharged for a separable cause or because of their concerted activity for collective bargaining or other mutual aid or protection purposes.

      (1) In this case, the Board found that the nine offenders were discharged for sponsoring and distributing the handbill and further, that their attack was related to none of D's labor practices. The attack was not an appeal to the public for support in a pending labor dispute.

   c) Therefore, the nine offenders' attack was no more defensible than the act of sabotage and they were properly discharged for cause.

4) **Dissent** (Frankfurter, Black, Douglas, JJ.). Section 10(c) does not obviate this Court's determining whether, under section 7, the distribution of the handbill was a legitimate tool in the labor dispute, which determination the Court has failed to make. This decision affords no guidance for future

Labor Law - 95

cases, other than that which the specific facts may afford. The notions of "loyalty" and "discipline" are imprecise and leave the door wide open to individual judgment by Board members and judges.

5) **Comment.** Either an unlawful object or the use of improper means may take concerted activity out of protected status. [*See* Elk Lumber Co., 91 N.L.R.B. 333 (1950)]

NLRB v. Mackay Radio & Telegraph Co.

c. **Employer refusal to rehire strikers--NLRB v. Mackay Radio & Telegraph Co.,** 304 U.S. 333 (1938).

1) **Facts.** The union went on strike to modify an existing collective bargaining agreement. In order to maintain service, Mackay Radio and Telegraph Company (D) hired replacements. After the strike failed, most of the strikers were allowed to return to work. However, D had offered permanent employment to 11 of the replacements and five had accepted. Five of the strikers were not rehired. All five were very active in the union. The NLRB ordered reinstatement. The court of appeals refused to enforce the Board's order, and the Supreme Court granted certiorari.

2) **Issue.** May an employer refuse to rehire employees because of their union involvement?

3) **Held.** No. Judgment reversed.

a) Although an employer may replace strikers with permanent replacements in order to carry on his business, he may not discriminate against employees when reinstating them because of their union involvement.

b) An employer may replace strikers with permanent replacements and only reinstate strikers into vacant positions.

c) But an employee remains an employee while striking, and may not be the object of discrimination in reinstatement. The Board was justified in finding that D selected the five strikers not to be rehired from a list of the most active union members.

4) **Comment.** A presidential Executive Order designed to deny federal government contracts to employers who permanently replaced economic strikers was invalidated. [Chamber of Commerce of the United States v. Reich, 74 F.3d 1322 (D.C. Cir. 1996)]

NLRB v. Erie Resistor Corp.

d. **Employer discrimination against strikers--NLRB v. Erie Resistor Corp.,** 373 U.S. 221 (1963).

1) **Facts.** When the collective bargaining agreement between Erie Resistor Corporation (D) and the union (P) expired, negotiations were unsuccessful and P went on strike. D managed to keep its plant open for the first month of the strike at a reduced rate of production. After the first month, D offered 20 years of "additional seniority" for purposes of lay-off only to all

strikers who returned to work and to all replacements. Many strikers returned to work under the offer, and consequently, the strike failed. Nearly all of the strikers were rehired, but when lay-offs proved necessary, those without the super seniority were laid off first. P claimed the action violated section 8(a)(3) and the NLRB held so; however, the court of appeals refused to enforce the NLRB holding. The Supreme Court granted certiorari.

2) **Issue.** Was D's offer of super seniority, which was not found to have been motivated by a discriminatory intent, an unfair labor practice?

3) **Held.** Yes. Judgment reversed.

  a) Some employer conduct is so inherently discriminatory against concerted union activity that an intent to discriminate should be inferred, since discrimination between strikers and nonstrikers is an inescapable consequence of the action. Super seniority discriminates by (i) affecting the tenure of strikers and nonstrikers differently and (ii) inducing those with little seniority to refrain from concerted activity thereby undermining the employees' mutual interest and dividing them into camps.

  b) Even though D's offer of super seniority may have been motivated by a legitimate business interest in keeping production up, by its nature it worked to discriminate between strikers and nonstrikers and thereby discouraged membership and participation in the union and its collective actions.

4) **Comment.** In *NLRB v. Truck Drivers Local Union No. 449 (Buffalo Linen)*, 353 U.S. 87 (1957), the Supreme Court recognized that employer lockouts in response to selective "whipsaw" strikes against an employer bargaining association are not a violation of sections 8(a)(1) and (3). The Court deferred to the Board's expertise in categorizing such activity as "defensive" lockouts.

e. **Employer lockout--American Ship Building Co. v. NLRB,** 380 U.S. 300 (1965).

  1) **Facts.** American Ship Building Company (D) operated four shipyards on the Great Lakes. D, following a bargaining impasse and fearing a strike, gradually laid off most of its employees, as available work diminished. The NLRB held that D's conduct had constituted an unfair labor practice by coercing the exercise of the employees' section 8(a)(1) bargaining rights. The court of appeals affirmed, and D appeals.

  2) **Issue.** Is a lockout following an impasse which is solely to bring economic pressure in support of an employer's bargaining position an unfair labor practice?

  3) **Held.** No. Judgment reversed.

    a) There is no evidence that D used the lockout to achieve an improper bargaining objective or that it was hostile to the union.

American Ship Building Co. v. NLRB

b) Nothing indicates that the lockout will destroy the union's capacity to effectively represent the employees.

c) There is no improper motivation shown and D's conduct was not so inherently prejudicial to the union's interest or devoid of economic justification as to dispense with proof of animus.

d) The right to strike is nothing more than that and the Board should not try to redress the balance of bargaining power between the parties.

e) The Act contemplates that lockouts will be used in the bargaining process in some fashion. The Board's opinion is entitled to the greatest deference, but its position is inconsistent with the structure of the Act and the sections it relies upon.

4) **Concurrence** (White, J.). Avoiding a strike that will occur at a particularly disadvantageous time is justified. Bad motive should not necessarily be required. The Board should be permitted to use its expertise in weighing the conflicting interests in the first instance.

5) **Concurrence** (Goldberg, J.). This was a defensive lockout and thus justified. The Court should not adopt a per se rule.

f. **Employer burden to show legitimate objectives--NLRB v. Great Dane Trailers, Inc.,** 388 U.S. 26 (1967).

1) **Facts.** Great Dane Trailers, Inc.'s (D's) employees went on strike on May 16, 1963. The collective bargaining agreement had expired on March 31. On July 12, 1963, a number of strikers demanded their accrued vacation pay. D refused, stating that all contractual obligations had been terminated by the strike. Shortly thereafter, it announced that all employees who reported to work on July 1 would be given vacation pay. D stated that this was a new policy, and was not based on the old collective bargaining agreement. The union (P) charged that sections 8(a)(3) and (1) were violated. The trial examiner found for the union, as did the Board. The court of appeals found that there had been no showing of anti-union animus on the part of D, and reversed the Board. The Board took the case to the Supreme Court.

2) **Issue.** Once it has been shown that an employer has engaged in discriminatory conduct, does the employer bear the burden of establishing that such conduct was motivated by legitimate objectives?

3) **Held.** Yes. Judgment reversed.

a) It is clear that D discriminated against striking employees by not giving them vacation pay.

b) However, a section 8(a)(3) inquiry does not stop there. It must further be determined whether the discriminatory conduct was motivated by an anti-union purpose.

(1) If the employer's conduct was *"inherently destructive"* of important employee rights, no proof of anti-union motivation is needed.

(2) If the adverse effect on employee rights of the discriminatory conduct is "*comparatively slight*," then anti-labor motivation must be proven *if* the employer has come forth with evidence of legitimate and substantial business justification for the conduct.

c) Either way, D has the burden to show that it was motivated by legitimate objectives. In this case, D did not meet this burden. We find that the Board's conclusions were supported by substantial evidence.

4) **Dissent** (Harlan, Stewart, JJ.).

a) The "legitimate and substantial business justification" test that the Court has announced may be interpreted as only burdening the employer to come forth with a nonfrivolous business purpose to shift the burden to the union to show the employer's anti-labor motive. In that case, D is being punished only for not anticipating this Court's holding.

b) On the other hand, use of the word "substantial" in the formulation of the rule may be construed as changing the rule that employers have always been free to take reasonable measures to discourage a strike by pressuring the economic interests of employees, including the extreme pressure of hiring permanent replacements, without any inquiry into the "substantiality" of the business justification. If the Court means to change this rule, it should do so only after hearing arguments on both sides.

5) **Comment.** Part of the reason for the Court's holding is that proof of the employer's motivation is most accessible to it.

g. **Strikers applying for reinstatement--Laidlaw Corp.,** 171 N.L.R.B. 1366 (1968).

Laidlaw Corp.

1) **Facts.** Laidlaw Corporation's (D's) employees went on strike after being warned that any striking employees would forever lose their jobs. The strike began January 12. On January 14, a striker named Massey applied for reinstatement and was refused. On January 18, Massey was offered a job, but as a new employee (with no seniority, lower wages, etc.); he refused this job. D did hire a number of striker/applicants, but reinstatement applications were considered *only* by the date of application. When openings arose, D did not check to see if a striker/applicant had previously applied for the job. The union (P) protested this. The trial examiner found that Massey was not entitled to his old job on January 14, as his job had been filled by a permanent replacement. However, the trial examiner also found that Massey was entitled to full reinstatement when he reapplied at a time when a position was vacant. Thus, it was found that the former strikers were discriminated against when D hired new employees rather than offer the jobs to strikers who had applied for reinstatement. D appeals.

2) **Issue.** Are permanently replaced strikers who apply for reinstatement entitled to job openings that subsequently arise?

3) **Held.** Yes. Trial examiner's conclusion confirmed.

   a) In *NLRB v. Fleetwood Trailer Co.*, 389 U.S. 375 (1967), the Supreme Court held that, by virtue of section 2(3), strikers remain employees if they have not obtained other regular or substantially equivalent employment and that an employer refusing to reinstate a striker (when job openings are available) must show that it had legitimate and substantial business justification.

   b) Furthermore, under *Fleetwood*, the basic right to jobs cannot depend on job availability as of the moment the applications are filed.

   c) Thus, Massey remained an employee even though he rejoined the strike after his January 14 attempt at reinstatement. D's offer to rehire Massey as a new employee was wholly unrelated to its economic needs and served only to punish Massey for engaging in concerted activity.

   d) D's conduct was inherently destructive of employee rights and it thus violated sections 8(a)(3) and (1).

   e) The burden is on employers in these situations to show legitimate and substantial reasons for failure to hire strikers.

4) **Comment.** *Laidlaw* has been endorsed by courts of appeals. In *T.W.A. v. Independent Federation of Flight Attendants*, 489 U.S. 426 (1989), the Supreme Court held that when taking back strikers, the employer need not displace junior employees who stayed on the job during the strike.

h. **Employee refusals to cross picket lines.** Employees who refuse to cross a picket line at their own employer will be protected against discipline under section 8(a)(1). However, if the picket line is an illegal one, under the Act an employee will be deemed to be engaging in an unprotected activity and may be disciplined. The most troublesome situation is a refusal to cross a picket line at a third-party employer. The Board has tended to regard such activity as protected unless waived by the bargaining agreement. Some federal courts have considered it not to be. Respecting the picket line would seem to be joining others in concerted activities. Those courts which have deemed it unprotected emphasize a similarity to a secondary boycott or a breach of the employment contract.

i. **Employer discipline of union officials--Metropolitan Edison Co. v. NLRB,** 460 U.S. 693 (1983).

   1) **Facts.** Metropolitan Edison (D) on previous occasions had punished union officials more severely than rank and file employees for their participation in work stoppages in violation of a general no-strike clause in the labor contract. Twice union officials filed grievances and in both cases arbitrators sustained the disparate treatment. In a later work stoppage, D again punished union officials more severely because they had not followed D's directions about the steps they should take to abate the strike. An unfair labor practice charge was filed and the Board found the selective discipline to be a section 8(a)(3) violation. It rejected D's arguments that the union

leaders had a general duty to ensure compliance with the terms of the collective agreement or in the alternative that the union had agreed to harsher sanctions by acquiescence in the arbitration awards. The court of appeals affirmed, and the case was taken to the Supreme Court.

2) **Issue.** Is it a violation of the Act for an employer to give additional discipline to union officials for failing to take the steps unilaterally defined by the employer and deemed by it to be necessary to abate a strike?

3) **Held.** Yes. Judgment affirmed.

   a) The facts of this case do not present the question of whether an employer may impose stricter penalties on union officials who take a leadership role in an unlawful strike or who engage in unprotected activity. We defer to the Board's conclusions that D's conduct adversely affects protected employee interests. D's disciplinary action inhibits qualified employees from holding office.

   b) If the employer comes forward with a business justification for its action, the Board would have to strike the proper balance between the justification and the invasion of employee rights.

      (1) D argues that there is an implied duty for union officials to uphold the terms of a labor agreement.

      (2) There is some authority for D's proposition, but even so, it does not follow that an employer can unilaterally define the actions that must be taken. Neither management nor labor's representatives may coerce each other in the performance of their official duties.

   c) A union may bind its officials to take affirmative steps to end an unlawful stoppage, but such a waiver of a statutory right would have to be clear and unmistakable. There is nothing to indicate that the parties intended to implicitly incorporate the rule of the two arbitration decisions into their subsequent labor contract.

4) **Comment.** Such strikers are afforded more protections by the Board. Replacements of U/L/P strikers may not vote in an election, and they may be protected even though the strike is technically unprotected or contrary to the CBA.

C. **CONSTITUTIONAL LIMITATIONS**

1. **Introduction.** Two constitutional doctrines restrict the power of state or federal government in controlling concerted activity to enforce the demands of a labor union against an employer, employees, or a competing labor union.

- a. **Due process.** The Fifth Amendment due process provision, applicable to the federal government, and the Fourteenth Amendment, applicable to state government, provides that "life, liberty, or property" shall not be taken "without due process of law."

- b. **Freedom of expression.** The First Amendment guarantees freedom of speech against federal or state interference, affirming the social value placed upon the expression of competing ideas.

2. **The Right to Strike.**

    - a. **A qualified right.** Neither due process, free speech, nor the Thirteenth Amendment's injunction against "involuntary servitude" guarantees an absolute "right to strike." There is, however, a right to strike to further "lawful labor objectives" and provisions in sections 7 and 13 of the NLRA affirm this right—"Nothing in this Act, except as specifically provided for herein, shall be construed so as to . . . interfere with . . . the right to strike. . . ." Lawfulness must be determined, of course, with reference to statutory and decisional law.

        1) In *Dorchy v. Kansas*, 272 U.S. 306 (1926), the defendant, a union official, ordered a strike in order to compel the employer to pay a stale claim of a former union employee. The defendant was arrested and convicted under a state statute prohibiting unlawful conspiracies with intent to suspend mining. The Supreme Court held that there is no unqualified right to strike protected by due process or the common law. A strike may be illegal because of its purpose, however orderly it is conducted. Here, the statutory prohibition of the strike is a constitutional one, and the collection of a stale claim was not a justifying purpose.

        2) The interests of employees in bettering their economic positions and bettering their working conditions must be taken into account, and their freedom to withhold personal services in concerted action would seem to be recognized under the Fifth and Fourteenth Amendments within the principles of "liberty" and "freedom of association." The interests of the employer and of employees must be accommodated and may be reasonably regulated in ways essential to the public welfare.

    - b. **Unlawful strikes.**

        1) **Determination.** A strike may be unlawful because of its purpose, or it may be unlawful because of the manner in which it is carried out. A strike judged unlawful per se would be one called for a purpose which has been defined as against the law, such as forcing an employer to commit an unfair labor practice. It has been held that neither sit-down strikes (in which employees remain in the plants effectively denying the owner of the plant access to it) nor strikes accompanied by violence are protected by the NLRA.

        2) **General rule.** Strikes in violation of a "no-strike" clause as well as "wildcat" strikes in which a minority of employees acts without prior

authorization from the majority union are held to be illegal. Certain other strikes also are generally held unlawful, including some strikes for economic betterment (*e.g.,* where no prior notice has been given to the employer), strikes in defiance of an existing union certification, and jurisdictional strikes (those called in competition for work with another union).

    3) Violation of federal statute. If the intent of a strike is to induce the violation of an existing, valid federal statute (and some state statutes), it will be held unlawful. For example, the practice of "featherbedding" (*e.g.,* maintaining positions that have no duties) is prohibited by the NLRA. Hence, a strike that takes as its object the inducement of that practice will be deemed illegal.

3. **Sources of Claimed Constitutional Right to Strike.** The Supreme Court has never determined whether there is an absolute constitutional right to strike. The sources for such a right might be the following:

    a. **First Amendment.** The First Amendment guarantees of free speech, press, and assembly.

    b. **Fifth Amendment.** The prohibition in the Fifth Amendment against deprivation of life, liberty, or property without due process of law.

    c. **Fourteenth Amendment.** Those provisions of the Fourteenth Amendment that make the First and Fifth Amendments applicable to the states.

    d. **Thirteenth Amendment.** The prohibition in the Thirteenth Amendment against slavery and involuntary servitude.

4. **The Right to Picket.** As with the strike, picketing will be termed unlawful only on consideration of its purpose and the manner in which it is conducted. The recent trend of federal legislation has moved in the direction of stricter regulation of picketing activities.

5. **Regulating the Means by Which Picketing Is Carried Out.** NLRA section 8(b)(1)(A) prohibits both mass picketing, which deters employees from entering or leaving a plant, and picketing accompanied by threats or violence.

    a. **Obstructing entrances.** Thus, obstructing plant entrances with the intent of prohibiting nonstrikers from entering or leaving is unlawful, whether or not the attempts are successful.

    b. **Mass picketers.** Note, however, that the mere presence of mass picketers who do not obstruct entrances or exits does not in and of itself violate section 8(b)(1)(A).

    c. **Isolated misconduct.** And minor, isolated instances of misconduct along a picket line will not necessarily amount to the degree of violence prohibited by the Act.

International Brotherhood of Teamsters, Local 695 v. Vogt, Inc.

    d. **State injunction against picketing--International Brotherhood of Teamsters, Local 695 v. Vogt, Inc.,** 354 U.S. 284 (1957).

        1) **Facts.** The union (D), attempting to organize 15 to 20 employees at a Wisconsin gravel pit, picketed the pit and consequently substantially damaged the business by interrupting or delaying shipments. The employer (P) filed suit in state court, which enjoined the picketing. D appeals.

        2) **Issue.** Does a state have the right to enjoin picketing that is occurring in the absence of a labor dispute (and is, in essence, coercing the employer into helping the union organize) when picketing for such reasons is against state law?

        3) **Held.** Yes. Judgment affirmed.

            a) States have the power to enjoin picketing that is against federal or state law.

            b) The cases have established a broad field in which states may prohibit or regulate picketing in furtherance of some state policy, whether legislative or common law. In this controversy, picketing, although peaceful, was for the unlawful purpose (in Wisconsin) of coercing the employer into helping the union organize.

        4) **Comment.** Thus, picketing may be enjoined when it violates federal law (*e.g.*, an unfair labor practice), or state legislation or judicial decisions. Cases which enjoin picketing often concern the violation of state laws which are equivalent to the NLRA; *i.e.*, the activity in question would be prohibited by the NLRA, but occurs in some area beyond the coverage of the Act (*e.g.*, purely *intrastate* commerce). (State/federal interrelations are treated in more detail in chapter VIII of this outline.)

    e. **Secondary picketing.** Note also that secondary picketing (where the site of the picketing activity is somewhere other than that of the primary labor dispute) has been severely restricted. This subject is discussed in more detail *infra*.

Edward J. DeBartolo Corp. v. Florida Gulf Coast Building & Construction Trades Council

6. **Handbilling at Shopping Mall--Edward J. DeBartolo Corp. v. Florida Gulf Coast Building & Construction Trades Council,** 485 U.S. 568 (1988).

    a. **Facts.** The Edward J. DeBartolo Corporation (P) owned a shopping mall at which H.J. Wilson Company planned to build a store. Wilson contracted with H.J. High Construction Company to do the work. Neither P nor any of the 85 mall tenants were involved in Wilson's selection of a contractor. The union (D) became involved in a dispute with High over substandard wages and benefits, and began distributing handbills at the mall entrances asking customers not to shop at any of the mall stores.

There was no picketing and no attempt to bring about a secondary strike by mall workers. After D refused to change the wording of handbills or to restrict the location of activity, P filed a complaint with the NLRB charging an unfair labor practice under section 8(b)(4). The case eventually reached the Supreme Court, which concluded that the handbilling did not fall within section 8(b)(4)'s proviso exempting publicity intended to inform the public that a primary employer's product was being distributed by a secondary employer. Because the lower courts had not made findings on whether the handbilling was covered by section 8(b)(4) in the first place and whether the First Amendment was implicated, the Supreme Court remanded the case. On remand, the Board found that the handbilling constituted coercion and was proscribed by section 8(b)(4)(ii)(B), and stated that it would presume the NLRA constitutional. The court of appeals refused enforcement, concluding that consumer publicity is not prohibited. The case again reached the Supreme Court.

b. **Issue.** Is stationary handbilling requesting a general consumer boycott of a mall because a tenant is using contractors who pay substandard wages contrary to section 8(b)(4)?

c. **Held.** No. Judgment affirmed.

1) Section 8(b)(4)(ii)'s prohibition of secondary boycotts requires a showing of threats, coercion, or restraint. This is in contrast to section 8(b)(4)(i)'s prohibition of secondary strikes, which requires only a showing of inducement or encouragement.

2) The Board found that the handbilling "coerced" mall tenants by attempting to inflict economic harm on them. This interpretation is too broad. Under this interpretation, a union could not even urge its own members not to shop in the mall. The legislative history of the 1959 amendments to the NLRA does not reveal an intent to bar boycotting appeals other than picketing. The proviso allowing publicity to inform consumers that a secondary employer is distributing a primary employer's product should be viewed as a clarification of section 8(b)(4)'s meaning rather than as an exception to a general ban on consumer publicity.

3) Because we view section 8(b)(4) as not reaching the handbilling involved in this case, it is unnecessary to decide the First Amendment issue.

7. **Exclusion of Pickets from Shopping Mall--Hudgens v. NLRB,** 424 U.S. 507 (1976).

   Hudgens v. NLRB

a. **Facts.** Union members who were shoe warehouse employees (located elsewhere) peacefully picketed in front of one of the company's retail stores in an enclosed, privately owned shopping mall. The mall manager threatened the picketers with arrest for criminal trespass unless they left the mall. The picketers' union (P) filed a complaint with the NLRB against Hudgens (D), the owner of the mall, alleging that the threat of prosecution for trespass was an unlawful labor practice and an infringement of their First Amendment rights of free speech and assembly. The NLRB found for the picketers, and the court of appeals affirmed. D appeals.

b. **Issues.**

   1) Did the exclusion of picketers from an enclosed privately owned shopping mall infringe their rights to free speech and assembly?

   2) Was the threat of prosecution for criminal trespass an unfair labor practice?

c. **Held.** a) No. b) Possibly. Judgment vacated and case remanded.

   1) The First Amendment guarantees the rights of free speech and assembly only against governmental interference, not against private action, as in the present case. The Constitution does not require the owner of private property who opens that property to private commerce to dedicate that property to public use. A shopping center is not the equivalent of a company-owned town, and *Amalgamated Food Employees Union Local 590 v. Logan Valley Plaza, Inc.*, 391 U.S. 308 (1968), which suggested that malls were similar to municipalities for First Amendment activities, is expressly overruled.

   2) Although the activity was not protected by the First Amendment, the case is remanded for the Board to determine whether, under section 7, the activity was appropriate taking into account: (i) the lawful, peaceful nature of the picketing for economic strike activity rather than organizational; (ii) the fact that the picketers were employees, not outsiders; and (iii) the fact that the picketing impinged upon the property rights of an individual who was not the employer.

d. **Dissent** (Marshall, Brennan, JJ.). The case could be disposed of on a nonconstitutional ground by applying the *Babcock & Wilcox* rule, *supra*. There were not effective alternate means of communication available to the employees.

   1) The owner of a modern shopping center is able to exercise a monopoly over places for effective communication. Consequently, access may be as essential for effective speech as are the streets and sidewalks of a municipality or a company town.

   2) The *Marsh v. Alabama*, 326 U.S. 501 (1946), criteria (control by the owner of all places essential for communicating about activities related to the shopping center) is the proper way to deal with these cases.

e. **Remand.** On remand to the NLRB, the Board considered that the economic activity in this case deserved as much protection as the organizational activity in *Babcock & Wilcox*. It concluded that D had violated section 8(a)(1). It emphasized that the picketers were employees of the company whose store was being picketed. It found no other reasonable means of communication to publicize the facts of a labor dispute of one store in the mall. Finally, the Board characterized D as an "agent" for the lessees and concluded that, in leasing to other merchants, D had submitted his own property to the incidents of lawful labor-related activity directed at the merchants.

f. **Comment.** Picketing is not protected constitutionally to the same extent as communication by spoken word. It is recognized that regardless of the message being communicated, the mere presence of a picket line may induce violent action, even though the picket line itself is conducted in a peaceful manner. Consequently, the entire setting must be peaceful in order to bring constitutional guarantees into play.

8. Shopping Center Organizational Picketing. In 1988, the Board developed a three-part test for evaluating organizational picketing in front of a store located inside of a private shopping center. The Board considered: (i) the strength of the section 7 interest, (ii) the strength of the property interests, and (iii) the availability of alternative means for the union to communicate with the employees. [*See* Jean Country, *supra*] Later, in *Lechmere, supra,* the Supreme Court rejected this test with respect to nonemployee union supporters.

D. THE NATIONAL LABOR RELATIONS ACT

1. Union Unfair Labor Practices Affecting Organization.

   a. Section 8(b)(1)—restraint or coercion.

   1) **Unlawful activities.** Violence, threats, and other coercive activity in the course of an organizing drive or in connection with a strike by a labor union are unlawful. The NLRA provides remedies against these unfair practices and the NLRB is empowered to take whatever steps may be necessary to implement the remedy selected.

   2) **Prohibited activities.** Compare section 8(a)(1) (applicable to employers) to section 8(b)(1) (applicable to unions). The restriction placed upon unions does not include the word "interference." Hence, the NLRB has much greater latitude in finding an unfair labor practice with respect to employers than with respect to unions. For unions, there must be a finding that goes so far as to constitute "restraint" or "coercion" (or of activities that tend to restrain or coerce). Thus, the same act a union may perform with impunity might give rise to a charge against an employer. For example, an employer's effort to spy on her employees' organizing activities might be held coercive, while the same activity by a union would be approved as a necessary aspect of its campaign (*i.e.*, securing information without which it could not proceed). Section 8(b)(1) may, in the final analysis, be directed only at those union activities that involve violence, threats, or excessive intimidation.

      a) **Physical coercion.** Actual or threatened physical restraint or coercion is a violation (*e.g.*, where threats of violence are made against nonstriking employees as they enter a struck plant).

      b) **Economic coercion.** Economic coercion may be a violation. For example, it is unlawful at an organizational meeting for a union official to threaten an employee by saying that those who do not join the union will eventually lose their jobs.

    c) **Other forms of unlawful coercion.** Harassing employees during working hours, breaking up an employees' meeting not sponsored by the union, etc., may constitute unlawful coercion.

    d) **Picketing.** While *peaceful* picketing may violate another section of the NLRA (such as section 8(b)(7), discussed *infra*), the Supreme Court has held that it does not violate section 8(b)(1). It may, of course, become unlawful coercive activity. [*See* Vogt, *supra*]

3) **Employee coercion.** Note that this section mainly deals with union coercion of employees, not coercion of supervisors or management. Hence, a threat by a union representative to a company officer of "trouble" if she attempts to break a strike would be permissible if no employee were present. If, however, an employee is present or is likely to hear about or be influenced by the statements made, such a threat might be termed "coercive" under the terms of this section. In *United States v. Enmons*, 410 U.S. 396 (1973), the Court held (5-4) that violence by union members (*e.g.*, blowing up a substation, firing rifles at three transformers, draining oil from a fourth, etc.) did not support the government's prosecution under federal law for conspiracy to extort, since the union's end was the legitimate objective of higher wages for employees and the force was therefore not wrongful under federal law (although the individuals could be prosecuted under state criminal statutes).

b. **Organizational and representational picketing.**

1) **Legality.** In *C.S. Smith Metropolitan Market Co. v. Lyons*, 16 Cal. 2d 389 (1940), a union picketed the employer's premises to get the employees to join and to get the company to hire only union members. The company had never discriminated against the union and none of its employees had shown any interest in the union. The picketing caused a loss of business and the company obtained an injunction. The union appealed. The picketing was held to be legal. The California court ruled that the right to carry on business without interference was not absolute and that the union interference must be judged by its objectives. The court held that under a state statute similar to the NLRA, the union had a legitimate interest in the employment relations of an unorganized employer since they affected working conditions and bargaining power of employees throughout the industry.

2) **Limitation in the NLRA.** Section 8(b)(7) is a 1959 amendment to the NLRA which limits the right of unions to picket interstate businesses for "organizational purposes."

    a) **Uncertified union.** In certain instances, section 8(b)(7) declares it an unfair labor practice for an uncertified union to picket in order to force an employer to grant recognition or to bargain with it or to require employees to accept it as their bargaining agent. This condition applies where (i) another union has been recognized and under section 9(c) no question of representation can be raised; (ii) a valid election has been conducted within the preceding 12 months; or (iii) where picketing has continued for an "unreasonable time" not to exceed 30 days and no petition for representation has been presented to the Board. Note, however, that peaceful picketing for the purpose of "informing the public that an employer does not hire union workers" is permissible if the claim is truthful and it does not induce employees or other employers from refusing to continue their normal services with the picketed employer (*e.g.,* pickup and delivery, etc.).

b) **Board priority.** Charges of section 8(b)(7) violations receive priority by the NLRB. The Board must seek an injunction against the unlawful picketing unless a section 8(a)(2) charge (employer domination of a union) has been filed and appears to be true. In the latter event, an injunction will not lie.

c) **Problems.**

(1) The term "picket" is not defined by the statute. The decision as to what constitutes picketing is made on a case-by-case basis. In one case, for example, the courts held that signs tacked on a tree by union people who then remained in their cars across the street from the employer's premises did *not* constitute picketing. [*See* NLRB v. United Furniture Workers, 337 F.2d 936 (2d Cir. 1964)]

(2) In order to constitute a violation, picketing must have as one of its purposes "organization or recognition." Hence, "picketing" to protest a substandard working condition does not come within the section. Neither would picketing to persuade an employer to abandon racially discriminatory hiring practices.

3) **Petition for certification not filed within thirty-day limit--Hod Carriers Local 840 (Blinne Construction Co.),** 135 N.L.R.B. 1153 (1962).

a) **Facts.** The employees signed cards designating the union as their representative, but the employer (D) refused recognition, transferring employees to reduce the majority. The union (P) picketed. P filed an unfair labor practice charge without a request for certification within the 30-day limit. After the 30-day period had expired, the NLRB denied part of the charge; P then filed a petition for certification. On hearing before the Board.

b) **Issue.** Is it a violation of section 8(b)(7) where a union has failed to make a timely petition but where it had a majority union, and the employer committed an unfair labor practice during the time of the picketing?

c) **Held.** Yes. No exception will be made for unions not certified but having majority status.

(1) Even where the employer has committed an unfair labor practice by not recognizing the majority, if a charge has been filed, a valid election cannot be held until the unfair labor practice charged has been disposed of.

Hod Carriers Local 840 (Blinne Construction Co.)

(2) However, the union still must file a certification petition within 30 days of the beginning of picketing in order not to violate section 8(b)(7).

4) Publicity or informational picketing. The other proviso in section 8(b)(7)(C) deals with "informational picketing." Where no union has previously been certified and no valid election has been held within the past 12 months, picketing can be used as a method of informing the public and no petition for certification need be filed within 30 days. In 1961, the Board held that picketing, to be protected by the proviso, had to be "purely" informational (*i.e.*, the picketing union must not be demanding immediate recognition). [Local Joint Executive Board of Hotel Employees, 130 N.L.R.B. 570 (1961)] The Board, upon a change of membership, reversed itself in the same case. To be protected, the following conditions have to be satisfied: (i) the information has to truthfully state that the employer does not employ union members or have a contract with a union; (ii) there must be no present intent to attain recognition; and (iii) the picketing must not interrupt deliveries or performances of services.

a) **Interruption of deliveries--NLRB v. Local 3, International Brotherhood of Electrical Workers,** 317 F.2d 193 (2d Cir. 1963)

(1) **Facts.** Local 3 (D) decided to protest the awarding of a post office renovation contract to Picoult (P). D picketed the building, including side and rear delivery areas, and on two occasions turned away deliveries to P by employees of other companies. D claimed its object was to have the subcontract let to a company that recognized it or, if that failed, to simply oust P. The Board found the picketing to violate section 8(b)(7)(C), and D appeals.

(2) **Issue.** Is picketing that has as its purpose to signal economic action backed by organized labor groups permissible?

(3) **Held.** No. Case remanded for further consideration by the Board.

(a) Permissible picketing, as defined by section 8(b)(7), is designed to influence members of the unorganized public, as individuals. It is picketing "where an object thereof is forcing or requiring an employer to recognize or bargain" and "for the purpose of truthfully advising the public."

(b) The "advising the public" requirement was not intended to be so broadly construed as to "include organized labor groups which, at a word from the picketers, would impose economic sanctions upon the employer," by group discipline, thereby tending to coerce employees in their freedom to accept or reject union membership (since they stand to lose their jobs when the employer goes out of business).

(c) The case is remanded to the Board for the determination as to whether the picketing in this case was for "advising the public" or whether it was the union's tactical purpose to signal economic sanctions backed by organized labor groups.

2. **Secondary Pressure—Regulation of Boycotts.** Section 8(b)(4) also applies to union action aimed exclusively at secondary employers. A "secondary boycott" is defined as union pressure—in the form of strikes, picketing, threats, or other coercion—aimed at an employer or other person with whom the union has no labor dispute, with the object of persuading or coercing that neutral party to stop dealing with a primary party with whom the union has a dispute, and thus ultimately of persuading the primary party to meet union demands.

   a. **Activities proscribed.** Section 8(b)(4) proscribes two types of activity: (i) engaging in a strike, refusing to handle goods, or inducing another individual to strike or refuse to handle goods; or (ii) threatening or otherwise coercing an employer for any of the illegal objects discussed below, including purely verbal threats.

   b. **Illegal objects.** Both types of secondary activity described above are prohibited by section 8(b)(4) if they are undertaken for any of the following purposes:

      1) *Section 8(b)(4)(A)*—to force an employer to enter into a "hot cargo" agreement.

      2) *Section 8(b)(4)(B)*—to force a third party to cease handling the employer's goods, or to force the third party to cease doing business with the employer.

      3) *Section 8(b)(4)(D)*—to compel an employer to assign work to one union rather than another. Section 8(b)(4)(D) is analytically distinct from the other provisions of section 8(b)(4) and it is treated separately below.

   c. **Judicial interpretation of section 8(b)(4).** Legislative history clearly shows that section 8(b)(4) was designed to curtail secondary pressure. Yet, the statute itself never refers directly to secondary pressure. Moreover, it does not clearly specify which activities are prohibited thereby. If the section were to be enforced literally, it would prohibit almost all strike activity, since one object of any strike is to induce or prevent persons from doing business with the primary employer.

      1) **Introduction.** Interpreting section 8(b)(4), the Supreme Court has held only that the section is limited to protecting an innocent secondary employer from the effects of a labor dispute involving another employer. In other words, the statute does not apply to strike activity unless the employees of a secondary employer are induced to strike (or to use other economic weapons) against their employer in order to aid a union striking another employer. [Local 761, International Union of Electrical, Radio & Machine Workers v. NLRB, *infra*—the "General Electric Co." case] The fact that the boycott which affects secondary employers is politically motivated will not prevent it from violating section 8(b)(4). [ILA v. Allied International, Inc. 456 U.S. 212 (1982)]

         a) **No broad rules.** The Supreme Court in *General Electric, infra,* however, refused to promulgate any broad rules beyond the

Labor Law - 111

foregoing. The Court indicated that in the absence of a specific legislative standard for determining whether particular secondary activity is prohibited by section 8(b)(4), the Board and the courts must develop the substantive law on an *ad hoc*, case-by-case basis.

2) **Refusal to cross a picket line.** A qualification attached to section 8(b) provides that secondary effects of primary strikes or picketing (*i.e.*, directed against the employer with whom its employees have a dispute) do not constitute an unfair labor practice where (i) the picketing is an outgrowth of a strike by the pickets against their employer, (ii) the strike is authorized by the employees' union, and (iii) the union involved is duly entitled to recognition by the employer. When each of these conditions is met, employees of secondary employers who have been sent to the struck place of business in the ordinary course of dealings may refuse to cross the picket line and the effect will not be an unfair labor practice on the part of those involved in the primary strike effort. [*See* NLRB v. International Rice Milling Co., 341 U.S. 665 (1951)] Note, however, that it has been held that the secondary employer whose employees refuse to cross the primary picket line can fire those employees and the employer later has no obligation to rehire them. [NLRB v. L.G. Everist, Inc., 334 F.2d 312 (8th Cir. 1964)]

3) **The "primary action" proviso.** The primary action proviso, added in 1959, states that "nothing in this clause (B) shall be construed to make unlawful, where not otherwise unlawful, any primary strike or primary picketing." Note that section 8(b)(7), discussed above, indicates several situations in which primary picketing is not lawful, and section 8(b)(4)(C) notes one situation (there are others) when a primary strike is not lawful.

4) **Publicity other than picketing.** Another proviso to section 8(b)(4) protects "publicity" designed to inform the public of a labor dispute with the primary employer or producer where the primary employer's products are "distributed" by a secondary employer against whom the publicity is primarily aimed. The protected sphere, however, includes only publicity "other than picketing" and then only on the condition that the effect of such publicity is not to bring about a work stoppage at the secondary employer's place of business.

   a) **Picketing of secondary employer.** The Supreme Court has held that notwithstanding the "other than picketing" condition applied to this "publicity proviso", picketing of the secondary employer to produce a consumer boycott of a struck primary employer firm's product is lawful. since the restriction applied only to that situation in which the object was to produce a boycott against all products handled by the picketed secondary employer (*i.e.*, the distributor), thus forcing him to cease dealing with the primary employer. Taking this distinction, it should be noted that the NLRB held a union in violation of the NLRA when, in the course of a dispute with a newspaper, the union picketed a restaurant hoping to force the restaurant to cease advertising in the newspaper. Because of the nature of the secondary employer's business, the logical intent of the "advertising" could only be to enforce a boycott of the firm's entire business.

   b) **Handbilling.** The Supreme Court has also held lawful handbilling to the public as well as handbilling to retailers seeking to induce them not to handle products distributed by struck workers. The NLRB has specifically rejected the claim that the same rules should apply to handbilling as to picketing at a secondary site. Hence, with respect to other forms of publicity, there is not the same "all products" limitation that applies to rule out picketing.

5) **Actions other than boycotts.** Section 8(b)(4) prohibits strikes, inducements to strike, threats, and coercion in certain areas other than that of secondary boycotts.

   a) **Secondary situations.** Where an action is directed to the creation of a "hot cargo" agreement in violation of section 8(e) or is intended to force an employer by secondary pressure to recognize a union not certified by the NLRB, it is held unlawful.

   b) **Primary situations.** Where such action is of a primary nature and is intended to (i) force an employer or self-employed person to join a labor or employer organization; (ii) force an employer, in defiance of another union's prior certification, to recognize the competing union; or (iii) compel an employer to make specified work assignments not stipulated by an NLRB order of certification, such action is held unlawful.

   c) **Note.** In all of these instances, the rules defining strikes, inducements, and other coercion apply as well as the provisos that privilege certain publicity other than picketing and the refusal to cross a picket line. The "primary action" proviso, however, will apply *only* to secondary boycotts and to secondary action seeking the recognition of an uncertified union. Primary action for recognition of an uncertified union is governed by section 8(b)(7) (as noted above) and is not a primary right. Section 13 preserved the primary right to strike.

6) **Changes made by the Labor-Management Reporting and Disclosure Act of 1959.** This Act substantially enlarged the scope of section 8(b)(4), which had to this point defined certain unlawful objectives and prohibited strikes and inducements to strike for those ends. As amended, however, the section prohibits a work stoppage directed toward "any individual employed by any person" covered by the Act, as well as threats against "any person engaged in business covered by the Act." The prohibitions now include coercion of employers and the inducement of work stoppages by supervisors, railroad workers, farm laborers, and others rather than just those technically covered by the Act's definition of an "employee" (as had previously been the case). The 1959 amendments also enlarged the number of objectives made unlawful by including "hot cargo" agreements in violation of section 8(e) within its coverage.

d. **Contractor-subcontractor relationships in construction industry.**

1) **Introduction.** Construction sites present particularly difficult problems in separating legal secondary activity from illegal conduct, due to the presence on most sites of a general contractor and several different subcontractors. Each subcontractor may have a different degree of independence from the general contractor, and there may be complicated relationships among the various subcontractors.

NLRB v. Denver Building & Construction Trades Council

2) **Picketing entire site is illegal--NLRB v. Denver Building & Construction Trades Council,** 341 U.S. 675 (1951).

   a) **Facts.** In 1947, Doose & Linter (P), a general building contractor constructing a commercial building and using all union employees, awarded a subcontract for electrical work to Gould & Preisner, a firm employing nonunion workers. Gould & Preisner was involved in a long-standing dispute with the local union. The union advised P that if Gould & Preisner's employees continued to work, the site would be picketed. The picket went into effect after P refused to release Gould. All union employees did not report to work and as a result, P ordered Gould & Preisner off the job. Section 8(b)(4)(A) forbids striking to force an employer to cease doing business with another business. The Board ruled that the object of the strike, if not the only object, was to force P to cease business with Gould & Preisner and that the union placard was merely a signal tantamount to a direction to strike and had no significant application to free speech. The court of appeals ruled the activity to be primary and refused to enforce the Board's decision. P appeals.

   b) **Issue.** Does a union commit an unfair labor practice if it strikes a construction site to force a union contractor to terminate a contract with a specific subcontractor with whom it has a dispute?

   c) **Held.** Yes. Judgment reversed.

      (1) The contractual agreement between P and Gould & Preisner defines the relationship as that of two employers doing business, not of employer and employee.

         (a) This is not like *International Rice Milling, supra,* where the appeal was to two employees not to cross a picket line in the traditional way.

      (2) Thus, D's argument that it engaged in a primary dispute with P is not valid. Striking to force an employer to cease business with another is forbidden in section 8(b)(4)(A). Operations at a common situs do not alter the legal relationship between the two employers.

      (3) Section 8(c), which safeguards freedom of speech, is inapplicable in this instance, as the placard was a mere signal to engage in an unfair labor practice.

   d) **Dissent** (Douglas, Reed, JJ.). The use of union and nonunion workers on the same job is a long-standing concern of trade unionism. D was not out to destroy the contractor because it was anti-union. The action was not carried to other sites. All D was doing was to protest the requirement to work alongside nonunion workers on the job. The action would be a proper primary activity. The presence of a subcontractor does not alter the realities of the situation.

e. **Application of section 8(b)(4) to specific problems involving secondary pressure.**

1) **Common situs situations.** Where more than one employer occupies the same physical location (*e.g.,* plant site, construction site, etc.), it may be difficult to determine whether a union is engaged in illegal secondary action because any strike activity directed toward one employer at the site may affect all.

   a) **Conflicting interests involved.** The most frequent common situs problem develops where the union and the secondary employer each have legitimate but opposing interests that deserve protection—the union must be able to reach the primary employer at a place where its picketing and other economic activity will have an effect upon that employer. At the same time, the secondary employer has an interest in avoiding the dispute between the union and the primary employer; as a neutral (and innocent) third party, he should not be put "in the middle" or forced to suffer economic harm as a result of the primary dispute.

   b) *Moore Dry Dock* rules--**Sailors' Union of the Pacific (Moore Dry Dock Co.),** 92 N.L.R.B. 547 (1950).

   Sailors' Union of the Pacific (Moore Dry Dock Co.)

   (1) **Facts.** Samsoc contracted with Kaiser Gypsum to transport product from Mexico on a Samsoc ship (Phopho), which was in the Moore Dry Dock (P) to convert it for this purpose and to replace its American crew with a Greek one. P agreed to the training of the Greek crew on board for two weeks before completion of conversion. When the Sailors' Union (D) learned of this arrangement, it demanded bargaining rights on the ship, but was refused. D picketed the ship and successfully persuaded P's employees not to work on the "hot" ship, although they worked on others at the dock. P charged secondary strike activity in violation of section 8(b)(4)(A).

   (2) **Issue.** Does the right to picket follow an ambulatory situs while it is on the premises of a secondary employer when the only way to picket that situs is at the secondary employer's premises?

   (3) **Held.** Yes. Order for D.

   (a) The right of neither the union to picket nor of the secondary employer to be free from picketing can be absolute.

   (b) Normally the premises of the primary employer is the situs, but it may be ambulatory. The enmeshing of premises and situs qualifies both rights.

   (c) Picketing of premises of the secondary employer is primary (i) if the picketing is limited to times when the situs of dispute is on the secondary employer's premises, (ii) if the primary employer at that time is engaged in its normal business at the situs, and (iii) if picketing is limited to an area close to situs and the picketing clearly discloses the dispute is with the primary employer.

   (d) When the picketing began, the entire crew of the Phopho had been hired and various members of the crew commenced work painting, cooking, cleaning, and oiling. They were serving purposes of Samsoc and not P since they were getting the ship ready for sea. Phopho was engaged in normal business.

- (e) The picketing was as close to Phopho as permitted. Picketing was careful to indicate dispute was with the primary employer, not with P. Since the conditions for permitting picketing on P's premises were met, the picketing is allowed.

(4) Comment. Ownership of the job site apparently is not a relevant factor. These same rules have subsequently been applied to picketing at a site owned by the primary employer.

Douds v. Metropolitan Federation of Architects

c) **Picketing subcontractor of employer--Douds v. Metropolitan Federation of Architects,** 75 F. Supp. 672 (S.D.N.Y. 1948).

(1) Facts. Regional Director Douds (P) filed suit to enjoin Metropolitan (D) from engaging in certain activities alleged to violate section 8(b)(4)(A). Ebasco Services, Inc., had been in the business of providing engineering services since 1905. In 1946, Ebasco began subcontracting some of its work to Project Engineering Company. In 1947, D struck Ebasco; consequently, Ebasco transferred more of its work to Project. D then began picketing Project's offices, calling Project's employees "scab", "louse", and "rat", and demanding that Project no longer accept work from Ebasco. This suit followed.

(2) Issue. For purposes of section 8(b)(4)(A), is a subcontractor "doing business" with the primary employer when it begins to perform the same services that striking employees had done?

(3) Held. No. Judgment for D.

- (a) From the legislative history, it is evident that section 8(b)(4)(A)'s "doing business" language had as its purpose preventing secondary boycotts. Secondary boycotts are those which injure the business of a third person who is wholly unconcerned in the disagreement between an employer and his employees.

- (b) Here, Project cannot claim to be unconcerned in the disagreement between Ebasco and the union. Some of the factors indicating this are: (i) Ebasco did not retain Project's services; rather, Ebasco paid Project its employees' wages plus an amount for overhead; (ii) Ebasco directly supervised Project's employees who worked on Ebasco projects; and (iii) the economic effect of using Project's services on Ebasco's employees was the same as if Ebasco hired strikebreakers to work on its own premises.

- (c) Corporate ownership or insulation of legal interests between two businesses cannot be conclusive as to neutrality or disinterestedness in a labor dispute.

2) **"Separate gate" cases.** When labor disputes occur at premises occupied or serviced by more than one employer, attempts are frequently made to isolate the employees and employer involved in the dispute from other employers at the

location. The device most commonly used is the creation of separate gates or entrances to the premises, one for employees of the primary employer and another (or others) for the remaining employees. The theory is that any picketing can then be confined to the gate reserved for the primary employer.

a) **Gate used by employees of independent contractor--Local 761, International Union of Electrical, Radio & Machine Workers v. NLRB (General Electric Co.),** 366 U.S. 667 (1961).

    (1) Facts. The union (D) peacefully picketed at General Electric's (P's) Appliance Park, a large manufacturing facility, because of 24 unsettled grievances with the company. All five entrances to the plant were picketed, including Gate 3-A, which was ordered by P to be used solely for entrance of employees of independent contractors. Normally, those employees alone would use Gate 3-A, although rarely a General Electric employee was allowed to pass by the guard in violation of company instructions. Because of the picketing, almost all of the employees of the independent contractors refused to enter. The Board found a section 8(b)(4)(A) violation, and the court of appeals enforced its order. D appeals.

    (2) Issue. Is a union's picketing of a gate used exclusively by employees of independent contractors a violation of section 8(b)(4)(A)?

    (3) Held. Yes. Case remanded.

        (a) There is no bright line for this problem. The *Moore Dry Dock* standards, *supra,* have been applied to picketing at the situs of the primary employer. The union must minimize the impact on secondary employers.

        (b) The key to the problem here is in the type of work being done by the independent employees. A separate gate must be reserved for persons doing work unrelated to normal operations of the employer.

        (c) The case is remanded to the Board for determination of a newly raised question of mixed use of the gate; if the employees of the independent contractor performed conventional maintenance work necessary to the normal operation of the company, the use of the gate would be a mixed use falling outside the bar of section 8(b)(4)(A).

    (4) Comments.

        (a) Employers should not be allowed to use the separate gate device to defeat the traditional objectives of a strike.

        (b) Typical examples of work related to operations of the primary employer include making deliveries for the primary employer and making repairs on the employer's plant or equipment. Construction of capital improvements likely would not be included.

        (c) In all other situations, however, picketing at a separate gate is ***prohibited*** if the separate gate is ***clearly marked*** as being for outside employees only.

b) Relatedness of work. In *Markwell & Hartz, Inc. v. NLRB*, 387 F.2d 79 (5th Cir. 1967), Markwell & Hartz ("M & H") was the general contractor at a site on which it did 80% of the work. Its employees were represented by UMW; it used two subcontractors for the rest of the work who were represented by the Trades Council. The Council demanded recognition for M & H employees and picketed the project. M & H built four separate gates, three for the subcontractors, their employees and supplies, and the fourth for itself. The Council picketed all four gates. M & H filed a section 8(b)(4)(B) charge. The Council argued that its picketing was protected under *NLRB v. General Electric Co., supra*. The Board concluded that *General Electric* did not control since the struck employer was not the owner of the premises. Because the subcontractors were to be considered neutrals, it applied *Moore Dry Dock* rules, *supra,* and found the picketing improper. The court of appeals affirmed. Judge Wisdom, in dissent, could find no basis for an "ownership of premises" distinction in *General Electric*. He argued that the crucial issue should be "relatedness" of the work, and that the rule should be the same for all businesses including the construction industry.

f. Exceptions to section 8(b)(4). There are two express provisos to section 8(b)(4), which exempt certain types of conduct from the ban on boycotts:

1) Requests not to cross picket lines. Activity that may cause employees of a neutral employer not to cross a picket line to make deliveries at the premises of the primary employer where a strike is in progress is specifically permitted. To comply with this exception, however, the union doing the picketing and carrying on the strike must be duly certified, and the strike must be an authorized one (ratified by the members of the union). This is often referred to as "signal picketing".

2) The "publicity proviso." Another exception to section 8(b)(4) allows the union to advise the public, by "means other than picketing," that a "product or products" are being "produced" by an employer with whom the union has a dispute, and that such products are being distributed by another secondary employer. [§8(b)(4)(i)] (*Example*: Newspaper advertisements or handbills asking the public to refrain from buying farm produce packed by nonunion growers and distributed through supermarkets.)

a) Limitation. There is no protection if the "publicity" induces a work stoppage or interferes with deliveries to the secondary employers. A union having a dispute with an employer who was constructing a new department store in a mall was not allowed to picket the mall's owner and tenants. [*Edward J. DeBartolo v. NLRB, supra*]

[*NLRB v. Fruit & Vegetable Packers & Warehousemen, Local 760 (Tree Fruits)*]

b) Secondary picketing of retail store--NLRB v. Fruit & Vegetable Packers & Warehousemen, Local 760 (Tree Fruits), 377 U.S. 58 (1964).

(1) Facts. Local 760 (D) called a strike against fruit packer firms in Yakima, Washington, that sold Washington state apples to Safeway, a retail chain. D instituted a consumer boycott against the apples in support of the strike and bills were distributed to customers of Safeway. Picketing was peaceful but placards appealed to customers not to buy Washington state apples being packed by struck firms employing nonunion workers in substandard wage scale and working conditions. The NLRB issued a cease and desist order against D for consumer picketing in front of a secondary establishment, a violation of section 8(b)(4). The court of appeals set aside the Board's order since Safeway was not likely to suffer a substantial economic impact and remanded the case to the Board to determine if Safeway had been "threatened" or "coerced."

(2) **Issue.** Does a union's peaceful and limited secondary picketing of retail stores appealing to customers not to buy specific products of firms that the union is striking constitute a labor violation?

(3) **Held.** No. The court of appeals reversal of the Board's order was proper.

  (a) Section 8(b)(4) forbids coercive picketing against secondary employers. A picketing directed only at a struck product and not going beyond the primary dispute and not against the secondary establishment is legal.

  (b) The question of whether Safeway was likely to suffer economic loss is not the governing factor in establishing a violation of section 8(b)(4)(ii)(B).

(4) **Concurrence** (Black, J.). Based on the analysis of the legislative history set out in the dissent, I conclude that the activity in this case is in violation of section 8(b)(4)(ii)(B). However, the section abridges freedom of speech under the First Amendment.

(5) **Dissent** (Harlan, Stewart, JJ.). Nothing in the Act justifies the fine distinction drawn by the Court between general and limited product picketing. The Act speaks of "threatening, coercing, or restraining any person." The distinction between lowering the purchases of a struck product and ceasing to purchase the product because of consumer refusal to buy a product is not a realistic one. The legislative history does not support the Court's position about the meaning of the Act. Only handbilling, not consumer picketing, is permitted.

c) **Who is a "producer."** There has been considerable litigation over which employers can be regarded as the "producer" of a product, so as to permit union publicity urging a boycott against persons dealing with that employer. Basically, the courts hold that a "producer" is anyone who enhances the economic value of the product ultimately sold or consumed, meaning that the union may in effect urge a public boycott against anyone in the marketing chain.

  (1) For example, the term "producer" encompasses a wholesaler of the product, thus allowing the union to boycott by handbilling against a retailer supplied by that wholesaler.

  (2) Likewise, an electrical subcontractor is considered a "producer" because its services enhance the value of the project on which it is working. This permits the union to boycott the prime contractor by placing the electrical subcontractor on an "unfair list."

(3) A general contractor may be a "producer" as to the department store for whom it is constructing a store building, but not as to a shopping mall owner or mall tenants.

d) **"Means other than picketing."** Despite the apparent ban in section 8(b)(4)(ii)(B) on picketing as a means of publicizing a dispute, the Supreme Court in *Tree Fruits, supra*, held that Congress had not intended to ban all picketing at secondary sites. Only picketing which unduly coerced the secondary employer was prohibited, so that noncoercive picketing is also protected by the publicity proviso. In *Tree Fruits*, for example, the Court held that peaceful picketing of retailers selling apples produced by the primary employer with whom the union had a dispute was lawful, since it was designed to induce the consumers to cease purchasing the apples (*i.e.*, the product), rather than to cease dealing altogether with the retailer.

(1) **Rationale.** The Court stated that in employing the term "means other than picketing" in the publicity proviso to section 8(b)(4), Congress had not used the "requisite clarity" necessary to effect a broad ban against peaceful picketing that limits first amendment guarantees of free speech.

(2) **Impact—product boycotts by picketing.** The union may lawfully picket a secondary employer for the purpose of imposing a partial, as opposed to a total, consumer boycott; *i.e.*, a boycott aimed at the struck product rather than at all of the products sold by the secondary employer.

e) **What constitutes a "product" boycott.** Picketing a secondary employer to effectuate a product boycott may be unlawful if the appeal to the consumer is so broad that it amounts to a total boycott of the secondary employer.

(1) Thus, union picketing of a secondary employer with signs urging consumers not to buy "products produced by nonunion manufacturers" is unlawful because there is no identification of the manufacturer or product. Since the effect is to induce a stoppage of all trade with the secondary employer, such picketing is not protected under the decision in *Tree Fruits, supra*.

(2) A more difficult problem occurs when the "product" of the primary employer is integrated into the total product sold by the secondary employer. The courts and the Board have differed on this issue. In *K & K Construction Co. v. NLRB*, 592 F.2d 1228 (3d Cir. 1979), the union had a dispute with a carpentry subcontractor on a housing project. It stationed pickets at the main entry of the project where prospective customers came to view the houses and at the developer's sales office at a shopping mall. The Board found no violation since there was no product "merger." The court of appeals found the Board to be in error and concluded that consumers could not separate the carpentry from the developer's product. It found the picketing in effect was asking customers not to deal with the developer.

f) **Main product picketing.** In *NLRB v. Retail Store Employees Union, Local 1001 (Safeco Title Insurance Co.)*, 447 U.S. 607 (1980), the Supreme Court sustained the Board's basis for enjoining picketing of five local title insurance companies that derived 90% of their gross income from sale of Safeco Insurance. The primary dispute was with Safeco. The Supreme Court ordered enforcement, emphasizing the *Tree Fruits, supra,* distinction between picketing that shuts off all trade with the secondary employer and that which merely asks customers not to buy a struck product. In this case, the picketing left the customer with "no realistic option other than to boycott the title companies altogether." Product picketing that threatens neutral parties with ruin or substantial loss are not within the purpose of section 8(b)(4)(ii)(B). The Court distinguished the case of a product making up a major portion of the neutral's business but still substantially less than a single dominant product, in which case neither *Tree Fruits* nor *Safeco* would control.

g. Hot cargo clauses.

1) **Background.** Before the amendment of the NLRA in 1959, the statutory secondary boycott prohibitions applied only to "forcing or requiring" one person to stop doing business with another. Hence, an employer might "voluntarily" agree in a bargaining agreement with a union not to deal with certain persons in the event of a union strike against that person, although a union could not lawfully attempt to enforce such an agreement by strike action. It was not certain how "voluntary" an employer's participation in such an agreement could be.

2) **Section 8(e).** In 1959, Congress passed section 8(e) banning "hot cargo" agreements.

3) **"Work preservation" versus "work acquisition"--National Woodwork Manufacturer's Association v. NLRB,** 386 U.S. 612 (1967). *Natural Woodwork Manufacturer's Association v. NLRB*

   a) **Facts.** Frouge (P), a general contractor working on a housing project in Philadelphia, in spite of agreeing to the terms of a local collective bargaining agreement with the carpenters union prohibiting use of prehung doors, ordered 3,600 prefitted doors. Members of the union (D) were ordered not to handle the doors, and P charged the "will not handle" provision in the agreement to be in violation of section 8(e). P also charged a violation of section 8(b)(4)(B). The Board concluded that section 8(e) was designed to protect jobs of on-site carpenters and found no violation. The court of appeals reversed, and D appeals.

   b) **Issue.** Does a collective bargaining agreement provision violate sections 8(b)(4)(A) and 8(e) if its purpose in forbidding employer's use of certain products is to preserve job functions for on site workers?

   c) **Held.** No. Judgment reversed.

   (1) The purpose of these sections is to prohibit the use of secondary strikes to bring pressure on employers and to prevent a neutral employer from becoming involved in such a dispute.

   (2) Section 8(b)(4)(A) returns to the regime of *Duplex, supra.* Section 8(e) closed the loophole presented by *Local 1976, United Brotherhood of Carpenters & Joiners v. NLRB (Sand Door)*, 357 U.S. 93 (1958). They do not apply to a dispute between an employer and its employees involving job function preservation. The decision is not directed at the door manufacturer.

d) **Dissent** (Stewart, Black, Douglas, Clark, JJ.). It is a violation of section 8(b)(4) if the "result" of the activity is to force one person to cease using the products of another. This is what has occurred here. Product boycotts have antitrust overtones and are likely to be more permanent than most strikes and boycotts, which are related to a particular labor dispute. Congress enacted section 8(e) to ensure that section 8(b)(4) would not be circumvented by employing employer agreements. The Court is simply substituting its own concepts of desirable labor policy for those of Congress.

e) **Comment.** The test is not an easy one to apply. In *NLRB v. Enterprise Association of Steam & General Pipefitters, Local No. 638 (Austin Co.),* 429 U.S. 507 (1977), the union had a lawful work preservation clause in its labor agreement with a subcontractor. The union refused to install certain plumbing units purchased and required to be installed by a general contractor. The Board, while recognizing the general legality of the work preservation agreement, concluded that it was an improper secondary pressure in violation of section 8(b)(4)(B) because the union was asking the subcontractor to do something not within its control. The pressure, in effect, would force the subcontractor from doing business with the general contractor. The Supreme Court enforced the Board's order, finding that it was not erroneous as a matter of law. Thus, even a valid work preservation agreement may have an unlawful aspect in application.

4) **Subcontracting provisions that protect jobs--Meat & Highway Drivers, Local Union No. 710 v. NLRB,** 335 F.2d 709 (D.C. Cir. 1964).

a) **Facts.** Local 710 (D) represented truck drivers employed by Wilson, Armour, Swift, and other Chicago meat packers. Since at least 1944, the meat packers used employees represented by D to deliver meat products in the Chicago area. As the meat packers moved their operations outside of the Chicago area the number of truck drivers decreased from 330 to 80. These drivers were covered by a bargaining agreement. Several clauses of the bargaining agreement were set aside by the Board: (i) a ***work allocation clause*** (a clause requiring all deliveries in the Chicago area to be done by local employees covered by the agreement); (ii) a ***union standards clause*** (a clause stating that, in the event subcontracting was necessary, the packers would hire a subcontractor which paid its employees at least union wages); and (iii) a ***union signatory clause*** (a clause requiring that when subcontracting was necessary only subcontractors employing employees represented by D would be hired). The Board found all three clauses violative of sections 8(e) and 8(b)(4)(A) or (B). D appeals.

b) **Issue.** Are contract provisions that properly protect jobs that are fairly claimable by a local bargaining unit secondary in nature and hence forbidden by section 8(e) and section 8(b)(4)(A) or (B)?

c) **Held.** No. Judgment reversed in part and case remanded.

(1) Subcontracting clauses that are secondary in nature are not permitted by section 8(e) or section 8(b)(4)(A) or (B).

(2) Regardless of whether shipments originate inside or outside the Chicago area, the ***work allocation clause*** is not secondary in nature

since it directly protects fairly claimable jobs. This is because here D is trying to retain and recapture jobs for its members, not acquire new jobs from union members in general.

(3) The *union standards clause* may also be permissible. It partially deters the employers from the temptation of using nonunion labor through substandard nonunion contractors. Thus, it appears that this clause's goal was to aid D's local unit's members rather than union members generally (the latter would be an impermissible secondary purpose). However, since the Board did not have the benefit of our cases enunciating the proper standard, this point is remanded to the Board.

(4) The *union signatory clause* bears only a tenuous relation to the legitimate economic concerns of the employees in the unit, is secondary in nature, and hence impermissible.

d) **Comment.** Clauses secondary in nature are those which benefit the local bargaining unit's members only indirectly (*i.e.,* "secondarily").

5) **Clothing and construction industry provisos.**

a) One proviso to section 8(e) exempts the clothing industry from section 8(b)(4)(B). This permits employees in the clothing industry to negotiate clauses not to subcontract to nonunion shops because of the integrated relationships among manufacturers, subcontractors, and jobbers. It is also lawful to use work stoppages to attain such a provision or to cease doing business with a nonunion contractor.

b) Another proviso allows "hot cargo" provisions in the construction industry that prohibit nonunion work to be done on the job site. A work stoppage to attain such a provision is lawful, but not one to force an employer to cease using a nonunion contractor. Such provisions may be enforced only by grievance or by suit. The Supreme Court has held that the construction industry proviso does not extend to the picketing of a "stranger general contractor" by a union that had no interest in organizing the employees of the general contractor being picketed. However, if the employer and the union are in a bargaining relationship, it is proper to seek a contract provision to that effect.

3. **Jurisdictional Disputes.**

a. **Introduction.** Section 8(b)(4)(D) covers a variety of situations touching on the issue of work assignments disputes. These may occur in the following ways: (i) a single union may seek to compel an employer to substitute one of its members to perform work being presently performed by an unorganized employee; (ii) two unions involved with the same parent employer may enter a jurisdictional dispute (*i.e.,* a contest to determine which employees of which union will fulfill a given assignment); (iii) unions involved with diverse employers may enter a similar dispute; or (iv) independent, unaffiliated organizations may contest with those already recognized by an employer.

1) **Failure of employer to conform.** This section declares strikes, work stoppages, attempts to induce a work stoppage, or any threat or coercion an unfair labor practice where a labor organization or its agents seek thereby to force or require an employer to assign particular work from employees in a particular union, craft, trade, or class to employees in another union, craft, trade, or class, *unless* the employer is failing to conform to an order or certification of the NLRB determining the bargaining representative from employees performing such work. A simple demand that work be reassigned is not unlawful. Threatening to strike or picketing to force a work stoppage as a means of compelling the assignment of work, however, is unlawful.

b. **"No raid" agreements.** A number of unions have entered into "no raiding" pacts as a means of preventing jurisdictional disputes from arising. These are private, voluntary agreements not necessarily binding on the Board.

1) **Express agreements.** The NLRB will not give substantial weight to an inter-union agreement unless it specifically covers the disputed work and the parties have agreed to be bound.

2) **Employer agreement.** Section 10(k) provides that if, within 10 days after a section 8(b)(4)(D) charge is filed, all parties to a jurisdictional dispute submit evidence to the Board of a voluntary settlement, the NLRB will dismiss the section 8(b)(4)(D) charge. However, section 10(d) requires that "all parties" must agree to the settlement, and this includes the employer. Thus, a voluntary settlement between the rival unions does not resolve the matter, unless the employer also goes along with it.

3) **NLRB functions under section 10(k).** The Board's initial position was that it was not required in the course of a work dispute to determine specific work assignments. Only in the event that a job came within the Board's description of a bargaining unit which a particular union had been certified to represent, *or* when the representational contract provided that the union represent certain specific employees, did the Board then make particular work assignments. In all other cases, the Board reserved decision on work assignments to the employer.

4) **NLRB settlement of jurisdictional disputes--NLRB v. Radio & Television Broadcast Engineers Union, Local 1212 (CBS),** 364 U.S. 573 (1961).

a) **Facts.** CBS (P), having collective bargaining agreements with both a technician union (D) and a stage employee union, neither of which clearly apportioned the work of providing lighting for telecasts away from the home studio, suffered from constant disputes. P chose to divide the disputed work. In so doing, it satisfied neither union. D's refusal to work caused a major telecast to be canceled following P's awarding of the lighting work to the stage employees. P charged a violation of section 8(b)(4)(D). The NLRB held that a section 10(k) hearing was required to determine the dispute. Its decision was that D was not entitled to have the work assigned to its members. D refused to comply, urging that the Board's duty was to make a final determination of which union was entitled to do the work. The Board issued a cease and desist order. The court of appeals refused to enforce the order since the Board had failed to make the required determination, and P appeals.

- b) **Issue.** Does section 10(k) require the NLRB to settle jurisdictional disputes?

- c) **Held.** Yes. Judgment affirmed. Under section 10(k), it is the Board's responsibility to make a final determination as to which of two unions is entitled to specific job assignments.

- d) **Comment.** After this decision, the Board indicated that it would follow a case-by-case approach. Among the criteria it would consider were skills and work involved, Board certifications, company and industry practice, agreements between unions and between companies and unions, arbitrator awards, joint board awards and AFL-CIO awards, efficiency of operation, and other relevant factors. [Machinists Local 1743 (J. A. Jones Construction Co.), 135 N.L.R.B. 1402 (1962)]

5) **Enforcement of work-assignment awards.**

- a) **Board resolution.** The Supreme Court considered the nature of a section 10(k) Board order in *NLRB v. Plasterers' Local Union No. 79*, 404 U.S. 116 (1971). The Court said that the order alone binds no one, but will serve to determine the outcome of a section 8(b)(4)(D) proceeding. If the losing union were to persist in picketing, it would be found guilty of a section 8(b)(4)(D) violation. If the company, having lost, persists in the proscribed assignment, it would have no section 8(b)(4)(D) protection against picketing by the successful union. Since section 10(k) awards are not "final orders," they cannot be reviewed directly, but in a consequential section 8(b)(4)(D) case, the validity of the section 10(k) order could be tested. [*See* NLRB v. International Longshoremen's & Warehousemen's Union, Local No. 50, 504 F.2d 1209 (9th Cir. 1974)] In this case, the court of appeals criticized the Board's case-by-case approach and its failure to "articulate any decision making standards," which made "judicial review virtually impossible."

- b) **Private resolution.** One of the problems with resolving "jurisdictional" or "work assignment" cases by private tribunals (arbitration hearings or AFL-CIO National Joint Board proceedings) is that not all "parties" to the dispute are before the decision maker. In *NLRB v. Plasterers' Local Union No. 79, supra*, the Supreme Court concluded that a National Joint Board award did not preempt the Board from considering the rival claims anew in a section 10(k) hearing or enforcing a redetermination in a section 8(b)(4)(D) proceeding. The rival unions had participated in the National Joint Board proceedings, but the company had refused to participate or agree to be bound. In an arbitration hearing, one of the unions will likely be the missing "party."

4. **Featherbedding and Make-Work Arrangements.**

   a. **Definition.** Featherbedding and make-work arrangements refer to practices that create an artificial increase in labor costs. This may include the unnecessary spreading of work, establishment of jobs where they are not necessary to efficient operations, or blocking efficient technological progress (*e.g.*, by requiring that work be done by hand when more efficient machines are available to do it).

   b. **NLRA provision.** Section 8(b)(6) defines as a union unfair labor practice any attempt to cause an employer to pay or deliver or agree to pay or deliver any money or other thing of value, in the nature of an exaction, for services that are not performed or not to be performed. This section has been so narrowly construed that it has proved almost worthless.

      1) **Example.** For example, it has been interpreted so as to exclude situations where the union is attempting to seek employment for its members, even if the employer does not want or need such employees. Thus, section 8(b)(6) applies only where the union is insisting on someone getting paid for doing nothing.

      2) **Requiring local performers to appear with national performers-- NLRB v. Gamble Enterprises, Inc., 345 U.S. 117 (1953).**

         a) **Facts.** The musician's union (D) refused to allow national bands to appear at a local theatre unless a local orchestra was paid to appear at the same time (even though the employer (P) did not want or need the local orchestra). P filed a complaint with the NLRB claiming that the union's conduct was in violation of section 8(b)(6), which prohibits unions from coercing employers to pay for work not done. The NLRB held no violation, but the court of appeals reversed.

         b) **Issue.** Did requiring a local orchestra to be paid every time a national band appeared in a local theatre violate section 8(b)(6)?

         c) **Held.** No. Judgment reversed. The union's proposal must be seen as contemplating some actual services (*e.g.*, fill-in or back-up orchestration) and consequently it is not violative of section 8(b)(6).

         d) **Comment.** Almost any actual or conceivable work will suffice to defeat the proscription of section 8(b)(6).

      3) **"Setting bogus."** In *American Newspaper Publishers Association v. NLRB*, 345 U.S. 100 (1953), American Newspaper Publishers Association requested the NLRB find inclusion of a system known as "setting bogus" in employment contracts to be "featherbedding" as defined in section 8(b)(6). "Setting bogus" means making duplicate forms for all local advertisements even when a competitor had already completed the work and distributed these to other publishers for little or no cost. The Board refused to rule in the Association's favor. The Supreme Court ruled that section 8(b)(6) forbids a union to exact pay from an employer for services not performed or not to be per-

formed. Even useless work done with the employer's consent must be compensated. Featherbedding occurs when a union requires money for employees not working.

5. **Violence and Union Responsibility.** Picketing is protected under the Act. But any violence that may flare up during picketing or a strike is not protected, and individual perpetrators and their union may be enjoined or damages may be assessed in a state court action. Employees may be subject to discipline or discharge, and finally the union may also be subject to a section 8(b)(1) unfair labor practice charge. The ordinary rules of agency are applied to determine union responsibility. The Board will issue cease and desist orders in cases of responsibility, but it will not order reimbursement. Damages action must be brought in a state court. The Board may seek an injunction under section 10(j).

6. **Remedies for Union Unfair Labor Practices.** Unions have become subject to two types of injunctions since 1947. Under section 10(l), a regional director may seek a federal injunction in cases of secondary boycotts, hot cargo agreements, strikes supporting work-assignment demands, and protracted recognition picketing. Other types of union misconduct (and company misconduct as well) may be reached under section 10(j). In these instances, an unfair labor practice complaint must have been issued and the Board must authorize the regional director to seek the injunction. The federal courts require proof of need for an injunction to issue. Finally, section 303 of the Taft-Hartley Act creates a federal tort in cases of section 8(b)(4) violations. Compensatory (but not punitive) damages may be sought by an injured "neutral" or a "primary" employer and by third persons who have suffered direct and foreseeable injury. The action is independent of an unfair practice proceeding and courts have assessed damages in cases in which the Board has found no unfair labor practice. [NLRB v. Deena Artware, Inc., 198 F.2d 645 (6th Cir. 1952); United Brick Workers v. Deena Artware, Inc., 198 F.2d 637 (6th Cir. 1952)] The doctrine of collateral estoppel has been applied where the union has been administratively found to have breached section 8(b)(4).

7. **Jury Trials.** The Supreme Court recently held that a contempt proceeding for breach of an order against violent activity was in the nature of criminal contempt, thus allowing the union to request a jury trial. [United Mine Workers v. Bagwell, 114 S. Ct. 2552 (1994)]

V. ADMINISTRATION OF THE COLLECTIVE AGREEMENT

A. INTRODUCTION

The establishment of the collective agreement does not end the duty of collective bargaining. That duty also includes bargaining over the interpretation and application of the agreement. Settlement of disputes arising under a collective bargaining agreement can take three forms:

1. **Grievance Discussions.** The parties may settle the dispute informally through grievance development and discussions between management representatives and union representatives.

2. **Arbitration.** The issue may be determined by arbitration if the grievance procedures do not resolve the dispute and the agreement provides for arbitration or the parties make a special submission to arbitration.

3. **Judicial Resolution.** The issue may be taken to court if there is no agreement to arbitrate, or more importantly, if there is a dispute over whether the matter is subject to arbitration.

B. NATURE OF THE AGREEMENT AND OF THE GRIEVANCE PROCESS

1. **The Collective Bargaining Agreement.**

   a. **The object of the agreement.** The object of collective bargaining is a written agreement between the employer and the union. It will define the relationship between the two parties, the important relationships between the employer and its employees, and the relationships among the employees themselves. The agreement will also provide machinery for disposing of disputes arising under it or which arise while it is in effect. The collective agreement is not an employment contract, but serves to fix the terms of the employment relations as employees are hired or are continued in their hire.

   b. **Nature of the collective bargaining agreement.** The collective bargaining agreement should be distinguished from the ordinary voluntary commercial contract. It is the product of a relationship compelled by law; it deals with a complex, ongoing relationship that determines the parties' rights (subject to periodic negotiations) for a considerable time into the future. It cannot be expected to be a detailed guide for all existing circumstances and future contingencies. The CBA is sometimes analogized to a constitutional document. A common assumption is that the collective bargaining agreement also encompasses informal agreements and concessions not reduced to writing and established customs and practices. The written collective bargaining agreement may contain intentional ambiguities, generalities, and gaps concerning items about which the parties could not reach particular agreement.

   c. **Who is involved.** A number of different decision makers, responsible for different aspects of the labor-management relationship, will be concerned with the construction and application of the collective bargaining agreement; these include the NLRB, the courts (state and federal), arbitrators, and other federal agencies.

2. **The Grievance Procedure.**

   a. **The hierarchy.** The vast majority of collective bargaining agreements provide for the resolution of disputes by the use of a private internal system rather than by the courts. "Grievances," as defined in the collective bargaining agreement, will be processed through a series of grievance "steps" (usually three or four) and may be submitted to final and binding arbitration if the matter cannot be resolved between the parties. The first step is usually rather informal, with the aggrieved employee or the union orally presenting the complaint to the immediate first line supervisor. If it cannot be resolved at that level, the grievance will be reduced to writing and carried through steps involving successively higher echelons of supervision and union representatives.

   b. **Defining the "grievance."** Often the collective bargaining agreement will define this term very broadly (*i.e.*, "any dispute, disagreement, or difference arising between any employee, union, and the company"). More often, grievances are described as disputes relating in some manner to a proper interpretation and application of the agreement. This does not mean that a grievance must involve a matter explicitly defined by the statement, however. An agreement is very much like a statute because its meaning often can be established only through the resolution of concrete problems.

   c. **Providing for the procedures.** Usually the contract will attempt to provide answers to the following questions:

      1) Who may initiate a grievance?

      2) Who will evaluate the grievance? (Usually a number of continually higher levels of consideration are provided for, with the last step being an arbitration proceeding.)

      3) How rapidly must the grievance be processed?

      4) When must the grievance be reduced to writing?

      5) What special provisions will be made to facilitate the work of the union representative in processing grievances?

   d. **What the grievance procedure can do.** A well drafted and administered grievance procedure can provide an effective way of peacefully settling disputes and improving the climate of labor relations. It can serve to pinpoint ambiguities, gaps, and trouble spots in the written agreement. It can help identify problems of supervision and personnel policy. Grievance processing may be also used to extend the scope of the written agreement and to gain leverage at the bargaining table. Grievance procedures establish a system of "industrial due process." The principle of "obey, and then grieve" has been recognized as indispensable for the success of any grievance procedure.

3. **Grievance or "Rights" Arbitration.**

a. **Introduction.** Grievance arbitration is the process by which disputes arising under a collective agreement are adjudicated by persons who have been selected by the parties for that purpose. This distinguishes the process from arbitration to fix wages or other benefits prospectively ("interest" arbitration), where the primary basis is something other than an agreement between the parties. Also distinguished are the situations where the parties are forced to arbitrate (compulsory arbitration), such as where the government compels the parties to submit their differences to resolution by a third party.

1) **Widespread Use.** The use of grievance arbitration is very widespread. This is due to the fact that unions generally feel that they can get a better break from arbitrators than they can from the courts (a reflection of their continuing distrust of the courts, dating back to the early days of the labor movement). Also, management tends to accept it as the best alternative available, particularly since the judicial process is time consuming and expensive and a strike is an intolerable way to resolve contract disputes.

2) **Arbitration Clauses.** Arbitration clauses vary in many respects—in the scope of the power given to the arbitrator, in the range of subjects which are committed by the agreement to potential arbitration, etc. The process of arbitration may itself differ in different situations. Sometimes a tripartite board is used, or a single arbitrator may be chosen ad hoc for each grievance or, possibly, the procedure will call for the appointment of a permanent umpire or panel of arbitrators.

3) **Procedure.** The procedure during arbitration is usually nontechnical and informal. Strict rules of evidence are not generally used when examining witnesses. The arbitrator will receive evidence at a hearing, listen to the parties' arguments, find facts, interpret the CBA, apply the CBA to the findings of fact, and decide the case and the appropriate remedy.

b. **Review of arbitrators' decisions.** In framing a decision, the arbitrator is not entirely free from possible judicial review and reversal, but has much greater leeway than a trial judge. Although arbitration agreements do not deprive the NLRB of jurisdiction of disputes covered by them, the NLRB has stated that it will decline such jurisdiction where the arbitration proceedings are fair and regular, all the parties agree to be bound, and the decision is not clearly repugnant to the NLRA. Judicial review is restricted and narrow.

This relative freedom of the arbitrator raises a number of questions: Should the selected method of analysis differ from that used by a court? Does the arbitrator have the power to look beyond the agreement in order to find a basis for decision (*e.g.,* a social policy)? What is the role of precedent?

c. **The duty to arbitrate.** When a union seeks to submit an unresolved grievance to arbitration, the company will occasionally object on the ground that the agreement excludes the issue in question from arbitration, or that the procedural steps of the grievance machinery have not been complied with, etc. In many cases management will allow the case to proceed to arbitration and will raise its objections before the arbitrator. On the other hand, management may simply refuse to arbitrate. In this event, the law is clear that the union may bring an action in a state or federal court under section 301 of the Labor-Management Relations Act to require the employer to arbitrate. The employer may then press objections before the court to convince the judge that no order to arbitrate should issue. The court can refuse to order arbitration only on certain very limited grounds. Therefore, in the normal case the company may choose to arbitrate and present its objections to the arbitrator for consideration.

d. **Complexity of issues.** The nature of the CBA is unique because of its origin and because it covers an ongoing, complex situation. The imperatives of compelled bargains and the possibilities of a strike lead to gaps, generalities, and ambiguities (some not unintended).

e. **Discipline and discharge.**

1) **Discipline of employees--Mallinckrodt, Inc.,** 83-2 CCH Arb. ¶8358 (Seidman 1983).

   Mallinckrodt, Inc.

   a) **Facts.** Three employees (Ps) were discharged for violating a company work rule. They were observed by a security guard as they smoked a marijuana cigarette in the isolated millroom during a break. None of Ps had been disciplined previously for such an offense. The matter was grieved and taken to arbitration by the union.

   b) **Issue.** Was there just cause for discharging the grievants? If not, what is the proper remedy?

   c) **Held.** No. Discipline should be reduced.

   (1) The officer testified truthfully about what he saw. The testimony of the grievants explaining their presence in the dark, dank, and dismal millroom is unbelievable.

   (2) Although they shared a joint, they were not under the influence as to be unfit to continue their work. Although they were smoking in a no-smoking area, their smoking presented no threat of fire or explosion. None of the grievants had been disciplined previously for use of intoxicants or drugs. However, the grievants were guilty of violating a company rule.

   (3) The reasonableness of the penalty must be considered. The company has used progressive discipline before in alcohol cases. Alcohol in industry is more debilitating and costly than the use of marijuana. The conduct of the employees during a break created no threat of harm to self or others. This is not a case of selling drugs or possessing a large cache. This was simple recreational use. The state is increasingly decriminalizing the use of the drug and first offenders are placed on unsupervised probation. Discharge was too severe a penalty.

   (4) However, in this case, the grievants lied about their activities. To get justice, one must act justly. Their discipline should be reduced to a five-day suspension. They should be reinstated without loss of seniority, but with no back pay.

2) **Discharge for drug use--Walker Manufacturing Co.,** 81 L.A. 1169 (C. Morgan 1983).

   Walker Manufacturing Co.

- a) **Facts.** The grievant (P) was discharged for smoking marijuana on company property. Work Rule 6 made possession, consuming, or being under the influence of a "controlled substance" an infraction subject to "discharge, suspension, or a written or an oral reprimand as appropriate." The matter was grieved and taken to arbitration.

- b) **Issue.** Was there just cause for discharging the grievant? If not, what is the proper remedy?

- c) **Held.** Yes. Grievance denied.

    (1) Not all offenses require progressive discipline; theft, for example, would not. Progressive discipline is used to correct relatively minor problems such as tardiness, carelessness, AWOL, etc.

    (2) In this case what grievant was doing was wrong, even in the absence of a work rule. It is not necessary for the company to show that this offense adversely affected its business—but neither would the company have to show this for a fist fight in the lunchroom.

    (3) The grievant had a clean work record, but he admitted that in his 11-month tenure on the job that he had violated the rule "a number of times." Clemency is not for the arbitrator, who is only to review whether the penalty is too severe under the circumstances.

    (4) I reject the union's contention that the rule has not been administered uniformly. The company has discharged summarily drug dealers and persons who have breached the rule five or more times, while suspending lesser violations. The fact that Ohio has seen fit to decriminalize the use does not prevent the company from enforcing reasonable rules against drug use on its premises.

3) **Arbitrary distinctions among employees.** If a company selects some employees for discipline and lets others off when many employees have committed the same infraction, or if fines are imposed more heavily on some employees than on others, the company must show some reasonable basis for making the distinctions.

4) **Two views on the discipline question.**

    a) The *majority view* is that absent any qualifying bargaining agreement provision or facts that show a contrary intent, the arbitrator must be satisfied that: (i) the employee in fact committed the offense of which he or she is accused; (ii) punishment was warranted under the circumstances; and (iii) the degree of punishment imposed was just (*i.e.*, that the penalty fit the crime).

    b) The *minority view* holds that the arbitrator does not have the authority to substitute his or her judgment for that of management as to the degree of punishment. Only the first two questions, therefore, lie within the realm of the arbitrator's authority.

5) Guides for decision. Because of the open nature of the CBA, arbitrators must often rely on their sense of fairness, past practices, national labor policy, and good industrial practice.

f. Subcontracting.

1) **Introduction.** In recent years, the question of subcontracting rights under a collective agreement has assumed increasing significance. The problem is particularly difficult for the arbitrator, since contracts often fail to contain provisions specifically permitting or prohibiting subcontracting. Arbitrators have taken a variety of approaches in solving disputes over this matter.

   a) **Disengagement.** Subcontracting often involves the removal of jobs from employees who are covered by a collective agreement; the employer, in effect, is disengaging from the terms of the contract some plant function. This disengagement may occur in connection with (i) converting to automatic equipment, (ii) having some outside independent contractor do work formerly done by company employees, (iii) transferring a department to another plant of the employer, (iv) removing a plant to another location, or (v) shutting a plant down altogether.

   b) **Competing forces.** Any of these occurrences presents an apparent collision between the interests of the employer and the interests of the employees and their union. The employer, of course, desires to maintain or lower overhead in order to compete more effectively. On the other hand, the employees want to protect their job security, and the union its bargaining agent.

2) **The requirement of good faith.**

   a) **Application of good faith requirement--Allis-Chalmers Manufacturing Co., 39 Lab. Arb. 1213 (1962).**

   Allis-Chalmers Manufacturing Co.

   (1) **Facts.** Allis-Chalmers Manufacturing Company (D) contracted out work. Since the agreement limited the referee's jurisdiction to disputes between the "company and the employees on matters covered by the agreement," the company argued that the union's (P's) claim of a violation could not be heard since it did not rest on a specific provision of the agreement (there was no subcontracting provision). D argued that the labor agreement itself gave rise to an implied, unqualified prohibition on contracting out work customarily performed by employees of the bargaining unit.

   (2) **Issue.** May an employer in good faith subcontract work usually done by unit employees?

   (3) **Held.** Yes. Grievance denied.

      (a) The referee's jurisdiction is not confined to considering only the explicit terms of the agreement.

(b) The recognition clause, the wage schedule, and the seniority provisions do not absolutely prohibit the contracting out of unit work. However, there is an implied limitation on the absolute discretion of management to contract out work. This is a condition of "good faith"; that is, the decision to do so must be made on the basis of factors related to conduct of an efficient, economical operation and be done with some regard to the interests and expectations of the employees involved.

(c) Each case must be decided on its own facts, especially with regard to the considerations underlying the managerial decision. Here, there was no bad faith or deception practiced by the employer, and the considerations of management were at least partially economic and related to operational efficiency and were not arbitrary or unreasonable.

b) **Implied good faith clauses.** Some arbitrators take the view that even if nothing is specifically mentioned in the agreement, the recognition, wage, and seniority clauses taken together imply a good faith clause that is violated if the work that is covered by the agreement when signed is later assigned to a noncovered employee or an independent contractor. To permit such a transfer would take work to those not covered by the agreed-upon standards, thus subverting the contract and destroying the meaning of the collective bargaining relationship.

c) **Established company practices.** If there have been numerous instances of subcontracting over a considerable length of time without protest and with no modification of the contract language, the practice may be sustained as proper under the collective bargaining agreement. [Carbide & Carbon Chemicals Co., 24 Lab. Arb. 158 (1955)]

d) **Management prerogative.** Other arbitrators hold that absent statutory restrictions or specific limitations in the agreement, the employer has the right to so transfer work, as long as he is not acting to cripple or destroy the union. [Pure Oil Co., Lab. Arb. 1042 (1962)]

g. **The effect of past practice and public law.**

1) **Introduction.** Absent other specific restrictions on authority, the arbitrator acts according to the prevailing rules of arbitration law and the accepted practice and custom of the common law of industrial relations. Prior awards are not binding or conclusive; they have value only as a persuasive force. Generally, in grievance arbitration, the controlling law is the collective agreement signed by the parties. However, in some instances, the contract will contain standard clauses used by an industry, and the arbitrator may make use of customs prevailing in the industry.

Phillips Petroleum Co.

2) **Past practice--Phillips Petroleum Co.,** 24 Lab. Arb. 191 (1955).

a) **Facts.** For more than a decade, Phillips Petroleum (D) furnished, for a nominal cost, electricity to employees who worked at its DeNoya power plant and who either lived at the camp or near it. D decided to discontinue this practice and gave its affected employees notice to this effect. The union (P) protested, claiming that the unilateral act violated the labor agreement. D contended that the furnishing of electricity was not mentioned in or covered by the contract and was merely a gratuity that could be discontinued at any time.

b) **Issue.** Are existing plant practices, with respect to major conditions of employment, included within a collective bargaining contract?

c) **Held.** Yes. Grievance sustained.

   (1) One line of cases holds that plant practices that are not specifically embodied in collective bargaining contracts may be discontinued upon proper notice.

   (2) A second line of cases regards long-standing plant practices which are major conditions of employment to be incorporated into the CBA unless expressly negated. The basis for this position is that the contract is more than "words on paper," but is also all the oral understandings, interpretations and mutually acceptable habits that have grown around the contract over time.

   (3) A third group of cases holds that the employer cannot unilaterally discontinue the prior practice, although such practices are not held to be fully incorporated into the contracts. In such cases, the employer must negotiate with the bargaining agent before making the change.

   (4) The approach of the second line of cases is adopted here since negotiators work within the framework of existing plant practices.

   (5) Although the contract involved here did not expressly embody the practice, it alluded to it and contemplated its continuance. Thus, the company is bound to reinstate electric service for the nominal monthly fee, or pay the difference between the employees' electric bills and the nominal monthly fee.

3) **Public law.** There are two schools of thought concerning the extent that an arbitrator should consider and apply external public law in determining an arbitration case. The typical collective bargaining agreement may mention external, anti-discrimination laws, as well as other specific employee protective statutes that are incorporated by reference. Of course it exists in the midst of, and is subject to, the public laws. Some arbitrators insist that their authority is derived from the collective bargaining agreement itself and that their only function is to construe the contract and apply it to the case without regard to the greater question of legality or illegality (*i.e.*, to "respect the contract and ignore the law").

Others take the position that an award that is faithful to the collective bargaining agreement but which cannot be enforced is contrary to law. A middle position is that while an arbitration award may permit conduct sanctioned by the contract but forbidden by the law, it should not command conduct forbidden by the law. This of course requires that arguments and proof concerning the applicability and effect of external public law may have to be considered by the arbitrator. To the extent that an arbitrator interprets and applies external law, there will be temptation for the courts to scrutinize awards for "error."

4. **Judicial Enforcement of Collective Bargaining Agreements.**

   a. **Federal court jurisdiction under Taft-Hartley section 301.** Section 301 of the Taft-Hartley Act (Labor Management Relations Act) provides that suits between an employer and a labor organization representing employees in an industry affecting commerce, or between two such labor organizations, may be brought in any federal district court having jurisdiction over the parties, regardless of diversity of citizenship or federal jurisdictional amount.

      1) **Congressional intent.** In enacting this section, Congress intended to create a federal forum for determination of suits by or against unions involving alleged breaches of collective bargaining agreements. [Westinghouse Employees v. Westinghouse Electric Co., 348 U.S. 437 (1955)]

      2) **The right to sue.** Although section 301 expressly authorizes only "employers and unions" to sue one another for breach of the collective bargaining agreement, the Supreme Court held that individual employees may also bring suit against their employers to vindicate "uniquely personal rights" under the contract; *e.g.*, special conditions of employment or special rates of pay. [Smith v. Evening News Association, 371 U.S. 195 (1962)]

   b. **Judicial enforcement of agreements.** As previously discussed, collective bargaining agreements normally contain a grievance procedure—usually, a commitment by both parties to submit any unresolved grievance or dispute arising under the contract to binding arbitration by a third party and to abide by the decision of the arbitrator.

      1) **Prior law.** Before the enactment of section 301, the law of the collective bargaining agreements varied by state and was enforced in state courts. Furthermore, since unions were associations, they could not be sued as entities, and a class action against the members was usually the way to bring an action against the union. Execution would thus be against the individual members.

         a) Various theories have been formulated about the nature of the collective bargaining agreement: (i) they are merely moral undertakings and not enforceable; (ii) the members are recognized to be third-party beneficiaries; (iii) the union acts as a contracting agent for its members, or perhaps all employees;

and (iv) the agreement establishes a custom or a "schedule," which is incorporated into and defines the details of the individual employment contract.

b) None of these explanations are entirely free of theoretical problems. The Supreme Court has been rather eclectic about the whole matter. Judicial enforcement of collective bargaining agreements is now considered to be conducive to sound industrial relations.

2) **Exhaustion of remedies doctrine.** No action will lie to enforce any claim under the collective bargaining agreement by one who has not first exhausted the available remedies under the contract grievance procedure. [Republic Steel Corp. v. Maddox, 379 U.S. 650 (1965)]

3) **Court may compel specific performance of agreement to arbitrate.** However, where either party has refused to arbitrate as provided in the agreement, and the grievance procedure has been followed, the other party may maintain an action under Taft-Hartley section 301 to compel the former to arbitrate as per the agreement.

   a) **Federal court power to fashion remedies--Textile Workers Union v. Lincoln Mills of Alabama,** 353 U.S. 448 (1957).

   Textile Workers Union v. Lincoln Mills of Alabama

   (1) **Facts.** Textile Workers Union (P) had a collective bargaining agreement with Lincoln Mills (D), containing a no-strike clause and requiring arbitration of all irreconcilable differences. When such a dispute arose, P requested arbitration and D refused. An action was brought in federal court to enforce the arbitration clause. The district court, pursuant to section 301 of the LMRA, determined that it had jurisdiction and ordered D to arbitrate. The court of appeals reversed, holding that section 301 gives federal courts only the jurisdiction to hear cases between unions and employers or between two unions when they affect commerce, but does not give courts the power to fashion remedies like the injunctive relief given here. P appeals.

   (2) **Issue.** Does section 301 of the LMRA empower federal courts to fashion remedies that have the effect of creating new substantive federal law?

   (3) **Held.** Yes. Judgment reversed.

   (a) Federal courts are given not only the jurisdiction to hear such cases, but also the power to fashion new substantive federal law to enforce the agreements that are the substance of such suits.

   (b) The legislative history of the LMRA shows that sections 301(a) and (b) allow sanctions to enforce executory agreements to arbitrate (rejecting the common law rule to the contrary). It is not unusual for federal courts to fashion federal law where federal rights are concerned.

Labor Law - 137

(c) Courts may look to state law for examples of remedies which would effectuate federal policies, but the law to be applied is federal.

(d) The Norris-LaGuardia Act is not applicable since failure to arbitrate is not the sort of abuse against which the Act was aimed.

(4) Concurrence (Burton, Harlan, JJ.). Having jurisdiction over the suit, the court is not powerless to fashion an appropriate federal remedy. I do not subscribe to the conclusion that the substantive law to be applied is federal law. Some federal rights may necessarily be involved which can be upheld constitutionally as "protective jurisdiction."

(5) Comment. Enforcement of arbitration clauses is crucial to industrial peace, and specific performance is the most direct and immediate way of assuring such enforcement.

c. **Recourse to private judicial machinery.** Many issues that arise under the collective agreement will be handled by the parties themselves with no resort to outside procedures. However, without some procedure for settling major disputes, many grievances would erupt into strikes. The preferred recourse is to private judicial machinery (arbitration) rather than the courts. While the general power to determine the rights of parties under a union contract is entrusted to arbitrators or perhaps the courts, the Supreme Court has held that the NLRB may interpret a contract to the extent necessary to determine whether a statutory duty has been violated, especially where the contract makes no provision for final and binding arbitration.

d. **Judicial enforcement of "no-strike" agreements.** As part of the consideration of an employer's agreement to arbitrate any dispute or grievance arising under the contract, the union normally agrees not to strike (or cause any work stoppage or slowdown) because of a dispute or grievance. This "no-strike" obligation is such a necessary ingredient of the commitment to arbitrate that it will be implied, even in the absence of any express provision, on the rationale that it is the "quid pro quo" for the employer's agreement to arbitrate.

1) Jurisdiction of state courts. An action to enforce a CBA may be brought in either federal or state court. However, a state court for purposes of uniformity must apply federal law to the case. [Local 174, Teamsters v. Lucas Flour Co., 369 U.S. 95 (1962)] The Supreme Court implied a no-strike clause in a CBA which contained an arbitration clause, but without the usual promise not to strike during the term of the CBA. This result was considered necessary because of "accepted principles of traditional contract law" and basic labor law which promote the arbitral process over the strike. Justice Black wrote a strong dissent. More recently, the Supreme Court allowed judicial review of a grievance concerning the "just cause" of a discharge. The CBA provided that there be no discharge without just cause, but it contained no arbitration clause. The CBA also prohibited a strike until all negotiations had filed through the grievance system. After the grievance system produced no agreement, the union brought a section 301 action. The company resisted, arguing that the CBA reserved the strike as the exclusive remedy. The Court found the action justiciable and found that judicial review of the case was to be preferred over a strike, a power solution which is the antithesis of the rational and peaceful mode of resolving disputes contemplated by Congress. [Graves v. Ring Screw Works, 498 U.S. 168 (1990)]

    a) **Statutes of limitations.** Although federal substantive law applies, the statute of limitations is governed by state law (and this is true whether the action is filed in federal or state court, as there is no federal limitations period applicable to collective bargaining agreements).

5. **Judicial Enforcement and the Review of Arbitration Awards.**

   a. **Introduction.** The "hands off" attitude of the courts toward the arbitrability disputes also applies to the judicial review of the award made by an arbitrator. In the famous *Steelworker Trilogy* (three opinions issued on the same day involving the Steelworkers' Union), the Supreme Court held that the merits of either the grievance or the arbitration award are irrelevant, when a federal court is asked to enforce an arbitration agreement or award thereunder. Judicial review is limited to whether the parties agreed to arbitrate the dispute and whether the award "draws its essence" from the collective agreement. [United Steelworkers of America v. American Manufacturing Co., *infra*; United Steelworkers of America v. Warrior & Gulf Navigation Co., *infra*; United Steelworkers of America v. Enterprise Wheel & Car Corp., *infra*]

      1) **Determination of arbitrability.** Under this approach, it is always a question for the court to determine whether the dispute or grievance falls within the agreement to arbitrate (*i.e.*, "substantive arbitrability"). It is sufficient if the claim on its face falls within the scope of the arbitration agreement, and all inferences are drawn in favor of arbitrability. Moreover, the parties may voluntarily submit the issue of arbitrability to the arbitrator, in which case they *waive* any right to subsequent judicial review of arbitrability.

      2) **Rationale.** The rationale is that arbitration is the linchpin of federal labor policy for CBA enforcement, and this means that the courts cannot substitute their judgment or intervene where the parties have committed themselves to arbitration.

      3) **District court assessment of merits--United Steelworkers of America v. American Manufacturing Co.,** 363 U.S. 564 (1960).

          United Steelworkers of America v. American Manufacturing Co.

         a) **Facts.** An employee settled an injury claim with American Manufacturing (D) on the basis of permanent partial disability and then wanted to return to work, but the company refused. The agreement provided that management could discharge "for cause." Arbitration was provided for all disputes arising under the contract. The union (P) asked for arbitration, but D refused on the basis that this type of dispute was not covered under the arbitration clause. P filed suit in federal district court to compel arbitration. The district court held that the employee was estopped from claiming any employee rights by his acceptance of the settlement, and the appeals court affirmed. P appeals.

b) **Issue.** If a contract provides for compulsory arbitration, must all claims be arbitrated even if the claims may lack merit?

c) **Held.** Yes. Judgment reversed.

(1) The function of the courts is to determine whether the claim by the party seeking arbitration is covered by the contract (where the parties have agreed to submit all questions under the contract to arbitration).

(2) If it is so covered, the parties must arbitrate, irrespective of whether the court deems the claim to be meritorious (*i.e.*, the courts cannot interfere in the machinery decided on by the parties).

d) **Comment.** The arbitration process and final settlement of labor disputes would be hindered if courts could preliminarily screen arbitration cases. The arbitration of even meritless cases can have a safety-valve effect.

4) **Narrow reading of matters exempted from arbitration--United Steelworkers of America v. Warrior & Gulf Navigation Co.,** 363 U.S. 574 (1960).

a) **Facts.** The United Steelworkers of America (P) had a collective bargaining agreement with Warrior & Gulf Navigation (D) which included "no-strike" and "no lockout" provisions as well as a clause requiring all disputes over the "meaning" or "application" of the agreement to be subject to the grievance procedure, which culminated in final binding arbitration. Another clause provided that "matters which are strictly a function of management" would not be subject to arbitration. D contracted out maintenance work formerly done by its employees and laid off some employees. Some of the laid-off employees were later hired by the new contractor. P claimed that D had created a partial lockout; the grievance was not settled; and P demanded arbitration, which was refused (D claiming that strictly management functions were involved). P sued under section 301 of the LMRA to compel arbitration. The federal district court dismissed the complaint, and the court of appeals affirmed. P appeals.

b) **Issue.** Must an employer arbitrate a decision to lay off employees and contract out their work where the CBA exempts management matters?

c) **Held.** Yes. Judgment reversed.

(1) The clause exempting strictly management matters must be read narrowly to include only those management functions over which the contract gives complete control and unfettered discretion.

(2) Grievance machinery is at the "very heart of industrial self-government." An agreement to arbitrate is a significant factor in reducing labor unrest, and if the agreement is not read broadly, a management clause could exempt every employer's whim from arbit-

ration, thereby frustrating the purposes of section 301. The grievance procedure—not the strike—is the terminal point for a dispute.

- (3) In interpreting the collective bargaining agreements in a dispute, the court must look to the common law of the shop which forms the context of the agreement. Since contracting out is often a matter of arbitration, absent a clear expression to the contrary, the arbitration clause should be read to cover it.

- (4) Whether the contracting out violated the agreement is a matter for the arbitrator, not the courts.

d) **Concurrence** (Brennan, Harlan, Frankfurter, JJ.). As in *American Manufacturing, supra,* the issue here is whether the company agreed to arbitrate a particular grievance. Unlike in *American,* the agreement here excluded matter strictly a function of management. So, the court below should be able to examine evidence of bargaining history to determine whether contracting out was a function of management. The risks of a vague exclusion clause and a broad arbitration clause are shown by what the courts below did when they found the company was in no way limited by any implied covenants of good faith, which would allow the company to destroy the agreement by contracting out everything. The vagueness of the arbitration clause is an indication that the parties were looking for the arbitrator's judgment on this sort of matter. I do not understand that the principles of this case will depend on the presence of a no-strike clause.

e) **Dissent** (Whittaker, J.). I see nothing in the contract to indicate that the employer wished to submit to arbitration a grievance questioning its right to contract out. To the contrary, over the years the parties had considered contracting major repair work to be "strictly a function of management." For years the union had unsuccessfully bargained for the inclusion of a provision to the contrary.

f) **Comments.**

- (1) More recent decisions by the Supreme Court reaffirm this inclusive reading of arbitration clauses. For example, in *Operating Engineers Local 150 v. Flair Builders, Inc.*, 406 U.S. 487 (1972), a provision binding the parties to arbitrate "any dispute" was held to cover the issue of whether the union was guilty of "laches" in instituting the grievance procedure. And in *Gateway Coal v. United Mine Workers*, 414 U.S. 368 (1974), a provision requiring arbitration of "any local trouble of any kind" was held to encompass safety disputes involving falsification of records on safe air flow in mining operations.

- (2) The arbitrability of an issue is ultimately a question of law and is not foreclosed by the arbitrator's determination. Unless the collective agreement or a submission agreement specifically extends that power to the arbitrator, "arbitrability" is a matter for the courts.

5) **Arbitration after corporate statutory merger.** After a small organized corporation (along with its work force) was merged into a much larger unorganized corporation, the employees of the merged company claimed that they had

acquired certain vested rights under their labor contract. After the surviving company rejected the claims, the union brought an action to compel arbitration. The Supreme Court held that the disappearance of the company did not terminate all the rights of the employees covered by the contract. It noted that the employment had been continued in similar operations following the merger. In response to the company's argument that the union had not followed the grievance steps, the Court remarked that that was a matter of "procedural arbitrability," which was for the arbitrator to decide along with the substantive issues. The Court recognized that if procedural issues were subject to judicial determination, the delays and added costs would virtually eliminate the effectiveness of arbitration. [John Wiley & Sons v. Livingston, 376 U.S. 543 (1964)]

6) **Presumption of arbitrability.** In *Nolde Brothers, Inc. v. Bakery Workers,* 430 U.S. 243 (1977), employees were covered by an agreement that provided for arbitration of severance pay and vacation pay. The company and the union bargained over a new agreement beyond the expiration of the old agreement. Finally, upon rejection of its last offer, the company closed its bakery. It paid accrued wages and vacation pay but refused to pay for severance and refused to arbitrate the issue. The court of appeals ordered arbitration of the severance claim. The Supreme Court affirmed, holding that the duty to arbitrate survived the termination of the contract. The Court said that the claim, although it arose "*after* the expiration of the collective bargaining contract, clearly [arose] *under* that contract." It said the presumption favoring arbitrability "must be negated expressly or by clear implication." The dissent pointed out that the closing of the plant should make the federal policy favoring arbitration inapplicable.

Litton Financial Printing Division v. NLRB

a) **Expiration of the CBA--Litton Financial Printing Division v. NLRB,** 501 U.S. 190 (1991).

(1) **Facts.** Litton Financial Printing Division (D) ran a check printing plant which used both hot- and cold-type printing. Production workers were covered by a CBA that contained a "broad" arbitration clause and provided for lay-offs by seniority if ability and aptitude were equal. The CBA expired on October 3, 1979. After D questioned the majority status, the union won an election which was upheld by the Board, which then ordered bargaining. In the interim, D closed down the cold-type process without notifying the union. Laid off were 10 of 42 employees, including six of the most senior employees in the plant. The union filed grievances claiming violation of the lay-off seniority provision. D refused to submit the issue to grievance procedure and refused to negotiate over the lay-offs. The Board found section 8(a)(1) and (5) violations, and the court of appeals enforced, finding the refusal to submit to arbitration a violation even though the CBA had expired, citing *Nolde Brothers, supra.* The Supreme Court granted certiorari.

(2) **Issue.** Did the lay-off, which occurred well after the CBA had expired, "arise" under the CBA for purposes of arbitration?

(3) **Held.** No. Case remanded for other considerations.

(a) The Board for a long period has held that an arbitration clause does not automatically survive when a CBA is by law extended until impasse under *Katz, supra.* An arbitration clause may survive because the CBA so provides, but it will not survive by operation of law. Arbitration is also a consensual process.

(b) A duty to take unilateral action to modify the terms of an expired contract may also spring from the terms of the contract, as in *Nolde*.

(c) In *Nolde*, we agreed that when the solution of a claim hinges on the interpretation of a clause in an expired contract providing for severance pay, the dispute, although arising after expiration, clearly arises under the CBA.

(d) We recognize that although arbitration is a consensual contractual undertaking, it will not necessarily expire for all purposes when the CBA does. Pending arbitrations and claims arising under the CBA will survive to be arbitrated.

(e) We reject D's arguments that the CBA stipulation about expiration rebuts the presumption concerning the survival of any arbitration duty, and also that the expiration of the duty not to strike relieves the employer's quid pro quo duty to arbitrate. The CBA provides that the no-strike clause does not survive, the CBA provides for interest arbitration, and the arbitration is broad. The dispute in this case arises under the CBA and there is a duty to arbitrate even after its expiration.

(f) *Nolde* does not suggest that any grievance concerning terms and conditions of employment will transcend the contract. It must arise under the CBA; that is, it must involve (i) facts and occurrences that arose before expiration, or (ii) post-expiration actions that infringe a right that accrued or vested under the CBA. Although certain provisions of an expired CBA cannot be unilaterally changed until after bargaining to impasse, this is to protect the statutory duties to bargain, which are not grounded in the contract itself.

(g) Structural provisions, such as contract remedies, will also survive in order to enforce the duties arising under the contract.

(h) The lay-offs in this case took place almost one year after the contract expired. The right asserted in this case involves a residual element of seniority, which the union argues is a form of "earned advantage, accumulated over time," and a form of "deferred compensation." However, unlike severance pay in *Nolde*, lay-off seniority here is different.

(i) The lay-offs here depended primarily on aptitude and ability, before seniority comes into play. Aptitude and ability are personal attributes and change over time. We cannot say that the lay-off provision created a right that vested or accrued during the term of the CBA, or that it was a contractual obligation that carries over after expiration.

(4) **Dissent** (Marshall, Blackmun, Scalia, JJ.). I agree with Justice Stevens, but wish to emphasize that the majority mischaracterized *Nolde Brothers*. *Nolde* defined "arises under" the expired contract to be when the resolution of the claim hinges on the interpretation given to the contract. This should be given to the arbitrator rather than the courts to decide. The CBA contained a broad arbi-

ration clause. The dispute is arbitral because of the presumption of arbitrability, which has not been negated here.

(5) **Dissent** (Stevens, Blackmun, Scalia, JJ.). An employer's obligation to arbitrate post-contract grievances might arise by operation of law or by operation of the expired contract. The Court is correct in deferring to the Board's holding that a statutory duty does not automatically survive. I part company with the Court in its application of the contract survival rule to the facts of this case. I am convinced that whether a claim "arises under" the expired contract is ultimately a matter of contract interpretation. The Court errs in reaching the merits. The case should have been submitted to arbit-ration under the broad arbitration clause.

7) **Successor's duty to arbitrate.** The implications of *Wiley, supra,* were reined-in by the Court in two later cases. In *NLRB v. Burns International Security Services, Inc.*, 406 U.S. 272 (1972), the Court recognized the duty of a successor to bargain with a union that had represented the employees of the predecessor company. The successor company had hired a majority of employees in the old bargaining unit. However, the collective bargaining agreement did not survive. The Court emphasized the importance of the policy of section 8(d), which encourages the parties to set the terms of their contract themselves. The Court noted that *Wiley* was a section 301 arbitration case and that *Wiley* had gone through a statutory merger. In the second case, *Howard Johnson Co. v. Detroit Local Joint Executive Board, infra,* the company had employed only a small fraction of the predecessor's employees. The union claimed that the refusal to rehire the former employees was a violation of the agreement with the predecessor. The successor, Howard Johnson Company, refused to arbitrate the issue. The Court found that the successor had no duty to arbitrate. The Court emphasized that no merger had taken place in this case and that there was no "continuity of identity in the business enterprise" since there was no "continuity in the work-force."

United Steelworkers of America v. Enterprise Wheel & Car Corp.

8) **Court enforcement of arbitrator's award--United Steelworkers of America v. Enterprise Wheel & Car Corp.**, 363 U.S. 593 (1960).

a) **Facts.** United Steelworkers of America (P) had a contract with Enterprise Wheel & Car (D) providing for final binding arbitration as to the "meaning and application of the agreement." In discharge cases, if the arbitrator ruled that an employee had been wrongfully discharged, D was to reinstate and pay for the lost time. The agreement also provided that neither party would institute civil suits against the other for violation of the agreement. D fired one employee and then fired other employees who left work to protest the discharge. A grievance was filed by P, but D refused to arbitrate. P filed suit in federal district court and the court ordered arbitration. Before the arbitration could occur, the contract expired, but P continued to represent the employees. The arbitrator held that the expiration of the contract did not bar reinstatement of the employees and ordered them reinstated with back pay offset by a deduction for a 10-day suspension and for any sums earned during the period. D refused to comply, and the court of appeals held that the district court had jurisdiction to enforce the award, but that the failure to specify the exact amounts to be deducted rendered the award unenforceable. It also held that an award rendered after expiration of the agreement could not be enforced. P appeals.

b) **Issue.** May a federal court refuse to enforce an arbitrator's award if it disagrees with the arbitrator's interpretation of the contract?

c) **Held.** No. Judgment reversed in part.

   (1) The federal policy of settling labor disputes would be undermined if the courts had the final say on the merits of an arbitration award. Arbitration is an indispensable agency in a continuous collective bargaining process.

   (2) Arbitrators are commissioned to interpret and apply the bargaining agreement by bringing their informed judgment to reach a fair solution, especially in formulating remedies. Arbitrators must apply the agreement and do not sit to apply their own brand of industrial justice. They may look to many sources for guidance, yet the award is "legitimate only so long as it draws its essence from the collective bargaining agreement."

   (3) In the decision to grant back pay beyond the expiration date of the agreement, the award is ambiguous. It may have applied or followed legislation, which would be wrong, or the arbitrator may have resorted to law for guidance. To require opinions to be free of ambiguity may lead arbitrators to play it safe and write no opinions at all. This would be undesirable.

   (4) In this case, we see no reason to assume that the arbitrator has abused the trust that the parties confided in him and has not stayed within the proper areas for his consideration.

   (5) If the courts were to review each award for errors of contractual law, the finality provisions of submission agreements would be rendered meaningless. It was the arbitrator's interpretation of the contract that the parties bargained for.

d) **Comment.** Courts will not enforce an arbitration award which violates either enacted law or public policy.

9) **Setting aside awards on the basis of "public policy"--United Paperworkers International Union v. Misco, Inc.,** 484 U.S. 29 (1987).

   a) **Facts.** Misco (P) and the United Paperworkers International Union (D) were parties to a collective bargaining agreement that contained a provision for final arbitration of disciplinary grievances. An employee on the night shift operated a slitter-rewinder machine, which is hazardous and had caused injuries in the past. The city police had earlier searched the employee's house and found a quantity of marijuana, and he had been placed under police surveillance. That evening, the employee and two other men were observed to briefly enter his car on the company parking lot and then enter another car nearby. After the two men left, the police arrested the employee sitting in the back seat of the other car. There was marijuana smoke in the air and a lighted marijuana cigarette in the front ashtray. A search of the employee's car uncovered a plastic scales case and marijuana gleanings, and he was arrested. Later, the employee told the company that he had been arrested for possession at his home. The

United Paperworkers International Union v. Misco, Inc.

company investigated the matter and discharged him for possession of marijuana on the plant premises. At the time of the discharge, the company had become aware of the cigarette and the employee's presence in the other car, but it was not aware of the search of his own car. A grievance was filed against the discharge and the matter was taken to arbitration. The arbitrator refused to accept evidence about the gleanings found in the employee's car and found that the company had not proved use or possession on its premises. P filed in federal district court to vacate the arbitration award. The district court set it aside as being contrary to public policy. The court of appeals affirmed. The Supreme Court granted certiorari.

b) **Issue.** May an arbitrator's award be set aside on the grounds that it contravenes general concepts of public policy?

c) **Held.** No. Judgment reversed.

(1) The courts play only a limited role in reviewing the decision of an arbitrator. They do not reconsider the merits even on allegations of errors of fact or misinterpretation of the contract. It was not for the court of appeals to retry the evidence concerning the fact of possession, nor for it to consider the arbitrator's refusal to accept the evidence, since the refusal did not amount to gross misconduct. We have recognized that a court may not enforce a collective agreement that is contrary to public policy. But the agreement must violate "some explicit public policy" that is "well defined and dominant, and is to be ascertained 'by reference to the laws and legal precedents and not from general considerations of supposed public interests.'"

(2) In this case, the court of appeals made no effort to review existing laws and legal precedents to find a dominant public policy applicable to the circumstances. In any event, it extended itself into speculation in its attempt to connect a supposed use of marijuana and the actual operation of dangerous machinery.

6. **Injunctive Relief Available.**

a. **Introduction.** Following the Taft-Hartley Act of 1947, the Supreme Court first held that federal courts could award only damages against a union that violated a "no-strike" agreement (*i.e.*, that federal courts could not enjoin the strike). The rationale was that section 4 of the Norris-LaGuardia Act prohibited federal courts from issuing injunctions in labor disputes. [Sinclair Refining Co. v. Atkinson, 370 U.S. 195 (1962)] However, this left the employer with no real remedy against a union that breached its "no-strike" agreement. A damage award would not necessarily end the strike. Moreover, if the agreement contained a broad arbitration clause (covering employer grievances), the union could stay the damage action pending arbitration of the dispute over the union's right to strike, while the strike continued.

1) **Forum shopping after *Sinclair*.** As a result of these deficiencies, few employers bothered to sue in federal courts. This resulted in much forum shopping and litigation in state courts until the Supreme Court held that such state court actions could be removed to federal court. [Avco Corp. v. Lodge 735 IAM, 390 U.S. 557 (1968)]

2) **Federal courts can issue injunctions.** Later, the Supreme Court reversed itself and held that federal courts can enjoin a union from striking in violation of a "no-strike" clause in the collective bargaining agreement where the dispute is arbitrable under the contract.

3) **Rationale—Taft-Hartley "repeals" ban on injunctions.** The Court reasoned that section 301 of the Taft-Hartley Act, in conferring jurisdiction on federal courts with respect to breaches of the collective bargaining agreement, impliedly repealed the anti-injunction provisions of Norris-LaGuardia in this area.

4) **Enjoining a strike violating "no-strike" clause--Boys Markets, Inc. v. Retail Clerks Union, Local 770,** 398 U.S. 235 (1970).

   Boys Markets, Inc. v. Retail Clerks Union, Local 770

   a) **Facts.** Boys Markets (P) and Local 770 (D) were parties to a labor agreement providing that grievances relating to the application and interpretation of the contract should be resolved by adjustment and arbitration and that during the life of the agreement there would be no-strike and no lockout. The dispute arose when nonunion employees rearranged merchandise at the store and D insisted that the work be redone. When P refused, a strike was called. P went to the state court to seek an injunction, and D removed the case to the federal district court, where the strike was enjoined and the parties were ordered to arbitrate the dispute. The court of appeals reversed, holding that the anti-injunction provisions of the Norris-LaGuardia Act prevent a federal court from enjoining a strike in breach of a "no-strike" clause. P appeals.

   b) **Issue.** Do the anti-injunction provisions of the Norris-LaGuardia Act prohibit a federal court from enjoining a strike violating a "no-strike" clause?

   c) **Held.** No. Judgment reversed.

      (1) *Sinclair, supra,* was erroneously decided. That case coupled with *Avco, supra,* has tended to oust the state courts of their injunctive powers. We decline to extend the rule of *Sinclair* to the states.

      (2) The unavailability of equitable relief in arbitration cases is a serious impediment to the accomplishment of congressional policy for the peaceful resolution of labor disputes. Without an adequate remedy, the employer has little incentive to agree to a no-strike clause in exchange for a grievance/arbitration procedure.

      (3) Our holding is a narrow one and does not undermine the vitality of the Norris-LaGuardia Act. We deal only with an agreement containing a mandatory grievance-arbitration procedure. In this case, there is no question that the dispute is subject to grievance and arbitration

Labor Law - 147

under the terms of the contract and that the company is ready to proceed to arbitration. And there are proper grounds for granting an injunction.

- **d) Concurrence** (Stewart, J.). Originally, I subscribed to *Sinclair*, but I agree with the Court that *Sinclair* was erroneously decided and that subsequent events have undermined its vitality.

- **e) Dissent** (Black, J.). *Sinclair* was correctly decided and Congress has not seen fit to overrule it.

- **f) Comment.** *Boys Markets* has been held to apply only to strikes over an arbitrable issue. Thus, for example, a federal court may not enjoin a sympathy strike. [Buffalo Forge Co. v. United Steelworkers of America, 428 U.S. 397 (1976)] *Rationale*: The question of whether the strike violates the collective bargaining agreement may be arbitrable. However, the strike itself is not over an arbitrable issue so that the arbitrator will not be in a position to resolve the labor dispute.

b. **Showing required to obtain injunctive relief.** The holding in *Boys Markets, supra,* does not make injunctive relief available in every case. Rather, an injunction may issue only where the employer establishes all of the following:

1) A *mandatory* grievance and *arbitration* proceeding in the collective bargaining contract;

2) A *dispute* which is *arbitrable* thereunder;

3) A *likelihood of irreparable harm* to the employer if the strike continues; and

4) Injury to the employer which *will exceed any harm to the union* from being enjoined.

c. **Individual damages.** In *Atkinson v. Sinclair Refining Co.*, 370 U.S. 238 (1962), the company sought damages from the union under section 301 and from certain individual employees for breach of a no-strike clause. The Supreme Court ruled that although a union may be liable for damages for violation of a no-strike clause under section 301(b), its officers and members would not be. The rule has been extended to individual wildcat strikers.

d. **Union damages.** In *Complete Auto Transit, Inc. v. Reis*, 451 U.S. 401 (1981), several locals of District 17 of the United Mine Workers Union ("UMW") engaged in strikes in violation of a no-strike clause. The company sued the locals, the district, and UMW, claiming that the district and UMW had a duty to take reasonable efforts to stop the illegal strikes. The Court ruled that sections 301(b) and (e) supplanted the rules of responsibility in section 6 of the Norris-LaGuardia Act and section 2(2) of Wagner. It ruled that although the local might be, the district and UMW were not vicariously liable and had no duty to respond to the stoppages, and that they would be liable if they had instigated, supported, ratified, or encouraged the strikes.

7. **The NLRB's Role During the Term of the Agreement.** Many of the rights and duties under the Act may be modified or traded away, such as the right to strike or picket, which will be unprotected activity if done in violation of a no-strike clause. The duty to bargain may also be restricted by the terms of the agreement. During the term of the agreement, conduct may raise both unfair labor practice/representational issues and arbitrable issues; these include discriminatory discharge cases, representation, and work-assignment cases.

   a. **Union jurisdictional disputes.** Controversies between unions which make overlapping "jurisdictional" claims to particular jobs present knotty problems for arbitration. From one view, each union is trying to bring the job under the regime of its own bargaining agreement. From a different perspective, it may be seen as an attempt by one or the other of the unions to redefine its respective bargaining unit. The Board has specific authority to "clarify" a unit. The Board also can deal with a unit issue in a section 8(a)(5) proceeding. The Board would have jurisdiction under section 8(b)(4)(D) if the controversy generates a strike. On the other hand, if it is considered a work assignment problem, the issue is subject to an arbitrator's jurisdiction. The problem in this kind of controversy is almost invariably that the arbitrator will derive his or her jurisdiction from only one of the agreements and will have no power over the other union, and an award would not be binding on all of the relevant parties. When faced with the question of whether a court should order arbitration in this sort of situation, the Supreme Court directed that an order to proceed to arbitration was appropriate and should be ordered for its "practical" and "curative" effects even though one of the unions would not be bound. [Carey v. Westinghouse Electric Corp., 375 U.S. 261 (1964)]

   b. **Contract enforcement and unfair labor practices.** If the requirements for an injunction under section 301 are met, any strike that violates a "no-strike" agreement may be enjoined even though the strike itself (or the conduct to which it is a response) is also an unfair labor practice.

      1) **Rationale.** Parties that have agreed to submit their disputes to arbitration should be compelled to do so; they cannot be permitted to bypass such procedures by categorizing objectionable conduct as an "unfair labor practice" and calling a strike.

         a) **NLRB jurisdiction not exclusive.** NLRB jurisdiction over unfair labor practices is not exclusive, and it does not oust courts from the jurisdiction conferred by Taft-Hartley section 301 to enforce the terms of the collective bargaining agreement. Moreover, the NLRB policy is to refrain from exercising jurisdiction in such cases and to defer to contractual mechanisms for settling the dispute.

         b) **Interpreting terms of agreements by the Board.** In order to properly dispose of unfair labor practice issues, the Board on occasion must refer to the terms of a bargaining agreement and its negotiations background. The Supreme Court has approved this practice as necessary for the proper enforcement of the Act, but only so far as necessary to dispose of the statutory case. The Court noted that it would be cumbersome if the Board had to wait on an arbitrator to get an interpretation of the agreement before the Board could effectively deal with the statutory part of the case. [NLRB v. C. & C. Plywood Co., 385 U.S. 421 (1967)]

    c) **Employee violations.** A company's refusal to provide a union with requested information needed to prepare for bargaining or to process a grievance is a section 8(2)(5) violation. The Supreme Court found that such a Board action was not inconsistent with the grievance and arbitration process. [NLRB v. Acme Industrial Co., *supra*]

2) **Suits by individuals.** The Supreme Court has also ruled that the federal statutory provisions authorizing suits for violations of union contracts are not to be interpreted as limiting the right to bring suits for contract breaches to employers and unions but must be construed as authorizing individual employees to sue for breaches to vindicate uniquely personal rights. For example, if a union acts dishonestly or fraudulently in administering a contract and its action results in a breach of an individual employee's contractual rights, the employee may sue the union as well as the employer.

3) **Remedies in breach of contract suits.**

    a) **Damages.** The amount of damages awarded in breach of contract suits is usually measured by the loss sustained as a result of the breach. In some instances, both compensatory and punitive damages and attorneys' fees may be awarded. For example, punitive damages have been awarded where they were deemed necessary to deter a union from violating a contract by a repeated series of strikes. Note that a judgment against a union may be enforced only against the organization as an entity and its assets (as opposed to the entity's individual members).

    b) **Injunctions.** In addition to damages, injunctive relief may also be granted, subject to certain limitations. Thus, federal courts may order specific performance of contract arbitration clauses, but strikes in breach of contract may only be enjoined in federal courts under the conditions set forth in *Boys Markets*, *supra*. A federal appeals court has held that a state court may enjoin a breach of a no-strike clause under the theory that the injunction is only a question of the "remedy."

4) **Role of the NLRB.** Obligations that parties incur under bargaining agreements will sometimes overlap or conflict with duties imposed by the NLRA. In these situations, the Supreme Court has declared that the authority of the Board to deal with an unfair labor practice that also violates a collective bargaining contract is not displaced, but it is not exclusive and does not destroy the jurisdiction of the courts in suits under section 301. "If there are situations in which serious problems will arise from both the courts and the Board having jurisdiction over acts which amount to an unfair labor practice, we shall face those cases when they arise." [Smith v. Evening News Association, *supra*]

5) **NLRB deference to arbitration.** The Board has provided guidelines for accommodation and deference to arbitration awards in cases that also concern unfair labor practices. In *Dubo Manufacturing Co.*, 142 N.L.R.B. 431 (1963), the Board said it would defer when a similar contract dispute was pending in an arbitration proceeding that was likely to resolve the unfair labor practice

controversy. In *Spielberg Manufacturing Co.*, 112 N.L.R.B. 1080 (1955), the Board deferred to an arbitration award that was the product of a proceeding that appeared to have been "fair and regular, all parties had agreed to be bound" and the decision "is not clearly repugnant to the purposes of the Act." In *International Harvester Co.*, 130 N.L.R.B. 923 (1961), the Board said it would not reexamine the merits of sections 8(a)(2) and (3) disputes already resolved in arbitration.

6) **Board need not agree with arbitrator.** Even when the Board would not have reached the same conclusions as the arbitrator would have, as long as the proceedings are fair and the results are not in conflict with the NLRA, the arbitrator's awards will usually be recognized.

    a) **Board's present position on deference to arbitrators--Olin Corp.,** 268 N.L.R.B. 573 (1984).   Olin Corp.

        (1) **Facts.** Olin (D) entered a labor agreement with the union (P) which contained a no-strike clause providing that no officer would cause or permit a strike directly or indirectly. The president of P was fired for participating in a sick-out. A grievance was filed and taken to arbitration. The arbitrator sustained the discharge, ruling that the president had instigated or participated in the sick-out and made no effort to stop it, in violation of his implicit obligations under the agreement. The arbitrator also concluded that there was no unfair labor practice proved since it was not shown that the president was fired because of legitimate union activities. In a parallel unfair labor practice proceeding, the ALJ refused to follow the arbitrator's disposition of the unfair labor practice because it was not seriously considered by the arbitrator and the arbitrator was not competent to pass on the statutory ground. Nevertheless, the judge found on the merits that the president had violated his duties under the agreement and that the discharge was for cause and not a violation of sections 8(a)(3) and (1).

        (2) **Issue.** Should the Board defer to the arbitrator's disposition of the unfair labor practice?

        (3) **Held.** Yes. Complaint dismissed. Rather than consider the merits, we will defer to the arbitrator's award.

            (a) *Spielberg, supra,* established the principles of Board deference to arbitration awards. With respect to unfair labor practices, *Raytheon Co.*, 140 N.L.R.B. 883 (1963), further required that the arbitrator must have decided the unfair labor practice issue.

            (b) We adopt a new standard for deferral. We will find that the arbitrator has adequately considered the unfair labor practice issue if: (i) it is factually parallel to the contract issues, and (ii) the arbitrator was generally presented with the facts relevant to resolving the unfair labor practice issue.

            (c) We will not require the award to be entirely consistent with Board precedent.

(d) The party wishing to reject deferral bears the burden to show that the new standards have not been met.

(e) In the present case, the arbitration satisfies the new standard and the arbitrator's interpretation that the agreement waived the union leadership prerogatives was the opinion for which the parties bargained.

(4) Dissent (Zimmerman, Member). The new deferral standard is beyond the Board's authority. The new rule is an abdication of the Board's statutory obligation to prevent unfair labor practices and imposes an inequitable burden on the General Counsel. It may actually discourage resort to grievance and arbitration.

b) **Deference to settlement agreements.** A "proper cause" discharge was challenged under the CBA and an unfair labor practice charge was filed. While the charge was pending, the company and the international union reached an agreed settlement providing for reinstatement without back pay. The grievant and the local union objected. The ALJ refused to defer to the settlement and recommended reinstatement with back pay. The Board reversed and deferred to the settlement. Following *Spielberg-Olin* criteria, *supra*, the Board indicated that it would defer to a settlement agreement (i) which was reached through a fair and regular bargaining process, (ii) to which the parties had agreed to be bound, (iii) which was not "palpably wrong", and (iv) which was factually parallel to the unfair labor practice and both parties were aware of the relevant facts. The court of appeals found the Board's approach to be rational and consistent with national labor policy and that the statutory right being asserted was waivable. However, the court warned that this deferral policy in respect to prearbitration settlements had questionable theoretical underpinnings, especially where the Board required both parties to have made concessions. [Plumbers & Pipefitters Local 520 v. NLRB (C-Catalytic, Inc.), 955 F.2d 744 (D.C. Cir. 1992), *cert. denied*, 506 U.S. 817 (1992)]

c) **Deference in representation cases.** Because of the complexities of work assignment cases, the Board will give consideration to an arbitrator decision resolving a work assignment grievance but will not consider itself obliged to "defer to it entirely." [Westinghouse Electric Corp., 162 N.L.R.B. 768 (1967)] The Board noted that one of the competing unions was not a party to the proceeding and that the arbitrator could only apply the contract to the case and could not take into account unit determination criteria applied by the Board.

d) **Title VII discrimination cases.** In *Alexander v. Gardner-Denver Co.*, 415 U.S. 36 (1974), the Supreme Court held that a prior resort to arbitration did not amount to an election of remedies or a waiver of judicial relief in a Title VII discrimination case. It also ruled that trial courts did not have to defer to the arbitration decision, but that it could be admitted into evidence and accorded "such weight as the court deemed appropriate." [*See also* Barrentine v. Arkansas-Best Freight System, Inc., 450 U.S. 728 (1981)] Recently, the Supreme Court has become more tolerant toward arbitration of federal statutory rights. It allowed arbitration of an age discrimination claim under the Federal Arbitration Act brought by a securities salesman who, as a condition of employment, agreed to arbitration of all claims arising out of the employment. The court distinguished *Gardner-Denver*, saying in that case it was not an arbitration-duty-enforcement case; the employee had not agreed to arbitration; the arbitrator was not authorized to resolve such claims; the union, not the employee, presented the case; and it was not a Federal Arbitration Act case. [Gilmer v. Interstate/Johnson Lane Corp, 500 U.S. 20 (1991)]

e) **The *Collyer* doctrine.** In *Collyer Insulated Wire, supra*, the NLRB substantially broadened its deferral policies. Faced with an alleged employer violation of section 8(a)(5), the NLRB held that it would dismiss charges involving refusals to bargain filed prior to an arbitration award—even prior to submission of the dispute to arbitration—if the dispute is contractual in nature, the agreement calls for final and binding arbitration, and a "reasonable" construction of the agreement would preclude a finding that the disputed conduct violated the NLRA.

f) **Scope of the *Collyer* doctrine.** In a number of decisions since *Collyer*, the NLRB has further elaborated upon the areas in which *deferral* to arbitration is appropriate.

   (1) Where the dispute concerns a refusal to bargain, the NLRB has deferred to arbitration in virtually every case. Typical disputes in this area have involved unilateral wage changes, subcontracting, and reassignment of work; failure to implement agreed upon warning rules regarding employee discipline; and unilateral union orders to driver-members to cease cash collections (together with threats of intra-union discipline).

   (2) However, the Board has been much more cautious about deferral in employee discipline cases involving discrimination on the basis of union activity (section 8(a)(3) cases).

   (3) The NLRB has refused to defer to arbitration where deferral would "relegate the [charging employees] to an arbitral process authored [and] administered . . . by parties [both union and employer] hostile to their interests."

g) **1973 NLRB guidelines.** In 1973, the Board's General Counsel set out a uniform procedure to be followed by regional offices in cases raising the possibility of deferral.

   (1) The NLRB will defer to arbitration when the dispute is "susceptible of resolution under the contract arbitration machinery in a manner conforming to the purposes of the NLRA," whether the interpretation of ambiguous substantive contract provisions is involved in the dispute.

   (2) But there are exceptions—notably, disputes where the entire contract is at issue, where recognition of the union per se is involved, or where a "hostile" environment pervades the contractual arbitration machinery.

   (3) The basic policy was to defer on virtually all disputes giving rise to an unfair labor practice, whether the dispute is contractual or statutory in nature.

h) **1977 retrenchment.** In 1977, the NLRB had occasion in two cases to review the *Collyer* doctrine, *supra*, with a Board membership different from that when *Collyer* was decided.

(1) Section 8(a)(5) charge. In a case involving a charge of section 8(a)(5) refusal to bargain, the Board found that deferral under the *Collyer* doctrine was appropriate. [Roy Robinson, Inc., 228 N.L.R.B. 828 (1977)]

(2) Section 8(a)(3) charge. However, where a charge of discrimination under section 8(a)(3) had been brought, the NLRB refused to apply *Collyer* on the theory that deferral is not proper as to matters involving section 7 individual rights. [General American Transportation Corp., 228 N.L.R.B. 808 (1977)]

i) Present status of doctrine--United Technologies Corp., 268 N.L.R.B. 557 (1984). [United Technologies Corp.]

(1) Facts. An employee filed a grievance with a supervisor of United Technologies (D) that was denied at the first step. After the supervisor allegedly threatened to discipline the employee if she took it to the second step, a section 8(a)(1) charge was filed. D claimed that the Board should defer its case in favor of the grievance-arbitration procedures of the labor agreement.

(2) Issue. Should the Board defer to grievance and arbitration in 8(a)(1) cases where an employee has been discouraged from pursuing that process?

(3) Held. Yes. The Board will defer to contract grievance and arbitration procedures, but will retain protective jurisdiction.

(a) Arbitration has gained widespread acceptance and is firmly established in federal labor policy. *Collyer, supra,* established the deferral standards for section 8(a)(5) cases. *National Radio Co.*, 198 N.L.R.B. 527 (1972), further extended deferral to section 8(a)(3) cases. However, in 1977, this Board adopted a more restrictive approach to sections 8(a)(1) and (3) and 8(b)(1)(A) and (2) cases.

(b) We again extend the *Collyer* policy and apply it to this kind of case and to section 8(a)(3) and (2) cases. The issue in this case is clearly cognizable under the grievance and arbitration provisions of the agreement. D is willing to arbitrate the matter and the grievance and arbitration machinery continues to be used by the parties to resolve disputes.

(4) Dissent (Zimmerman, Member). The majority overstates the appropriateness of arbitration as a substitute for Board processes. Arbitration is not designed to protect employee statutory or public rights. Even under a broad deferral policy, deferral should not be applied in this case because prohibited means were applied to preclude access to the grievance procedures.

j) Deferral by the courts to arbitration. While the question of deferral to arbitration arises more frequently in connection with NLRB unfair labor practice charges, the courts, in accord with the general Board policy favoring arbitration, will on occasion decline jurisdiction on substantive matters where arbitrable issues are involved. [*See* Carey v. Westinghouse Electric Corp., *supra*]

k) **Application--Hammontree v. NLRB,** 925 F.2d 1486 (D.C. Cir. 1991) (en banc).

(1) **Facts.** Hammontree (P) was a truck driver for Consolidated Freightways. He drove short round-trips, called "peddle runs," which originally the company allowed drivers to choose from among all runs by seniority. However, drivers never knew the time of their runs and were tied to the phone. Later, the company and the union negotiated a verbal modification—only peddle run times would be posted. Subsequently, as the CBA was expiring, the new union president notified the company that all agreements became null and void on March 31. The new CBA failed to specify assignments for peddle runs and the prior arrangement had not been reduced to writing as required by the CBA. P later filed a grievance that his seniority rights had been violated on peddle runs. This grievance was heard by a "Multi-State Grievance Committee" of an equal number of union and management members. The Committee failed to resolve the grievance and it was taken to the Southern Area Committee, which found for P and awarded back pay. The company stopped posting departure times and P filed another grievance, which was denied by the first level committee. P then filed an unfair labor practice charge with the Board. The General Counsel filed section 8(b)(1) and (3) charges maintaining that D had been discriminated against for filing the first grievance. The ALJ rejected the company's argument that P should be confined to his grievance remedy because the two claims were sufficiently different so as not to require deference to the Committee's decision. The ALJ also ruled that since P was asserting an individual claim, he was not required to exhaust his grievance remedies. The Board accepted the first finding, but rejected the second and ruled that P must exhaust the grievance remedies. P seeks review of the Board's order.

(2) **Issue.** Must P exhaust his grievance remedies before the Board will consider his unfair labor charges?

(3) **Held.** Yes.

(a) The Board has two deferral policies, one by which it defers or delays hearing a charge when a grievance is pending. A second post-arbitral deferral policy is not involved in this case.

(b) We apply the *Chevron U.S.A., Inc. v. Natural Resources Defense Council*, 467 U.S. 837 (1984), two-step inquiry in reviewing the Board's action. We must determine whether Congress has spoken on the matter; if so, that legislative intent will be given effect. If Congress has not spoken or has done so ambiguously, we will defer to the Board's reading of the statute if it has a reasonable basis.

(c) We do not read section 10(a) to reflect any congressional intention to preclude the Board from requiring exhaustion. We do not read the provision to prevent the Board from diminishing the exercise of its authority.

(d) We also conclude that section 203(d) does not prevent the Board's deference in favor of the private dispute resolution procedures devised by the parties. P cannot nullify his contractual claim simply by filing a statutory claim.

- (e) There is no statutory prohibition against the Board's action, and we also conclude that the Board's action constituted a rational interpretation of the NLRA. We are not considering the precedential effect of arbitration upon statutory claims, but whether the Board has proper justification for requiring exhaustion of arbitration remedies. Deferral is not abdication; it merely delays P's right to a public forum. The Board properly has said it will not require financially burdensome or dragged out proceedings or deferral where the union's interests are antagonistic to the employee's interests.

- (f) We conclude that the Board's action represents a reasonable interpretation of the NLRA and LMRA.

(4) Concurrence (Edwards, J.). This is not a difficult question and there is established precedent commanding judicial deference to the Board's judgment. *Gardner-Denver, supra*, et al. are clearly distinguishable. Also, a union may waive certain statutory rights through the bargaining process.

(5) Dissent (Mikva, C.J.). This case involves the interaction of two congressional policies. This case does not require the application or interpretation of the CBA, and P never agreed to give up his statutory protections against discrimination under section 10(a). The statutory preference for arbitration under section 203(d) simply is not involved in a discrimination case when the employee has not voluntarily submitted his claim to arbitration. This was not an arbitration to a neutral third party. The joint committee system does not adequately protect the employee from management or union discrimination. Exhaustion should not be required here.

c. **Modifying or terminating an existing agreement—Union-employer bargaining duties.**

1) **Basic rule.** If the union or employer wishes to terminate or modify a collective bargaining agreement, that party must comply with all of the following steps:

   a) It must notify the other party in writing of this intention (i) 60 days prior to the expiration date of the contract, or (ii) 60 days prior to the time it proposes to terminate or modify if the contract contains no expiration date;

   b) It must offer to meet and confer with the other party for the purpose of negotiating a new contract or a contract containing the proposed modifications;

c) It must notify the appropriate federal, state, or territorial mediation agency within 30 days of the first notice, unless an agreement has been reached by that time; and

d) The terms and conditions of the existing contract must continue in full force and effect, without resort by any party to strike or lockout, for a period of 60 days after the first notice is given or until the expiration date of the contract, whichever occurs later. [NLRA §8(d)]

2) **Qualifications.** Section 8(d) provides two qualifications to the above procedure:

   a) **Certification of another union.** Where the NLRB certifies another union during the stated period, thereby superseding the contracting union, steps b), c), and d) above do not apply.

   b) **No duty to bargain where subject covered by existing agreement.** Neither party owes any duty to bargain as to a subject which is in fact covered by an existing agreement (*e.g.*, where the union seeks to modify some term or provision *before* the time provided in the contract for renegotiation). But a subject not covered by an agreement may be negotiated prior to the expiration of the agreement.

   c) **Subjects not covered in contract--Jacobs Manufacturing Co.,** 94 N.L.R.B. 1214 (1951).

   Jacobs Manufacturing Co.

   (1) **Facts.** In 1948, Jacobs Manufacturing (D) and its union (P) entered into a collective bargaining contract which allowed for a reopening of negotiations on wage rates in 1949 if either party desired. Bargaining over the company's health insurance plan occurred during the initial contract negotiations, but nothing pertaining to the health plan was included in the final contract, while pensions were not even discussed. In 1949, invoking the reopening clause, P notified D that it desired to renew wage rate negotiations, and also negotiations for total employer support of health insurance and the establishment of a pension plan. D refused to participate in health insurance and pension bargaining contending that these subjects were not part of the 1949 "wage rate" renegotiation provision. P filed with the NLRB against D for refusal to bargain in good faith.

   (2) **Issue.** Are subjects not included in a contract subject to the restrictions of section 8(d), which deals with the reopening of negotiations on subjects discussed in the contract?

   (3) **Held.** No.

      (a) It was a violation of section 8(a)(5) to refuse to bargain about pensions. The reopener did not impose a duty to discuss pensions or insurance; thus, the duty to bargain must be predicated on the Act. The bargaining agreement is silent about pensions; indeed, they were never discussed. Pensions are a mandatory subject.

      (b) Section 8(d) reaches only "modification of terms and conditions contained in a contract." It does not justify a refusal to negotiate during the term of a contract about bargainable matters which have not been made part of the agreement itself.

(c) A minority of the Board is of the further view that what we have discussed in this opinion leads to the conclusion that the employer was also required to discuss group insurance.

(4) **Concurrence** (Herzog, Chairman). D was not required to negotiate about group insurance. That subject had been fully discussed in negotiations. It is not explicitly mentioned in the agreement, but it is only reasonable to assume that the rejection of the union's discussion amounted to a part of the "contemporaneous bargaining" which the parties negotiated in 1948. Otherwise, the union could come back and demand to negotiate times without number.

(5) **Dissent** (Reynolds, Member). Section 8(d) does not require either party to bargain about anything else during the life of the agreement. In this way, the agreement stabilizes all rights and conditions of employment. This does not mean that no negotiations will go on, for the parties will do so in dealing with day-to-day grievances.

(6) **Dissent** (Murdock, Member). There was no violation here at all. The reopener clause required a discussion of wage rates only.

(7) **Comment.** Neither party is required to consider a proposal to modify an existing agreement where the modification would become effective prior to the time provided in the agreement for renegotiation, but only if the subject is covered by the agreement.

Johnson-Bateman Co.

d. **Unilateral adoption of drug and alcohol testing--Johnson-Bateman Co.,** 295 N.L.R.B. No. 180 (1989).

1) **Facts.** The Johnson-Bateman Company (D) announced its unilateral adoption of an alcohol and drug testing program for all employees who were injured on the job. The bargaining agreement contained a management rights clause which reserved to D all "rights, privileges, and prerogatives" it had except as "clearly abridged by express provisions of this agreement." The agreement also provided that possession or use of alcohol on the premises was a dischargeable offense. The union (P) filed unfair labor charges. D claimed that P had waived its right to bargain about the change.

2) **Issue.** Does a general management rights clause in a collective bargaining agreement justify unilateral adoption of a drug and alcohol program by the employer?

3) **Held.** No. Violation of bargaining duty made out.

158 - Labor Law

- a) Drug and alcohol testing is a mandatory bargaining subject. The Board has repeatedly held that generally worded management rights or zipper clauses will not be construed as waivers of statutory bargaining rights.

- b) Waivers may be shown by bargaining history, but such must have been fully discussed, consciously explored, and unmistakably waived.

- c) In this case, the management rights provision reserving the right to change company rules is couched in general language without any reference to any particular subject. This and the zipper clause are too general to amount to a waiver to bargain about the testing program.

- d) Nothing in the bargaining history is sufficient to sustain the company's position. Testing was not even discussed.

- e) The 1983 arbitration award which concerned overtime showed evidence of a waiver by P. It recognized the right to make rules to manage the plant only as broad as permitted by the bargaining agreement itself.

- f) P's acquiescence in the testing of new employees is not sufficient to amount to a past practice which would permit testing of existing employees.

e. **Partial transfer of operations for economic reasons--Milwaukee Spring Division of Illinois Coil Spring Co.,** 268 N.L.R.B. 601 (1984).

    1) **Facts.** Illinois Coil Spring (D) had three divisions. During the term of the collective bargaining agreement, D proposed to the union that scheduled wage increases at Milwaukee Spring Division be canceled and that certain operations be transferred to a nonunion division. The union would not agree and declined to bargain further. Thereafter, on the basis of economic considerations, certain operations were transferred to the nonunion division. The union filed unfair labor practice charges and initially the Board found that D had violated sections 8(a)(1), (3), (5), and (d) when it transferred the operations without the union's consent. Following a change of Board membership and while the matter was on appeal, the case was returned to the Board for further consideration.

    2) **Issue.** Is it improper under the Act to transfer part of a plant's operations to a sister plant for economic reasons without first obtaining the bargaining agent's agreement?

    3) **Held.** No. The original order is reversed and the case dismissed.

        a) The controlling principles in this case are (i) an alteration of the "terms and conditions" contained in a collective agreement cannot be done without the union's consent, and (ii) if the conditions altered are not "contained in" the agreement, then the employer need only bargain to impasse.

Milwaukee Spring Division of Illinois Coil Spring Co.

b) There was no violation of section 8(d) since the transfer did not change the wage and benefits paid at the Milwaukee facility, there was no modification of the recognition clause, and the agreement contained no work-preservation provision requiring that operations conducted at that facility must remain there.

c) The resultant lay-off of employees was not a section 8(a)(3) violation because there was no bargaining violation and D acted without anti-union animus.

d) Today's decision should encourage meaningful and realistic midterm bargaining about job transfers.

4) Dissent (Zimmerman, Member). There was a section 8(d) violation because D was trying to avoid the wage provisions of the agreement. There is no implied work-preservation provision in the agreement and I agree that the recognition clause does not impliedly prohibit job transfers.

f. **The collective bargaining agreement and bankruptcy.** In *NLRB v. Bildisco & Bildisco*, 465 U.S. 513 (1984), the Supreme Court, in determining the interaction between labor law and bankruptcy law, ruled that a collective bargaining agreement was an "executory contract" under the Bankruptcy Code which could be rejected by the bankruptcy court under section 365(a), applying a lenient "business judgment" test. It also ruled that the agreement became unenforceable from the date of the filing of the bankruptcy petition and could be rejected without bargaining to impasse. Congress promptly amended the Code and imposed stricter standards. Section 1113 requires the debtor or trustee to continue the agreement in effect and to propose to the union modifications which "must be necessary to permit the reorganization" of the debtor and which are fair and equitable. If a court finds that these requirements have been satisfied and that the union has rejected the proposal without good cause, the court can approve an application if the equities "clearly favor" rejection of the collective bargaining agreement. The courts of appeals have not agreed about whether "necessary" means that a contract change must be "essential" or something less.

VI. SUCCESSORSHIP

A. SUCCESSION OF UNIT, REPRESENTATIONAL STATUS, AND SURVIVAL OF THE BARGAINING AGREEMENT UPON CHANGE OF OWNERSHIP OF THE BUSINESS

1. **Survival of the Agreement and Representational Status.**

   a. **Duty of new employer to bargain—"contractual successorship."** Corporate mergers, combinations, and acquisitions are common in American business. Important questions are whether the new employer is bound by the terms of a preexisting collective bargaining agreement, and whether he must recognize and bargain with the existing union representative.

   1) **Assumption of existing contract.** Where the successor agrees to accept ("assumes") the existing contract as part of her acquisition of the business and there is no significant alteration of the work force, she is obviously bound by its terms and must also bargain with the designated representative.

   2) **Surviving corporation in statutory merger.** Where the successor is the survivor corporation in a statutory merger, the new employer may be bound as a matter of state corporation law to assume certain obligations of the disappearing entity. Moreover, the Supreme Court has held that the purchaser must bargain with the representative and must honor the grievance and arbitration procedures of the existing contract with respect to grievances arising out of the merger. [*See* John Wiley & Sons v. Livingston, *supra*]

2. **Survival of Bargaining Status But Not the Agreement.** A business may be taken over less formally than by statutory merger. The business, the assets, or the business name may change hands. The new owner may hire all, some, or none of the old work force, or the scope or nature of the business operations may be changed in varying degrees over time.

   a. **Retention of some of the work force.** When a new owner takes over a business with an existing organization without materially changing the type and scope of operations and existing job positions (that is, the bargaining unit jobs are not substantially changed) and the new employer hires a majority of the old work force, the Supreme Court has held that the successor must bargain with the incumbent union. However, the bargaining agreement with the former employer does not survive. Under these circumstances, a mere change in the ownership is not enough to ignore the wishes of the employees. However, the Court did not require demonstration that a majority of the retained employees did in fact support the union.

   b. **Circumstances which will destroy the duty to bargain.** The duty to bargain will not carry over if the successor recruits a new work force, the operational structure and practices are materially changed (even if the work force is retained), or the successor has a good faith reasonable doubt about the incumbent union's majority status.

Fall River Dyeing & Finishing Corp. v. NLRB

3. **The Effect of Delay--Fall River Dyeing & Finishing Corp. v. NLRB,** 482 U.S. 27 (1987).

   a. **Facts.** Sterlingwale was a long-established textile dyeing firm. The majority of its business consisted of finishing its own fabrics, but 30-40% was commission dyeing for other companies. Its employees had long been represented by the United Textile Workers (P). The most recent bargaining agreement expired in April 1982. The company experienced financial reverses and ultimately went out of business in the summer of 1982, making an assignment for the benefit of creditors. Former officers and employees organized Fall River Dyeing & Finishing Corporation (D) to do only commission work and began operations at the old business site in September, using the same production processes and job classifications. D began hiring a full shift from the ranks of former supervisors and employees of Sterlingwale. In October, after D had hired about one third of the shift and training operations had begun, P requested D to recognize and bargain with it. Upon refusal, P filed unfair labor practice charges against D on November 1, 1982. By January, the full shift had been hired and commission operations began. The large majority of supervisors and workers were former Sterlingwale employees. By April 1983, D had hired two full shifts and ex-Sterlingwale employees were now in the minority. The Board found that D was the successor of Sterlingwale and that D's duty to bargain arose in January because the former employees were in the majority then and because of the Union's request for recognition. The court of appeals enforced the bargaining order, and the Supreme Court granted certiorari.

   b. **Issue.** Will the presumption of majority support apply to a long-established union in a successorship situation where resumption of operations using former employees by the successor is delayed for several months?

   c. **Held.** Yes. Judgment affirmed.

      1) The presumption is based not so much on a certainty of actual majority status of the union as upon a policy that promotes stability in bargaining relationships. The presumption should be applied to long-established unions as well as recently certified ones. We approve the Board's test to determine successorship, which looks to the total circumstances including whether the new company has acquired substantial assets from the old company and has continued the old business operations without interruption or substantial change.

      2) The Board's determination is supported by substantial evidence. The seven-month hiatus in this case is only one factor in the determination of substantial continuity. The duty to bargain arises when the successor has employed a substantial and representative compliment of employees, which in this case occurred when the first full shift was recruited. The designated job positions were substantially filled, and the operation had reached substantially normal production.

      3) We also hold that the Board's continuing demand rule is reasonable. The duty to bargain arises only after a demand made by the union. The union has no established relationship with the successor and will

be unaware of the successor's plans for operation and hiring, and a bargaining duty may likely be premature. The reasonableness of the rule is demonstrated by the facts of this case. The union made a demand and D, rather than being confused about when a duty to bargain might arise, denied any obligation and stuck to that position.

d. **Dissent** (Powell, J., Rehnquist, C.J., O'Connor, J.). In this case, there was not substantial continuity. D was a completely separate entity. It came into existence many months after the old company ceased operations. D bought only tangible assets and took over only the smaller fraction of the old business. Also, the Board was wrong in its determination about a representative workforce. D had not completed its hiring plans with the first shift. Here, expansion was imminent and reasonably definite. The Court requires D to recognize a union that has never been elected or accepted by a majority of its employees.

4. **Successor's Responsibility for Prior Employer's Unfair Labor Practice.** In an action against the successor employer for reinstatement and back pay due to the prior business owner's unfair labor practice, the Supreme Court held both employers jointly liable. The Court recognized that section 10(c) allows remedial orders to apply to others than the actual perpetrator. It held that a bona fide purchaser who acquires the business with knowledge that the wrong remains uncorrected may be considered in privity with the predecessor employer. The Board properly exercised its discretion in this case where the new employer acquires substantial assets and continues without interruption or substantial change in the business operations. Employees may well view the successor's failure to remedy as a continuation of the predecessor's labor policies. [Golden State Bottling Co. v. NLRB, 414 U.S. 168 (1973)]

5. **Successor Employer's Duties Under Prior Employer's Bargaining Relationship--Howard Johnson Co. v. Detroit Local Joint Executive Board,** 417 U.S. 249 (1974).

    a. **Facts.** The Hotel and Restaurant Union (P) was the bargaining agent and had entered an agreement with the prior owner of a franchised motel and restaurant. Howard Johnson Company (D), the franchiser, bought the personal assets of the business and leased the premises from the prior owner. It continued the same business at the same location under the same name. D assumed none of the obligations of the prior business except for four contracts. It hired only nine former employees out of a total of 53 and used none of the previous supervision. P brought an action against D and the former owner to restrain them from continuing a lockout in violation of the bargaining agreement. The former owner agreed to arbitrate the matter and the federal district court found that D was also required to arbitrate the matter. The court of appeals affirmed, and the Supreme Court granted certiorari.

    b. **Issue.** Is a successor business operator who continues without material changes and who hires only a small fraction of the former employees required to arbitrate claims brought by the bargaining agent of the former employees?

Howard Johnson Co. v. Detroit Local Joint Executive Board

    c.   **Held.** No. Judgment reversed.

        1)   Both courts below relied mainly on *Wiley, supra,* which was our first encounter with the difficult issue of "successorship." The holding there that a corporate merger does not necessarily terminate all rights under a bargaining agreement was cautious and narrow.

        2)   The courts found tension between *Wiley*, an arbitration case, and *Burns, supra*, a substantive contract case, and determined that *Wiley* controlled here. But the "fundamental policies" outline in *Burns* should not be lightly disregarded. We do not find it necessary to decide whether the two cases are irreconcilable here.

        3)   Not even *Wiley* supports the decision below, which is an unnecessary extension of that case, which involved a merger. This case is only a sale of assets and the original employer is still in existence with substantial assets. P has a viable remedy with the original employer, who has agreed to arbitrate the claim. More importantly, in *Wiley*, the successor had hired all of the employees of the former employer. Here, only nine employees were retained and no supervisors.

        4)   We find nothing in federal labor policy requiring a successor purchaser of assets to hire all of the predecessor's employees. *Wiley* does not require D to arbitrate the issues of P's claim. Such an obligation requires "substantial continuity of identity in the business enterprise." There was no continuity of the workforce here.

    d.   **Dissent** (Douglas, J.). The principles of *Wiley* and *Burns* require affirmance. The agreement with the prior owner provided that successors should be bound. There was a substantial continuity of the business operation. D, as former franchiser, had previously exercised control over the business and continued the same business without interruption, at the same location, under the same name and almost the same number of employees. The only change was the replacement of the union members. *Burns* does not control; it was not a merger situation. It was not a suit to compel arbitration and there had been no prior identity between the two business entities. The present emphasis on the number of employees retained gives too much control to the successor to avoid arbitration.

6.   **Double-Breasted Employers.** In recent years, some organized subcontractors in the construction industry have organized a parallel unorganized counterpart to be in a position to bid on projects in which the general contractor invites bids from nonunion subs. Unions may treat the two entities as a common employer and file refusal-to-bargain charges. The Board has adopted a two-step approach. It first looks for signs of interrelated operations, common management, common ownership, and central control of labor relations and whether similar relationships would lead to comparable arrangements. The Board then will determine whether the two companies constitute a single bargaining unit by applying the community of interests test. This approach has been approved by the Supreme Court. The issue may also be tested in an action to compel arbitration under section 301.

VII. IMPACT OF THE ANTITRUST LAWS ON UNION CONCERTED ACTIVITIES

A. LEGITIMATE UNION ACTIVITIES EXEMPT FROM ANTITRUST LAWS

1. **Concerted Labor Union Activities Are Legitimate.** The Supreme Court has held that a union acting in its own self-interest and using only lawful means is not subject to attack under the antitrust laws. The basic policy favoring legitimate concerted activities, as expressed in the Norris-LaGuardia Act, was held to warrant this interpretation of the Sherman and Clayton Antitrust Acts.

2. **Accommodation of Antitrust and Labor Policies.** The basis for reconciling antitrust and labor policies was developed by Justice Stone in *Apex v. Leader, supra*. *Apex* and *United States v. Hutcheson, supra*, should be reconsidered at this point.

3. **Illegal Combinations.** Where a union contracts with all electrical manufacturers and contractors in a specific locality and uses those contracts to prevent the installation of equipment manufactured outside the area, there is a violation of the Sherman Act. [*See* Allen Bradley Co. v. Local Union No. 3, IBEW, 325 U.S. 797 (1945)]

4. **Present Judicial Interpretation of the Exemption.** Generally speaking, the antitrust laws are held to apply to a union only when (i) the union combines with nonlabor groups (*e.g.*, employers), and (ii) such combinations result in a restraint of interstate trade and commerce.

   a. **Union conspiring to eliminate competition--United Mine Workers of America v. Pennington,** 381 U.S. 657 (1965).

   United Mine Workers of America v. Pennington

   1) **Facts.** United Mine Workers Welfare Fund (P) sued to recover unpaid pension payments from Phillips Brothers Coal Company (D). D cross-complained against P and various large coal companies, claiming that they had entered into a combination to drive small coal companies out of business by setting wage rates above those which smaller companies could pay. The rationale behind this combination was to allow the large companies to mechanize in ways small companies could not. D also claimed that the union had set industry-wide wage and benefit standards so high that small producers would be forced out of business. The trial court found that a cause of action was made out by D, and the court of appeals affirmed. P appeals to the Supreme Court.

   2) **Issue.** Is a union immune from antitrust law when it combines and conspires with large coal producers with the purpose of eliminating competition by setting industry-wide wage and benefit standards which small producers could not afford?

   3) **Held.** No. Judgment reversed on other grounds.

a) *Allen Bradley, supra,* established that unions are not immune from the antitrust laws when they conspire to eliminate competition in an industry. Although the union may impose industry-wide wage and benefit standards, those standards may not be motivated by an intent to eliminate some employers from the industry.

b) The union could attempt to influence public officials to improve the wages and conditions of employment of its members, and may do so even by bargaining with a multi-employer bargaining unit, but it may not act to limit its freedom to bargain with all employers by conspiring with one set to eliminate others outside the bargaining unit.

4) **Concurrence** (Douglas, Black, Clark, JJ.). If the company can prove its allegations, both the union and the large employers have violated the antitrust laws.

5) **Dissent** (Goldberg, Harlan, Stewart, JJ.). Historically, antitrust laws have been used to frustrate labor's efforts, and the Court should not limit labor's exemption from these acts. Here, the union peacefully acted to improve conditions. Pattern bargaining is used in many industries. Judges and juries cannot appreciate the distinctions required by the majority rule.

6) **Comment.** This case presents the conflict between cooperation and conspiracy—it is difficult to demonstrate where one begins and the other one ends.

b. **Issues related to conditions of employment--Local Union No. 189, Amalgamated Meat Cutters v. Jewel Tea Co.,** 381 U.S. 676 (1965).

1) **Facts.** Amalgamated Meat Cutters (D) obtained, through multi-employer bargaining, a restriction from retailers limiting meat sales to the hours between 9 a.m. and 6 p.m. Jewel Tea (P) was one of two retailers who opposed the restriction, but it finally capitulated after a strike vote. P claimed that the restriction should be relaxed as to its prepackaged meats, which did not require a butcher's presence, and filed an action in federal court claiming that the restriction violated the Sherman Act, sections 1 and 2, since it was obtained through an alleged conspiracy to restrict P in the use of its property and in its marketing approach. The district court found the conduct exempted. The court of appeals reversed, and D appeals.

2) **Issue.** Is an issue that a union claims to be related to conditions of employment and which it attempts to obtain through normal negotiations exempt from the Sherman Act?

3) **Held.** Yes. Judgment reversed.

a) Where an issue is closely related to conditions of employment and sought to be obtained through bona fide negotiations to further union policies, it is exempt from the Sherman Act.

b) This is not a case which required the NLRB's primary jurisdiction, since courts may determine whether an issue is a subject of mandatory bargaining, and the NLRB usually adjudicates cases where there has been a refusal to bargain, not an agreement, as here.

    c) Jewel has failed to show that it was feasible to sell meat at night without using butchers or affecting their interests.

4) **Concurrence and dissent** (Douglas, Black, Clark, JJ.). The majority rule requires that *Allen Bradley, supra,* be either overruled or greatly impaired.

5) **Concurrence** (Goldberg, Stewart, Harlan, JJ.). Congress did not intend bargaining over mandatory subjects to be subject to the antitrust laws.

6) **Comment.** As long as the union and employer are bargaining over subjects as to which they were required to bargain (*i.e.*, wages, hours, terms, and conditions of employment), the activities are exempt from the antitrust laws.

c. **Extending the labor law exemption.** There has been confusion about the proper theory for extending the nonstatutory labor law exemption from the antitrust laws in organized professional football and basketball. In *Brown v. Pro Football, Inc.*, 116 S. Ct. 2116 (1996), the Supreme Court favored a broad application of the exemption. It found that Congress in the Clayton Act had "hoped to prevent judicial use of antitrust laws to resolve labor disputes." It approved multi-employer bargaining, noting that it was well established and that to terminate the exemption when the CBA lapses would create instability and uncertainty in the bargaining process.

d. **Union-subcontractor agreements.** The Supreme Court has distinguished a clause prohibiting union contractors from awarding jobs to nonunion subcontractors from the nonstatutory antitrust exemption recognized in *Jewel Tea, supra,* stating that *Jewel Tea* imposed direct restraints on competition among subcontractors which would not have resulted simply from eliminating competition based on differences in wages, hours, terms, and conditions of employment.

1) **Prohibiting dealings with nonunion subcontractors--Connell Construction Co. v. Plumbers & Steamfitters Local Union No. 100,** 421 U.S. 616 (1975).

    a) **Facts.** The union (D), representing Dallas workers in the mechanical and plumbing trades, entered a bargaining contract with 75 contractors which included a "most favored nation clause." In the contract, D agreed that if it extended a better contract to any other employer, all members of the multi-employer bargaining group would be offered those same terms. D insisted that Connell Construction (P), a general building contractor who dealt with union and nonunion subcontractors, enter into a contract with them. The contract prohibited P from working with subcontractors who were not under a collective bargaining agreement with D even though it had no intention of representing P's employees. P refused to enter the agreement and D picketed P's construction site, which resulted in 150 workers walking off the job. When P sued in state court to enjoin the picketing as a Texas antitrust violation, D removed the case to federal court, at which point P reluctantly entered the bargaining agreement and revised its complaint to allege Sherman Act violations. The district court held that federal

Connell Construction Co. v. Plumbers & Steamfitters Local Union No. 100

legislation preempted state antitrust law and held that P's agreement with the union was exempt from federal antitrust legislation on the basis of section 8(e). The court of appeals affirmed, and P appeals.

- b) **Issue.** Is a bargaining agent who obtains a contract prohibiting a "stranger" contractor from dealing with nonunion subcontractors protected by LMRA section 8(e) from antitrust regulation?

- c) **Held.** No. Judgment reversed in part and case remanded.

    (1) Although the language of section 8(e) is broad, it was Congress's intent to extend the provision to subcontracting agreements contained to work done at the construction site within the context of a collective bargaining relationship.

    (2) D's action could constitute a federal antitrust violation, as its agreement with P excluded nonunion subcontractors, eliminating not only competition which could involve below standard wages and working conditions, but also competition involving more efficient operating methods.

    (3) It is not an aim of federal labor regulation to restrict efficiency competition. Section 8(e) does not protect D from a federal antitrust suit, although federal law preempts state antitrust policy when state remedies look to control the organizational goals of union functions.

- d) **Comment.** Modern case law seems once again to employ a balancing of interests approach, with the employees' interest in jobs compared against the public's interest in a competitive economy.

2) **Setting rules for nonunion independent contractors.** In *American Federation of Musicians v. Carroll*, 391 U.S. 99 (1968), the Federation had a rule that required band leaders (who also usually played an instrument in the band) on one-time "club dates" to hire a minimum number of players, charge a minimum charge for each player, use a standard form contract, and charge a premium when playing outside the band's territory. Certain band leaders brought an antitrust action against these rules. The Supreme Court found that the union rules did not amount to a combination with a "nonlabor group" even though the band leaders were employers who acted as contractors. The Court reasoned that the band leaders performed work and functions that affected hours, wages, job security, and working conditions of Federation members. Hence, it was lawful to pressure the leaders to become members of the Federation and to impose the rules upon them. This the Court found to be consistent with the union activity exemption from the antitrust laws.

- a) **Comment.** The key to holding that the orchestra leaders were a "labor" group and parties to a labor dispute was the presence of job or wage competition (or other economic interrelationship) affecting legitimate union interests between the union members (in this case, the sidemen) and the independent contractors (here, the orchestra leaders).

VIII. FEDERALISM AND LABOR RELATIONS

A. THE ROLE OF STATE LAW IN LABOR-MANAGEMENT RELATIONS: THE PREEMPTION DOCTRINE

1. **In General.** State laws governing labor relations cover a wide variety of subjects. Some statutes expressly ban picketing and boycotting, and others (notably antitrust provisions) have been read to limit labor unions and union activities. Still other states have comprehensive labor relations statutes, comparable to the NLRA.

2. **Preemption Doctrine.** The interest in a uniform national labor policy clearly outweighs any recognized interest in state regulation. Hence, subject to certain exceptions discussed below, state statutes are preempted by federal labor law wherever the two areas overlap.

    a. **Scope of federal power.** The NLRA is interpreted very broadly. If an activity is even arguably regulated or protected by federal law, the states have no jurisdiction to regulate that activity.

    b. **Theories.** Two prominent theories have been used to explain restrictions on state powers in the field of labor relations. One, the "substantive rights" theory, is applied to prevent state interference with rights or privileges which Congress has created or protected by its enactment of the labor laws. The other, the "primary jurisdiction" theory, presumes that Congress created an administrative agency to define, adjust, or leave unregulated all of the myriad and delicate interactions of labor relations and that the policy determinations of this agency should be free of state interference.

    c. **State court attempt to exercise jurisdiction--San Diego Building Trades Council v. Garmon,** 359 U.S. 236 (1959).

    San Diego Building Trades Council v. Garmon

    1) **Facts.** San Diego Trades Council (D) was an uncertified union that sought but failed to obtain a union shop agreement from Garmon (P), who argued that D was not the employees' collective bargaining agent. D began peacefully to picket P's business. P contended that the purpose of the picketing was to dissuade customers from patronizing his business, while D claimed that its purpose was to educate the workers. P filed an action in a California state court to enjoin further picketing and for damages. The trial court held for P, finding that the activity was not privileged because it violated section 8(b)(2). On appeal, the California Supreme Court held that the picketing was not privileged. The Supreme Court granted certiorari and reversed, holding that the state injuction conflicted with the Board's authority. On remand, the California court sustained the damages on the basis of state law. The Supreme Court again granted certiorari.

    2) **Issue.** May state courts assert jurisdiction over concerted labor activity that is arguably regulated by federal law?

    3) **Held.** No. Judgment reversed.

Labor Law - 169

        a) When conduct is clearly or even arguably covered by the provision of the NLRB, state jurisdiction must yield. Federal preemption in the area of labor law is necessary to avoid conflict and to further national purposes.

        b) If the NLRB claims jurisdiction of either conduct protected by section 7 or prohibited by section 8, the states have no jurisdiction. If the Board clearly decides that the activity is not covered by sections 7 or 8, states may take the jurisdiction. Failure of the Board to take jurisdiction or to define the status of the activity does not leave it for the states to regulate.

    4) Concurrence (Harlan, J.). I concur because the conduct is arguably protected under section 7.

    5) Comment. There are few exceptions to the preemption doctrine. However, states may enjoin violent strikes, and some breach of contract or breach of fair representation cases may be heard in state courts.

  d. Matters of "peripheral" federal concern. The Supreme Court has also stated that the preemption doctrine does not apply where the matter is of only "peripheral" concern to federal labor policy.

    1) "Purely internal union matters." Normally, union disputes with members are regulated by NLRA sections 7 and 8, thus preempting state regulation thereof. However, the Court has recognized that some cases may involve "purely internal" union affairs which are of only peripheral concern to national labor policy, in which case state regulation and adjudication would be proper. However, this doctrine is extremely limited in its scope.

    2) Emphasis on conduct in question. In *Amalgamated Association of Street, Electric Railway & Motor Coach Employees v. Lockridge*, 403 U.S. 274 (1971), the collective bargaining agreement between the union and Western Greyhound had a union shop clause requiring employees to "remain members" of the union. Plaintiff Lockridge, a member of the union, obtained a release from his dues checkoff by Greyhound and fell two months behind in his dues. The constitution and general laws of the union provided that "where agreements with employing companies provide that members must be in continuous good financial standing, the member in arrears one month may be suspended from membership and removed from employment." The union asked Greyhound to remove Lockridge from employment, and Greyhound complied. Lockridge then sued in Idaho state court for breach of contract, arguing that his arrearage only resulted in loss of good standing in the union, not loss of membership. The court held that his suspension was contrary to the union's established practice and that neither the union shop agreement nor the union constitution justified his suspension. The court ordered reinstatement and back pay, and the state supreme court affirmed. The Supreme Court held that if the conduct sought to be regulated is arguably within the NLRA, the state courts may not take jurisdiction. The emphasis is on the ***conduct*** in question and not on the ***nature*** of the state court action. The present case deals with a one for preemption" uniquely within the Board's province. [Sears, Roebuck & Co. v. San Diego County District Council of Carpenters, 436 U.S. 180 (1978)]

3) **Activity unregulated by the NLRA--Lodge 76, International Association of Machinists v. Wisconsin Employment Relations Commission,** 427 U.S. 132 (1976).

Lodge 76, International Association of Machinists v. Wisconsin Employment Relations Commission

a) **Facts.** The collective bargaining agreement between the Machinists (D) and Kearney and Trecker (P) was terminated pursuant to an agreement in 1971. Thereafter, P instituted a number of unilateral changes in the conditions of employment provided in the former contract, including eliminating union dues checkoff, eliminating union lost time, and removing the union office from its premises. In March 1972, P announced that the work week would change from 37½ hours to 40 hours per week. D's response was a refusal to work any overtime in excess of 37½ hours per week. P filed a charge with the NLRB, which found that the challenged activity did not violate the NLRA. P then filed a complaint with the Wisconsin Employment Relations Commission, which held that the refusal to work overtime violated state labor laws and ordered D to cease and desist from such activities. The state court enforced the Commission's order. The United States Supreme Court granted certiorari.

b) **Issue.** Can partial strike activities which are not violative of the NLRA be regulated by state law?

c) **Held.** No. Judgment reversed.

(1) Federal preemption involves two considerations: (i) whether the activity is clearly or arguably within the primary jurisdiction of the Board and (ii) whether the activity is unregulated by the NLRA because Congress intended that the conduct be "controlled by the free play of economic forces." This case falls within the latter category, and state jurisdiction is consequently inappropriate.

(2) *Garmon, supra*, requires state courts to abstain when the conduct is arguably within the NLRA. In cases such as the present it is necessary to consider whether "the exercise of plenary state authority to curtail or entirely prohibit self-help would frustrate effective implementation of the Act's processes." There is no question here that the Act's processes of economic free play would be frustrated by the state's action.

d) **Concurrence** (Powell, J., Burger, C.J.). The opinion does not prevent states from enforcing "neutral" statutes that are not directed toward altering the bargaining position of employers and union. These would include tort or contract law.

e) **Dissent** (Stevens, Stewart, Rehnquist, JJ.). No legislative expression is to be found that indicates any congressional intent to leave the partial strike wholly unregulated. The partial strike is not so important to the bargaining process that the states cannot make it illegal.

B. **REPRESENTATION, BARGAINING, AND CONCERTED ACTIVITIES**

Direct state intervention into conduct that is subject to federal regulation will not be tolerated, even when the Board has not acted in a particular instance. Nor may a state act to resolve unfair labor practices whether committed by an employer or by a union. However, many state laws do not directly intrude into the organizational or bargaining processes but rather will have some effect upon them. The extent to which they may be permitted is explored in this part of the outline.

Brown v. Hotel & Restaurant Employees, International Union Local 54

1. **State Qualifications for Union Officers--Brown v. Hotel & Restaurant Employees, International Union Local 54,** 468 U.S. 491 (1984).

    a. **Facts.** Local 54 (P) represents workers employed in casino hotels in Atlantic City. New Jersey law requires annual registration with the Casino Control Commission (D) and disqualifies unions from collecting dues or administering welfare funds if their officers fail to meet specified personal qualifications. D found P's president and other officers disqualified and ordered their removal from office. D barred P from collecting dues until they were removed. P brought an injunction against D in federal court. The district court denied relief without considering the merits. The court of appeals reviewed the merits and concluded that D was preempted by section 7 of the Act from disqualifying elected union officers. The Supreme Court granted certiorari to consider the preemption issue.

    b. **Issue.** Is a state preempted from imposing qualification standards upon officers of unions representing employees in the casino industry?

    c. **Held.** No. Judgment vacated and case remanded with instructions.

    1) Section 7 confers various rights upon employees. Section 504(a) of the LMRDA, enacted in 1959, limits persons convicted of certain crimes from holding union office. To this extent, it limited the preemptive effect of section 7.

    2) Section 603(a) indicates that Congress did not intend to preempt the operation of all state regulation of union officials.

    3) The New Jersey regulation does not actually conflict with section 7 and so is not preempted. The statute goes only to the section 7 right of selecting officers and does not impact on employee rights to select a particular union as bargaining agent. Any remedy under such a state statute must not interfere with organizational or bargaining rights.

    4) We remand to develop the record concerning whether the state prohibition of dues collection will so incapacitate D that it cannot function as the chosen collective bargaining agent.

    d. **Dissent** (White, Powell, Stevens, JJ.). This state statute is not directed just at individuals; it also imposes sanctions on the union

174 - Labor Law

itself by prohibiting collection of dues. Therefore, it infringes on federally protected rights.

2. **State Court Injunction Affecting Wage Clause--Local 24, International Teamsters v. Oliver,** 358 U.S. 283 (1959).

   a. **Facts.** An antitrust suit was brought by Oliver (P) against the Teamsters (D). P owned and drove his own truck. When he was hired by interstate carriers, he was paid a wage (in accordance with a union scale) and a truck rental fee. D desired to abolish all owner/operators since they would, while charging a union wage, rent their trucks for less than their cost of actual operation, thereby using a portion of their wages to cover their truck expense. This allegedly allowed independent carriers to undercut union labor. For this reason, D and independent carriers, including P, had negotiated a minimum rental provision in the labor contract. The Ohio state court found that the agreement constituted a price fixing agreement between the union and a nonlabor group that restricted articles of commerce (the trucks) and barred truck owners from a reasonable return on their money. The Ohio court enjoined the use of the minimum rental clause. The United States Supreme Court granted certiorari.

   b. **Issue.** Is a minimum rental clause in labor contracts with independent carriers an illegal price fixing agreement which can be abated by state courts?

   c. **Held.** No. Judgment reversed.

   1) The object of the minimum rental clause is to protect the undermining of the negotiated wage scale. Here the clause is concerned with wages, not price fixing. It is part and parcel of labor's effort to improve working conditions. Thus, a minimum rental clause is something which is a proper subject for bargaining.

   2) Ohio state law cannot be applied in this case. To do so would wholly defeat the intent of Congress in enacting the Wagner and Taft-Hartley Acts. Thus, federal law preempts the Ohio law. The Ohio statute would frustrate the parties' solution to the wage problem.

   d. **Comment.** In a pre-ERISA, case the Supreme Court held that pension plans established by collective bargaining were not beyond the reach of state regulation, relying on section 10 of the Welfare and Pension Plans Disclosure Act of 1958. [Malone v. White Motor Corp., 435 U.S. 497 (1978)]

3. **State Regulation of Minimum Benefit Standards--Metropolitan Life Insurance Co. v. Commonwealth of Massachusetts,** 471 U.S. 724 (1985).

   a. **Facts.** A Massachusetts (P) statute requires that accident and health insurance policies contain specified minimum mental health care benefits. P brought an action against Metropolitan Life Insurance Company (D) and other companies to require inclusion of such coverage in their policies. D contends that the state law is preempted by the Act since insurance benefits are a subject of mandatory bargaining. The state courts granted relief, and

D appeals to the United States Supreme Court.

    b.   **Issue.** May a state under its police powers regulate the specific content of insurance policies that may be a subject of mandatory collective bargaining?

    c.   **Held.** Yes. Judgment affirmed.

        1)   Congress did not specifically consider whether state laws of general application that touch upon subjects of mandatory bargaining should be preempted.

        2)   The Act was intended to establish a procedure for more equitable bargaining, which is unrelated to local or federal regulation that establishes minimum terms of employment.

        3)   Such minimum standards are independent of the collective bargaining process, but rather touch upon employees as individuals and not as members of a collective bargaining organization. The Wagner Act was not intended to allow unions and unionized employers to exempt themselves from state labor standards that they disfavor.

4.   **State Plant Closing Law.** A state statute mandated severance pay for plant closings, but allowed modification of the state requirements in cases of contracts having express contractual severance pay provisions. The statute was attacked under ERISA and the Act. Applying the *Metropolitan Life* rule, *supra*, the Court sustained the state act as part of the state regulatory "backdrop" to negotiations. [Fort Halifax Packing Co. v. Coyne, 482 U.S. 1 (1987)]

5.   **Preemption of Contract Breach Actions.** In *Allis-Chalmers v. Lueck*, 471 U.S. 202 (1985), the collective agreement provided health insurance benefits that were subject to grievance and arbitration. Lueck suffered injury and filed a claim with the insurance carrier. Later, the carrier interrupted payments and this, according to Lueck, was due to the company's bad faith and harassment. Lueck brought a tort action in state court against the company and the insurance carrier. The state court found the action was not preempted since it was not based on the collective agreement, but upon state tort law. The United States Supreme Court found preemption. It stressed the need for predictability and uniformity. The Court, applying federal (rather than state) law, found that any implied duty on the part of the company to act in good faith was based on the labor agreement and thus was subject to federal law. It found that any effort to enforce the tort action would inevitably involve interpretation of the labor agreement. Such claims should be grieved and arbitrated rather than litigated in state court.

New York Telephone Co. v. New York Department of Labor

6.   **State Unemployment Benefits for Strikers--New York Telephone Co. v. New York Department of Labor,** 440 U.S. 519 (1979).

    a.   **Facts.** The New York unemployment insurance law allows payment of benefits to strikers after they have been off work for eight weeks. The insurance fund is financed primarily with employer contributions, based upon benefits paid to former employees in past years. The union engaged in a seven-month strike against the company and after the waiting period, more than $49 million in benefits were paid to 33,000 striking employees.

New York Telephone (P) sought a declaration that the payment of benefits under the New York statute conflicted with federal law. The United States district court enjoined disbursements and allowed recoupment. The court of appeals reversed, and P appeals.

b. **Issue.** Does the NLRA implicitly prohibit payment of state unemployment benefits to strikers?

c. **Held.** No. Judgment affirmed.

1) There is no claim that the state has sought to regulate or prohibit conduct that is protected under section 7 or prohibited under section 8.

2) *Teamsters v. Morton*, 377 U.S. 252, and *Lodge 76, supra*, did identify areas in which there was a policy of free play of economic forces between the parties free of state interference.

3) In this case, there is no attempt by the state to regulate or prohibit private conduct in the labor-management field or regulate bargaining relationships. The Social Security Act, which established federal participation in the unemployment system, and its legislative history indicate that Congress did not intend to restrict the freedom of the states to legislate in this area. The New York statute is entitled to the same deference that has been extended to analogous state laws to protect interests deeply rooted in local feeling and responsibility.

4) There is not sufficient evidence in the NLRA or its history to indicate an intent to preempt a state's power to make such a policy choice.

d. **Concurrence** (Blackmun, Marshall, JJ.). The crucial inquiry here should be whether the exercise of state authority frustrates the "effective implementation of the Act's processes," not whether the state's purpose was to benefit a class of citizens.

e. **Dissent** (Powell, Stewart, JJ., Burger, C.J.). The decision "substantially . . . alters the balance of advantage between management and labor" in the state of New York. The Court "substantially rewrites the principles of preemption." *Morton* and *Lodge 76* require preemption in this case.

f. **Comment.** The provision in the Federal Food Stamp Act denying food stamps to strikers and their families was held constitutional. The Supreme Court found no impairment of speech and held that it was not required that the protected right of association be maximized by government funds. The Court further concluded that the adverse effect was connected to three different valid congressional objectives. The dissent found that rather than being neutral, the statute amounted to a penalty on strikers.

7. **Permanent Replacements and State Regulation--Belknap, Inc. v. Hale,** 463 U.S. 491 (1983).

   Belknap, Inc. v. Hale

   a. **Facts.** During a strike, Belknap (D) hired a large number of permanent replacements under written employment contracts. These included Hale and 11 others (Ps). In the face of an unfair labor practice complaint, D reached a settlement with the union whereby it agreed to reinstate the striking workers. Ps were displaced as a consequence and brought contract and misrepresentation actions in state court. D argued that the actions were preempted by the Act, but the state court rejected this and tried the case. D appeals.

    b. **Issue.** Does the Act preempt state breach of contract and misrepresentation actions brought by permanent striker replacements who have been displaced by returning strikers?

    c. **Held.** No. Judgment affirmed.

        1) Two doctrines control state preemption cases: (i) *Garmon, supra,* ruled that state regulation is presumptively preempted if it concerns conduct that is actually or arguably prohibited or protected by the Act, unless it is of only peripheral concern or touches interests deeply rooted in local feelings and responsibility; and (ii) *Lodge 76, supra,* ruled that state regulation or actions concerning conduct that Congress intended to be unregulated is preempted.

        2) There is no indication that Congress intended to leave the strike replacement process unregulated.

        3) Neither the breach of contract nor the misrepresentation claims are preempted. They concern issues not identical with any that could be presented to the Board or which would interfere with the Board's determination of matters within its jurisdiction.

        4) The state interests outweigh any interference with the Board's function.

    d. **Dissent** (Brennan, Marshall, Powell, JJ.). These claims go to the core of federal policy and should not be subject to possible conflicts of federal and state regulation.

8. **Enforcement of Rights Under Bargaining Agreements.** The Supreme Court has ruled that actions to enforce the terms of a collective bargaining agreement may be brought in state court, but the federal law displaces the local state law. However, it has found that local tort law independent of the labor agreement will not be displaced. [Allis-Chalmers Corp. v. Lueck, *supra*—state law tort action for bad faith delay in paying disability benefits which had their origin in bargaining agreement was not preempted by section 301]

    a. **Retaliatory discharge--Lingle v. Norge Division of Magic Chef, Inc.,** 486 U.S. 399 (1988).

        1) **Facts.** Lingle (P) had been an employee of Norge Division of Magic Chef, Inc. (D) under a labor contract that provided a remedy for discharges without just cause. P was discharged by D for filing a workers' compensation claim that D asserted was false. P pursued an action for retaliatory discharge under Illinois workers' compensation law and recovered compensatory and punitive damages in federal district court. (The case had been removed to federal court under

diversity jurisdiction.) The court of appeals found that the action was preempted by section 301.

2) **Issue.** May a discharged employee pursue a state statutory tort remedy for discharge even though she also has a remedy under a collective bargaining agreement?

3) **Held.** Yes. Judgment reversed.

   a) We have already recognized that federal and state courts have concurrent jurisdiction over section 301 actions and that the controlling law must be federal. If the state claim depends on the meaning of the collective bargaining agreement, the application of state law is preempted.

   b) The Illinois tort of retaliatory discharge turns on the conduct of the employee and the motive of the employer. Neither inquiry turns on the meaning of the contract, and although there may be a factual overlap with any federal action, this case may be considered to be an "independent" state action. The disposition of this case will not interfere with the arbitration of labor contract matters.

9. **State Refusal to Process State Claims.** In *Lividas v. Bradshaw*, 114 S. Ct. 2068 (1994), the California Commission of Labor declined to enforce the state wage payment law if a claim involved the interpretation of a CBA containing an arbitration clause. A unanimous Supreme Court rejected this approach. It rejected application of preemption rules, stating that *Lueck* and *Lingle*, *supra*, did not go that far. *Lueck* and *Lingle* stressed that the legal character of the claim as an independent right outside the CBA is the determinative factor—not whether a grievance could be filed under the same facts. The Court held that when the meaning of the CBA's terms are not in dispute, the mere fact that the CBA will be consulted does not require that the state claim be extinguished. The Court also rejected arguments that the Commissioners' hands-off policy (i) would allocate scarce resources to the support of unorganized workers who would have no union to assist them, and (ii) would tend to encourage workers to organize and pursue arbitration.

10. **Retaliatory Lawsuits.** If a person brings a nonpreempted state lawsuit for the purpose of retaliating against the defendant for exercising protected rights, the action will not be enjoined as an unfair labor practice if the suit is "well-founded." [*See* Bill Johnson's Restaurants, Inc. v. NLRB, 461 U.S. 731 (1983)] The Court balanced the First Amendment rights of access to the courts and the rights under the Act.

11. **State Regulation of Activities of Supervisors.** Section 2(3) excludes "supervisors" (as defined in section 2(1)) from the coverage of the Act. At the same time, section 14(a) provides that supervisors are not prohibited from becoming or remaining members of a labor organization, but "no employer subject to this Act shall be compelled to deem individuals [defined as supervisors] as employees for the purpose of any law, either national or local, relating to collective bargaining."

a. In *Marine Engineers Beneficial Association ("MEBA") v. Interlake S.S. Co.*, 370 U.S. 173 (1962), picketing by MEBA was enjoined by a state, which rejected claims of federal preemption, holding that the members were supervisors and hence MEBA was not a "labor organization." The Supreme Court reversed, holding that the task of determining what is a "labor organization" required NLRB expertise. It ruled that courts should defer whenever a reasonably arguable case can be made that the union is a "labor organization" within the meaning of the Act.

b. In *Hanna Mining Co. v. District 2, Marine Engineers Beneficial Association*, 382 U.S. 181 (1965), Hanna Mining Company's employees, who were represented by MEBA, informed the company that a majority of them no longer wished to be so represented. Hanna broke off negotiations and petitioned NLRB for an election. The Board dismissed the petition on the ground that the engineers were "supervisors." Later, Hanna filed charges of illegal recognition picketing; these charges were dismissed on the same ground. Still later the state court dismissed an injunction action against picketing by MEBA on grounds of lack of jurisdiction. The Supreme Court reversed on the ground that the activity was not protected under section 7 and not prohibited under section 8(b). It concluded that *Garmon, supra*, did not require preemption. The Court rejected the union's argument that the enactment of section 14(a) indicated that Congress intended a hands-off attitude as far as state action was concerned.

c. In *Beasley v. Food Fair of North Carolina, Inc.*, 416 U.S. 653 (1974), supervisors brought a state "right-to-work" action against the company, which had fired supervisors who had joined a union. This time the Supreme Court found that state remedies were barred. The Court held that the Act gave supervisors no protection against discharge and inferred that an employer should be able to decline to deal with supervisors free from a fear of state damage actions.

IX. RECONSIDERING THE NLRA AND THE FUTURE

A. THE CONTEXT THEN AND NOW

1. **Labor Force Organization.** In 1935, at the time the NLRA was enacted, the percentage of the organized nonagricultural labor force stood at about 12%. A high of 35% was reached in 1952 and, after a continuous decline, it is now back to about 12%. This gives pause to consider whether the basic assumptions of the Act should be reconsidered, which were that:

   a. Organization is necessary to redress imbalance in bargaining power;

   b. Organization will promote industrial stability and industrial peace;

   c. Organization will increase purchasing power and benefit the economy;

   d. Organization will achieve industrial democracy; and

   e. Regulation of industrial democracy will promote the greater political democracy.

B. CHANGES IN CONTEXT

1. **Economic.** Globalization and mobility of capital has resulted in downward pressure on wages, and undercuts the key mission principles which supported the Act. Increased wages can as well be spent on imported goods as domestic. There is now a widespread belief that organized labor has priced itself out of the world market.

2. **Demographic.** The distribution of jobs in the world has shifted away from the blue collar industries which were the core of organization.

3. **Employer Practices.** The assumption that the employment relationship was long-term, full-time, and carrying with it continuing health insurance and pension benefits, which developed in the years of World War II, has been rejected. Employment arrangements are no longer static—part-time employment, short-term employment, and the use of temporary employees are quite common.

4. **The Law.** The legal status of the employment relationship has shifted from that of a full-range private contract to one of severe federal and state regulation. Examples are the FLSA (1938), Equal Pay Act (1963), Title IV of the Civil Rights Act (1964), Age Discrimination Act (1967), Americans with Disabilities Act (1990), Immigration Reform and Control Act (1987), OSHA (1970), ERISA (1974), and WARN Act (1993). The states also have added many protective and regulatory acts.

C. GAP BETWEEN EMPLOYEE PREFERENCES AND THE EXTENT OF ORGANIZATION

A 1984 survey ascertained that 41% of employees wished to be represented, while only 14% were in fact organized. Management hostility, which has become marked in the past decades, is said to be the reason for the gap between employee preferences and reality.

D. LABOR LAW REFORM

Four directions of reform have emerged.

1. **Strengthening the NLRA.** The Dunlop Commission in 1994 recommended the following:

    a. **Prompt elections.** Holding organizational elections within two weeks from the time employees have shown a sufficient interest. Legal challenges would be postponed until after the election. The rule in *Lechmere, supra,* should be reversed so that nonemployee organizations will have more ready access.

    b. **NLRB injunctions.** The NLRB should be required to seek injunctions to abate discrimination actions against employee organizers and during negotiations.

    c. **Use of bargaining ADR.** Greater assistance in bargaining the initial CBA, such as mediation and binding interest arbitration.

    d. **Counterindications.** Whether these approaches will help bridge the representation gap is uncertain. Identified weaknesses seem to be that (i) managerial resistance will likely not be mitigated and (ii) these approaches do not sufficiently counter the dynamic changes in the field since 1935.

2. **Allowing Wider Variety of Management/Employee Interaction.** The Dunlop Commission recognized the desirability of modifying section 8(a)(2) so that management/employee structures be permitted to discuss and deal with matters concerning quality, productivity, efficiency, safety, and health, short of bargaining or amending the NLRA.

3. **Employee Participation Committees.** An Employee Participation Committee ("EPC") is a single committee representing all employees in the plant and office, and would deal with a wide range of issues involving the employment relationship. Such a committee would work parallel to and in cooperation with the labor union. This organization is based upon the "works councils" which are mandated and have functioned well in Germany.

4. **Nonmajority Union Representation.** Nonmajority union representation would allow any two or more employees to organize and deal with their employer on their own behalf. There would be no petitions, elections, or campaigns. In England and Japan, "shop floor" issues are dealt with by these "members only" unions, while larger issues are handled by bargaining with other organizations on an industry-wide basis.

X. THE INDIVIDUAL AND THE UNION

A. UNION DUTY OF FAIR REPRESENTATION

1. **Introduction.** In the wake of union growth and prosperity, which had been greatly facilitated by the RLA and NLRA, Congress became concerned about the plight of the individual union member and evidences of union corruption. This led to the enactment of the Labor and Management Reporting and Disclosure Act.

    a. **The LMRDA.** The Act had three major aspects: (i) provisions to assure democratic procedures within unions; (ii) provisions to require periodic information about finance and internal operations; and (iii) provisions that prohibit certain kinds of actions by union officials, such as unauthorized expenditures and loans, and that also bar persons convicted of certain crimes from office.

    b. **Duty owed to all employees in unit.** NLRA section 9(a) provides that the union selected by the majority of the employees in the appropriate bargaining unit shall be the exclusive representative of all employees in the unit—whether members of the union or not. The union's right to exclusive representation of all employees in the bargaining unit carries with it the duty to represent all members fairly—including minority and nonunion members. The duty of fair representation extends not only to negotiation of the collective bargaining agreement but also to administration of the agreement (*e.g.* to grievance and arbitration procedures established by the agreement). [Conley v. Gibson, 355 U.S. 41 (1957)]

    c. **Racial discrimination cases.** A union's duty to represent all members was first recognized in cases where the union engaged in racial discrimination against union members and nonmembers. [*See* Steele v. Louisville & Nashville Railroad Co., *supra*; Brotherhood of Railroad Trainmen v. Howard, 343 U.S. 768 (1952)]

    d. **Inevitable differences.** In a case in which an employee protested a seniority system that gave credit for preemployment military service and had the effect of placing the plaintiff at a disadvantage, the Supreme Court held that the union had not breached its duty of fair representation. It said, "Inevitably differences arise in the manner and degree to which the terms of any negotiated agreement affect individual employees and classes of employees. The mere existence of such differences does not make them invalid." It went on to recognize that "a wide range of reasonableness must be allowed" subject "always to complete good faith and honesty of purpose in the exercise of its discretion." [Ford Motor Co. v. Huffman, 345 U.S. 330 (1953)]

    e. **Punitive damages.** In a later case, the Court held that a union is not subject to punitive damages for breaching its duty of fair representation. [IBEW v. Foust, 442 U.S. 42 (1979)] In this case, the Court indicated that the value gained from punitive damages would be more than offset by possible impairment of union financial stability and inhibitions that would be placed on union discretion. A concurring opinion protested the breadth of the stated rule and would leave open the possibility of punitive damages in cases of intentional racial discrimination or deliberate personal animus.

- **f. Fair representation and the NLRB.**

    - **1) Discrimination.** In 1962, the Board found that unions that had induced employers to discipline employees for nonmembership violated sections 8(b)(1)(A) and (b)(2). The Board found an implied right in an employee to be free from such pressure, which also tended to encourage union membership. [NLRB v. Miranda Fuel Co., 140 N.L.R.B. 181 (1962), *enforcement denied*, 326 F.2d 172 (2d Cir. 1963)] A minority of the Board, reading the legislative history of Wagner, Taft-Hartley and Landrum-Griffin, could find no statutory basis for such an implied unfair labor practice. The Fifth Circuit recognized the Board's authority in a racial discrimination case in 1967. [Local 12, United Rubber Workers v. NLRB, 368 F.2d 12 (5th Cir. 1967)] The Court noted that section 8(b)(1)(A) is not confined to discrimination that "encourages or discourages union membership." The Court also endorsed the Board's determination that fair representation is an "essential element" of section 7 rights. Since then, courts of appeals have recognized the duty and the Supreme Court in *Vaca, infra,* implicitly approved the proposition.

    - **2) Remedies.** The Board has revoked the certification of a union guilty of racial discrimination. [Independent Metal Workers, Local 1 (Hughes Tool Co.), 147 N.L.R.B. 1573 (1964)] It has refused to apply the contract-bar rule to a collective bargaining agreement that is discriminatory on its face. [Pioneer Bus Co., 140 N.L.R.B. 54 (1962)]

    - **3) Statute of limitations.** In *DelCostello v. International Brotherhood of Teamsters*, 462 U.S. 151 (1983), the Supreme Court applied a six-month statute of limitations to actions brought by individual employees asserting rights in the face of an arbitration award that they claimed was flawed due to a breach of the duty of fair representation. The Court drew from the NLRA rather than from analogous state law.

2. **What Constitutes "Breach" of Duty of Fair Representation.** The union will be held to have breached its duty of fair representation only when its conduct toward a member of the collective bargaining unit is shown to have been arbitrary, discriminatory, or in bad faith.

    - **a. Rationale.** The process of labor-management relations involves continuous dealings between the union and the employer, and it is inevitable that the union may propose changes in work conditions or terms of employment that will benefit some employees or classes of employees and prejudice others. Moreover, the union is constantly confronted with complaints and grievances by individual unit members. It is clear that broad discretion must be vested in the union, both in its dealings with management and its dealings with individual unit members.

b. **Examples.**

1) **Unfair labor practices.** Thus, a charge of union unfair labor practices cannot be predicated solely on the fact that the collective bargaining agreement negotiated by the union prejudices a particular employee or group of employees, as long as it appears that the union negotiated the provision in question in good faith.

2) **Invidious or arbitrary classification.** But there is a breach of the union's duty of fair representation where the union induces the employer to discriminate against the employee on the basis of an "invidious or arbitrary classification," such as race or citizenship.

3) **Sex discrimination.** Likewise, unions that determine membership solely on the basis of sex (and who refuse to process grievances on that basis) violate section 8(b)(1)(A). Any attempt to cause the employer to discriminate on the basis of sex would presumably violate section 8(b)(2).

4) **Intimidation.** Moreover, the union may breach the duty of fair representation where it acts for the purpose of intimidating nonunion members; *e.g.*, making an "example" of a nonunion employee to encourage other nonunion employees to join the union.

5) **Political expediency.** A breach of the duty occurs where the union acts solely out of political expediency.

6) **Duty of fair representation in bargaining--Air Line Pilots Association, International v. O'Neil,** 499 U.S. 65 (1991).

   a) **Facts.** Continental Airlines and the Air Line Pilots Association (D) were engaged in a bitter strike. All but 200 of D's 2000 pilots supported the strike, but by the time it ended, 400 of them had "crossed over" and went back to work. The company hired about 1000 replacements. At the end, there were 1600 pilots working and only 1000 pilots striking. For many years, the company had made route assignments by bid based on seniority. In September 1985, the company posted 441 route positions for bid. D, fearing this might lock out the striking pilots, authorized striking pilots to submit bids. After first accepting these bids, the company then announced that bids would be taken only from working pilots. Finally, an agreement was reached in October. Pilots were given three options: (i) certain striking pilots could submit bids for routes, (ii) pilots who elected not to work would receive severance pay, and (iii) striking pilots who retained job claims would be taken back after all of the first-option pilots had been reinstated. One hundred captain positions were awarded to working pilots, and the next 70 positions were awarded by seniority to option-one pilots. Thereafter, pilots in the two groups were offered positions on a one-to-one basis. O'Neil (P), a former striking pilot, brought action against D, claiming breach of its "duty of fair representation." The district court granted summary judgment in favor of D, finding that D had acted in good faith and without discrimination, and the court of appeals reversed. D appeals.

- b) **Issue.** Did D breach its duty of fair representation in the conduct of its negotiations and settlement?

- c) **Held.** No. Judgment reversed and case remanded.

    (1) D argues that "the duty of fair representation requires only that a union act in good faith and treat its members equally and in a nondiscriminatory fashion." D further argues that the duty does not require provision of adequate representation, contending that the courts cannot review the rationality of good faith, nondiscriminatory decisions.

    (2) The NLRA regulates only the process of bargaining and does not permit the government to regulate the substantive terms of negotiated bargains. But because unions have exclusive representational status, the courts can review their private agreements to determine whether or not a union fairly and adequately represented its constituency. The duty of fair representation is akin to that of trustees or corporate officers.

    (3) D argues that if a union does not adequately represent its members, the members have the power to vote them out. The cases cited by D were contract administration cases and not negotiation cases, but the statutory duty extends to nonnegotiation activities as well.

    (4) We doubt that a bright line between contract negotiations and administration can be drawn, and some union activities will not fall into either category.

    (5) We are satisfied that the appeals court correctly applied the tripartite standard of *Vaca v. Sipes, infra,* but its arbitrariness refinement interjected more judicial review of the contract substance than is consistent with labor policy. A court should not substitute its own notion of what a proper bargain should be.

    (6) Any review of the bargains struck must be highly deferential and recognize the wide latitude negotiators need for effective performance of their bargaining responsibilities.

    (7) The court of appeals placed too much stress on the fact that the deal struck by D was worse than the result would have been had the D simply called off the strike. Assuming that the settlement was indeed a bad one, it was by no means irrational. There was at the time some legal doubt about the status of the bid call under the RLA. Calling off the strike would raise the possibility of litigation over the bid call, and the settlement agreed to produce certain and prompt access to a share of new jobs. Also, almost one-third of the striking pilots chose severance pay.

    (8) No discrimination has been shown.

- d) **Comment.** The District of Columbia court of appeals has held it to be a breach of the duty of fair bargaining when a union, in an election campaign, vowed not to dove-tail seniority lists of two unions which were to be combined in a corporate merger. The court also held it to be a breach of bargaining duty for a union to adopt a procedure by which schedule changes would be approved by a vote of union members only. [Truck Drivers Local 568 v. NLRB (Red Ball

Motor Freight Inc.), 379 F.2d 137 (D.C. Cir. 1967); Branch 6000, National Association of Letter Carriers v. NLRB, 595 F.2d 808 (D.C. Cir. 1979)] Other circuits have not been as demanding.

3. **State or Federal Action Proper.** Suits by employees under section 9(a) may be brought in either federal or state court. [Humphrey v. Moore, 375 U.S. 335 (1964)] Since no federal limitations period specifically applies to such actions, the appropriate state statute applies in both forums.

B. THE INDIVIDUAL AND HER GRIEVANCE

1. **Right to Adjust Directly with the Employer.** Normally, individual grievances under the collective bargaining contract are presented to the union, and the union presses the claim on behalf of the employee. However, it is not essential that the individual employee go through the union.

    Section 9(a) specifically provides that she may seek to adjust any grievances directly with her employer—without the intervention of the union—as long as the adjustment is not inconsistent with the terms of the collective agreement, and the union is given the opportunity to be present at the adjustment.

2. **Right to Union Representation at Investigatory Interviews.** An employee is entitled to request to have a union representative present at an investigatory interview by the employer which the employee reasonably believes might result in disciplinary action. The employer's refusal of a request for such representation is a violation of NLRA section 8(a)(1). [NLRB v. J. Weingarten, Inc., *supra*]

3. **Employee's Right to Judicial Relief Against Employer.** The fact that an employee has the statutory right to present her grievance directly to the employer does not mean that the employer has to act upon it.

    a. **Exhaustion of contract remedies required.** If the employer fails or refuses to act on the grievance, the employee must first file a grievance or ask the union to institute whatever grievance procedure is provided in the collective bargaining agreement. The employee cannot sue the employer unless she has attempted to exhaust the remedies provided in the collective agreement.

    1) But the individual employee has no absolute right to have her grievance arbitrated under the collective bargaining agreement. She cannot compel the employer to arbitrate directly with her, nor can she compel the union to act on her behalf, unless the CBA would provide otherwise. [*See* Vaca v. Sipes, *infra*]

    b. **Contract action against employer.** If the union "arbitrarily" refuses to press an employee's grievance under the procedures outlined in the collective bargaining agreement or otherwise fails to represent her fairly, the employee may bring suit against the employer to enforce the collective bargaining agreement on the theory that, as a member of the bargaining unit, she is a third-party beneficiary of the agreement.

4. **Employee's Right to Judicial Relief Against the Union.** Moreover, if the union's failure to act on her behalf amounted to a breach of its duty of fair representation (*supra*)—*i.e.*, its refusal was "arbitrary, discriminatory, or in bad faith"—the aggrieved employee can (i) file a union unfair labor practice charge with the NLRB; (ii) file a private damages action against the union under Taft-Hartley section 301; or (iii) where applicable, initiate procedures under Title VII.

Vaca v. Sipes

a. **Action to obtain admission to the union--Vaca v. Sipes,** 386 U.S. 171 (1967).

1) **Facts.** Owens (P), an employee in a meat packing plant, suffered from high blood pressure and took half a year sick leave from his heavy labor job. He returned to work with a certification from his physician, but was permanently discharged on the recommendation of the company doctor. The union, following the grievance process of the bargaining agreement, processed P's grievance to the fourth step, sending P at its own expense to get a third medical opinion before proceeding to the next step, arbitration. The third doctor agreed with the company doctor's opinion, at which point the executive board of the union elected not to send the complaint to arbitration and recommended to P that he accept referral by the company to a rehabilitation center. P refused the offer, demanded that his case be arbitrated, and, when again refused, brought an action against the company and a separate class action suit under section 301 of the LMRA against the union in state court accusing the union of "arbitrarily" refusing to arbitrate his case. P was awarded damages by a jury. The union appealed on the grounds that the trial court lacked jurisdiction. The state court asserted jurisdiction and ruled that the case turned on whether P had been wronged by the company and not whether the union had exercised its duty of fair representation in deciding against arbitration of P's case. This decision was appealed by the union.

2) **Issue.** Is a state court's jurisdiction over an action by a union member against his union for not properly processing his complaint against an employer nullified by the Board's authority to hear cases alleging unfair union representation?

3) **Held.** No. Judgment reversed on the merits.

a) The preemption doctrine has never been applied to suits against breach of union fair representation. Handling such cases often involves delving into subjects outside of the Board's jurisdiction, such as negotiation and grievance processing, and substantive contract review.

b) The Board's concern is with the well-being of the labor body and not so much with individual interests. Under section 301, an employee may directly sue the union. As under this section, suits against employers allow evidence against union failure to process complaints to be brought forth.

c) Correct in its assertion of jurisdiction, the state court did fail to apply the proper rule to the case. A union is guilty of breach of duty only if its conduct was in bad faith, capricious, or discriminatory. The state court's ruling that disregarded the union's good faith in its processing of P's grievance was wrong.

4) **Dissent** (Fortas, Harlan, JJ., Warren, C.J.). Cases brought by an employee against his union for breach of the statutory duty of fair representation are under the jurisdiction of the NLRB.

5) **Dissent** (Black, J.). The Court opens slightly the courthouse door to an employee's incidental claim of fair representation against his union, but it shuts it against his more valuable breach of contract claim against the employer. The jury had found that P was fit for work, his grievance was meritorious, and the company had violated the agreement. P is now left remediless and the company is allowed to hide behind the union's conduct. P was not trying to completely sidestep the grievance procedure in favor of litigation. Either the employee should be able to sue his employer for breach of contract after trying to exhaust his contractual remedies, or the union should have an absolute duty to exhaust those remedies on his behalf. Now, the employee must take on both the employer and the union in a three-ring donnybrook.

6) **Comment.** In a more recent Supreme Court case, a union member was denied job referrals through a hiring hall operated by the union. The member brought an action in federal court claiming that he was denied referrals because he had opposed the union's leadership in a recent election. The district court and court of appeals each concluded that they lacked jurisdiction. The Supreme Court reversed, holding that the Board did not have exclusive jurisdiction over these matters and that it was not necessary that there be a claim of breach by the company. The Court indicated that "the duty of fair representation is not intended to mirror the contours" of unfair labor practices under the NLRA. [Breininger v. Sheet Metal Workers, Local 6, 493 U.S. 67 (1989)]

b. **Apportionment of damages--Bowen v. United States Postal Service,** 459 U.S. 212 (1983).

1) **Facts.** Bowen (P) was fired by the United States Postal Service (D) for fighting with another employee. The Postal Workers Union (D) declined to take his grievance to arbitration. P sued Ds for damages. The district court instructed the jury that it could apportion damages between Ds. The jury awarded damages against the Postal Service for lost wages up to the time that a hypothetical arbitration would have reinstated P and against the union for all losses afterwards. The court of appeals held that the union should not be liable for any part of P's lost earnings. The Supreme Court granted certiorari.

2) **Issue.** May a union that has breached its duty of fair representation be held liable for damages caused by an employer's wrongful discharge?

3) **Held.** Yes. Judgment reversed.

Bowen v.
United States
Postal Service

Labor Law - 189

a) Damages may be apportioned between the wrongdoers. The interests identified in *Vaca v. Sipes, supra,* provide a measure for apportionment. The employee must be made whole. The employer must bear the natural consequences of its breach. If the employer has not prevented access to the grievance-arbitration process, the union must bear responsibility for increases in the employer's damages caused by its breach of duty.

b) *Vaca* does not apply principles of ordinary contract law. The union plays a key part in the process and the employer must rely on the union's disposition of the employee's claim. If the union fails, the employer must be in the same position as if the wronged employee were in a position to take action on her own behalf.

4) **Concurrence and dissent** (White, Marshall, Blackmun, Rehnquist, JJ.). The union should not be liable for back pay. The natural consequences of the union's breach, for which it must be liable, are of a different nature. The majority's new rule will tend to cast the bulk of damages on the union. The union's failure does not make the employer's act any less wrongful. The union should only be secondarily liable for lost wages.

c. **Exhaustion of internal union procedures.** In *Clayton v. International Union, United Automobile Workers*, 451 U.S. 679 (1981), the Supreme Court held that an employee does not always have to exhaust internal union procedures (in contrast to labor agreement procedures) before bringing a section 301 action against the employer and the union. The Court said that exhaustion would not be required where the union officials are so hostile to the employee that a fair hearing could not be expected, where the appeals procedure could not reactivate the employee's grievance or give her the full relief sought, or where exhaustion would unreasonably delay the opportunity to obtain a judicial hearing on the merits.

C. DEVICES INSURING UNION SECURITY

Unions have long sought to extract agreements from employers that effectively make all workers in the bargaining unit members of the union. The basic argument is that compulsory membership and the "checkoff" of union dues (whereby the employer deducts union dues directly from the employee's paycheck and forwards them to the union) are necessary to secure the union's bargaining position.

1. **Federal Regulation of Compulsory Union Membership Arrangement.** NLRA section 8(a)(3) prohibits employer discrimination on the basis of union membership. The statute is qualified, however, to allow certain union security devices to be negotiated by the parties (*see infra*).

    a. **Background.** Under the original NLRA, union security agreements, including agreements for a "closed shop", were legal as long as the union had majority support. This led to serious abuses, including situations in which the union could dictate who would or would not be hired by controlling membership status.

b. **Present law.** To rectify such abuses, section 8(a)(3) and section 7 were amended by the Taft-Hartley Act in 1947, to provide that employees may refrain from union activity, except that if the union is the exclusive bargaining agent for the unit, the union may lawfully negotiate union security clauses (requiring union membership and/or the payment of union dues) after the employee has been hired. [NLRA §8(a)(3)]

c. **Types and legality of compulsory union membership agreements.**

1) **Closed shop.** In the closed shop, membership in the union is a condition of employment—that is, membership is required before hiring. This type of arrangement is illegal. [NLRA §§8(a)(3), 8(f)]

2) **Preferential hiring.** Preferential hiring requires the employer to hire only workers recommended or referred by the union.

   a) **Required union membership.** If this arrangement demands union membership before the employee is hired, it also is illegal.

   b) **Hiring halls.** However, a system of job referrals (hiring halls) operated by the union, or a system of union work permits, is legal provided that there is no discrimination in making referrals on the basis of membership or nonmembership in the union.

3) **Union shop.** Under the union shop arrangement, membership in the union is compulsory after employment. Such arrangements are legal as long as the negotiating union is the majority representative.

   a) **Grace period.** Section 8(a)(3) provides a 30-day "grace" period after hiring, before membership becomes mandatory. Thus, a collective agreement is lawful if it requires, as a condition of employment, that every new employee join the union "on or after" the 30th day of his employment.

   b) **Full membership not compulsory.** Under recent case law, full-fledged union membership cannot be required even though the collective bargaining contract contains a union shop clause (*i.e.*, only the payment of dues and initiation fees can be demanded).

      (1) In effect, this allows anti-union employees in a union shop to treat the agreement as if it created an "agency shop" (*see* below).

      (2) An employee can also resign membership and thereby avoid the union's power to assess fines and enforce rules.

4) **Agency shop.** The "agency shop" is also legal. Here, full membership in the union is not required but all employees must pay dues and initiation fees, regardless of whether they join.

NLRB v. General Motors Corp.

a) **Agency shop agreement in right-to-work state--NLRB v. General Motors Corp.,** 373 U.S. 734 (1963).

    (1) **Facts.** During negotiations, the union (P) proposed an agency shop provision. The plant was located in a right-to-work state, but an agency shop would not be contrary to the local statute. General Motors (D) refused to consider the proposal and P filed an unfair labor practice charge. The Board found that D had violated section 8(a)(5). The court of appeals refused to enforce the order, and the Board took the case to the Supreme Court.

    (2) **Issue.** Is it an unfair labor practice for a union and employer to enter an agency shop agreement in a right-to-work state?

    (3) **Held.** No. Judgment reversed.

        (a) Under federal law, an agency shop is not an unfair labor practice, and it was the responsibility of General Motors as an employer to bargain over such a proposal.

        (b) An agency shop allows employees the freedom to decline union membership, yet takes care of the problem of employees who receive union benefits, but do not want to contribute to the monetary support of the union.

        (c) The Taft-Hartley amendments to section 8(a)(3) are concerned with certain abuses of forced union membership, and the new proviso is for the prevention of the use of union security agreements for purposes other than getting employees to pay union fees. The meaning of "membership" has been whittled down to its financial core.

5) **Maintenance of membership.** Under the agency shop arrangement, union membership is not required but current members can renounce membership only within a time period fixed in the agreement. Any new employees who become members must retain their membership status for the duration of the agreement. Such arrangements are legal. The CBA provision must clearly inform employees of their option to reduce their "membership" to that of agency payments.

d. **Enforcement of union security clauses in the agreement.** Section 8(a)(3) provides for the enforcement of lawful compulsory union membership agreements. The employer (generally acting at the request of the union) has the right to discharge an employee for lack of union membership where a valid compulsory union membership agreement is in effect, provided that:

1) The employer is not aware of any reasonable grounds for believing that membership was unavailable to the subject employee "on the same terms and conditions generally applicable to other members;" or

2) The employee's union membership is denied or terminated for failure of the employee to tender the periodic dues and initiation fees uniformly

required of all persons as a condition of acquiring or retaining membership. [NLRA §8(a)(3)(A), (B); *and see* Radio Officers Union AFL v. NLRB, 347 U.S. 17 (1954)]

3) Note that employees need not become full-fledged members to be protected from discharge; they merely must tender dues and initiation fees. [NLRB v. Hershey Foods Corp., 513 F.2d 1083 (1975)]

e. **Authorization to negotiate union security agreements.** The union may negotiate union security agreements without explicit authority from employees in the bargaining unit. However, if employees wish to rescind the union's authority to negotiate a union security agreement, they may vote to do so in a special "deauthorization" election. [NLRA §8(a)(3)]

2. **State Regulation of Compulsory Membership Agreements—"Right-to-Work" Laws.** NLRA section 14(b) permits states to prohibit union security agreements otherwise legal under section 8(a)(3). Thus, agreements that are valid under federal law may still violate a more stringent state provision. (Note, however, that the RLA does not have a provision comparable to section 14(b); hence, federal law preempts any state right-to-work laws as to railroad or airline employees.)

   a. **Present legislative response.** Pursuant to section 14(b), a number of states have enacted "right-to-work" laws which either outlaw or restrict compulsory union membership arrangements.

   b. **State courts decide validity.** Whether a particular union shop or agency shop arrangement is prohibited by a state "right-to-work" law is to be determined by state courts. [*See* NLRB v. General Motors Corp., *supra*]

3. **Union Members May Not Be Compelled to Make Political Contributions-- International Association of Machinists v. Street,** 367 U.S. 740 (1961).

   International Association of Machinists v. Street

   a. **Facts.** The International Association of Machinists (D) and other labor unions entered into a union shop agreement under section 2, Eleventh of the RLA with the carriers of the Southern Railway System, which gives unions and carriers the power to require dues and initiation fees of employees not desiring union membership as a condition of continued employment. Some of D's members, including Street (P), brought a state class action suit to enjoin D from using their dues to finance candidates and political and economic ideas they opposed. The trial court enjoined the enforcement of the union shop agreement, ruling that section 2, Eleventh, which allowed the channeling of dues into the political arena, violated the First Amendment. The Georgia Supreme Court affirmed, and D appeals.

   b. **Issue.** Did Congress intend in section 2, Eleventh of the RLA to give unions the means of coercing employees into supporting political candidates and causes they object to?

   c. **Held.** No. Judgment reversed and case remanded.

Labor Law - 193

1) In harmony with the Court's policy of interpreting federal statutes in such a way as to avoid doubt of their constitutionality, section 2, Eleventh can be interpreted with all reason as prohibiting a union from funding political causes on an employee's objection from that employee's union fees.

2) Congress intended section 2, Eleventh to strengthen the bargaining power of the unions by allowing nonunion members benefiting from the union's bargaining activity to be subject to union dues. There is no evidence that Congress intended to permit unions to require employees to support political causes, as money spent in this manner does not defray bargaining costs. No constitutional question need be reached.

3) The injunction against enforcement of the union-shop agreement is too broad. It would also be improper to enjoin political expenditures generally. This too might be restrictive of the union's majority to state positions in respect to union affairs.

d. **Concurrence** (Douglas, J.). Forced collection for paying the costs of bargaining is one thing, but spending dues money for the promotion of political elections or social purposes is beyond the causes that gave rise to the need for group action in the first place, although the individual cannot prevent the use of the money to promote the causes of the group. Otherwise, *Railway Employees Department v. Hanson*, 351 U.S. 225, would be reversed *sub silentio*.

e. **Dissent** (Black, J.). The majority has rewritten section 2, Eleventh. To the extent that the section allows dues from protesting employees to be spent on political causes, it is in violation of the First Amendment.

f. **Dissent** (Frankfurter, Harlan, JJ.). Political expression is a valid trade union practice. P has not been deprived of his right to influence union policies or to take political stands.

g. **Comment.** The Court has extended the rule in this case to the use of agency fees under the NLRA on the basis that the later amendments to the RLA had been patterned after the Taft-Hartley amendments to section 8(a)(3). [*Communications Workers v. Beck*, 487 U.S. 735 (1988)]

4. **Adequacy of "Escape" Clauses.** In *Ellis v. Brotherhood of Railway, Airline & S.S. Clerks*, 466 U.S. 435 (1984), the Supreme Court ruled that a rebate scheme whereby employees could obtain rebates for objectionable uses of agency shop collections was inadequate. It found that the time consumed in obtaining the rebate was too long and that the forced "borrowing" was not justified by administrative convenience. The Court approved exactions for funding national conventions, publication of the union's monthly magazine, and litigation expenses connected with unit negotiations, grievance processing, fair representation, and jurisdictional disputes.

5. **Adequate Procedures for Escape.** In a consolidated case, the Board set forth some guidance concerning dues-reduction procedures for nonunion members in a national union who were covered by CBAs requiring payments in lieu of dues. The union published escape procedures in the December issue of its union

magazine. Objected expenditures had to be specified and sent by certified mail in January. Responding to the General Counsel's challenge to the rules, the Board required more information and detail in the notices. It found that the annual December notice was adequate for current employees, but that new employees must be notified at the time when they become obligated to pay. The Board also required that additional information be provided before an employee can be discharged for nonpayment. The certified mail requirement was deemed burdensome on employee rights. The Board finally allowed employees to be charged with national and district level expenditures which were germane and ultimately inured to the members of the local unions. [California Saw & Knife Works, 320 N.L.R.B. No. 11 (1995)]

D. UNION HIRING HALLS

1. **Background.** The 1947 Taft-Hartley Amendments to the NLRA were designed in part to limit union power to discipline its members and to "insulate" employees' job rights from their union rights and duties.

2. **Union Unfair Labor Practices.** The Taft-Hartley Amendments made certain union disciplinary actions unfair labor practices.

   a. **Union coercing employer to discriminate in employment.** NLRA section 8(b)(2) prohibits unions from causing (or attempting to cause) an employer to discriminate against any employee. Such discrimination would also be an employer unfair labor practice under section 8(a)(3).

      1) **Nondiscriminatory exclusive hiring hall--Local 357, International Brotherhood of Teamsters v. NLRB,** 365 U.S. 667 (1961). Local 357, International Brotherhood of Teamsters v. NLRB

         a) **Facts.** Local 357 (D) had a collective bargaining agreement with California Trucking Associations (D) that included a nondiscriminatory exclusive union hiring hall provision whereby union and nonunion casual employees were to be hired on the basis of seniority through union hiring lists. Slater (P), a union member, was hired by a member of the Association without going through a union hiring hall. When the union protested, P was discharged. P filed section 8(a)(1) and (3) charges against the Association and section 8(b)(2) and (1)(A) charges against the union. The Board found the hiring hall agreement to be per se illegal and the court of appeals affirmed. The Supreme Court granted certiorari.

         b) **Issue.** Is a nondiscriminatory exclusive hiring hall agreement invalid per se?

         c) **Held.** No. Judgment reversed.

            (1) Absent some express showing of discrimination, an exclusive hiring hall agreement may be enforced. However, if the hiring hall has a discriminatory effect

it can be invalidated, but there was no such evidence in this case. An example of such discrimination might include creating a "closed shop."

    d) **Concurrence** (Harlan, Stewart, JJ.). The natural consequence of such an agreement is to make employees and job applicants believe that the union is favored.

    e) **Dissent in part** (Clark, J.). An arrangement like an exclusive hiring hall is so closely allied to a closed shop that its effect is to weigh too heavily in favor of the union the advantages of such agreements.

   b. **Unfair financial practices.** NLRA section 8(b)(5) prohibits unions who negotiate a union security agreement from charging "excessive or discriminatory initiation fees." [*See* NLRB v. Television Broadcasting Studio Employees Local 804, 315 F.2d 398 (3d Cir. 1963)—union raised initiation fee from $50 to $500 to discourage new members]

E. BENEFITS FOR UNION OFFICIALS

1. **Superseniority.** Collective bargaining agreements often contain "superseniority" provisions in favor of certain union representatives. These provisions put them in a preferred status vis-a-vis rank and file employees.

   a. **Permissible and impermissible seniority discrimination--Local 900, International Union of Electrical Workers v. NLRB (Gulton Electro-Voice, Inc.),** 727 F.2d 1184 (D.C. Cir. 1984).

    1) **Facts.** The labor agreement between Local 900 (D) and Gulton Electro-Voice had long contained a clause granting superseniority as to lay-offs and recalls to a number of union officers, including the recording secretary and the financial secretary, neither of which offices was directly connected with contract negotiations or administration. During a lay-off, the superseniority of the recording secretary caused some employees to be laid off. Charges were filed claiming that the preferences given the two officers unjustifiably discriminated on the basis of union involvement. The ALJ dismissed the complaint, but the Board reversed. D seeks review.

    2) **Issue.** Is it an unfair labor practice to grant superseniority to union officers whose duties have no direct connection with the negotiation and administration of a collective agreement?

    3) **Held.** Yes. Order enforced.

      a) Section 7 protects the right to engage in concerted activities and protects the right to refrain therefrom. Discrimination based on the exercise of section 7 rights can be a violation of section 8(a)(3) or (b)(2) unless it furthers other substantial statutory or business purposes.

b) Since 1975, the Board has recognized the justification of superseniority for union stewards with respect for lay-offs, but not for overtime, vacation, shift, or other types of preferences. Lay-off superseniority was justified because it furthered effective administration of bargaining agreements to keep stewards on the job.

c) In 1977, the Board adopted a rule extending superseniority to a wider range of union officials. In the present case, the Board reverted back to its original rule.

d) The Board is justified in its judgment that lay-off superseniority is not necessary for general categories of union officials since they, unlike stewards, can still perform their functions while away from the plant on lay-off or they can be replaced without undue disruption of union affairs.

e) There is no indication that the members of the local intended to waive complaints about the broad superseniority treatment when they voted to approve the collective agreement.

F. DISCIPLINE OF UNION MEMBERS UNDER THE NLRA

1. **Union Restraint and Coercion of Employee Rights.** Section 8(b)(1) prohibits unions from restraining or coercing employees in the exercise of rights guaranteed them by section 7—namely, the rights to (i) self-organize, (ii) bargain collectively, (iii) engage in concerted activities for the purpose of collective bargaining, and (iv) refrain from any of the above activities.

   a. **Power of union to adopt and enforce internal rules.** However, the protection of section 8(b)(1) is limited by a proviso granting the union "the right . . . to prescribe rules with respect to the acquisition or retention of membership in the union."

   b. **Fines for failure to honor strike--NLRB v. Allis-Chalmers Manufacturing Co., 388 U.S. 175 (1967).**

   NLRB v. Allis-Chalmers Manufacturing Co.

   1) **Facts.** Allis-Chalmers Manufacturing (P) and the union (D) were parties to a collective bargaining agreement which allowed employees who did not desire to be full union members to be members only in the sense that they paid the monthly union dues. When some full union employees crossed the picket line to work for P during an authorized strike against P, D fined each of these employees $20-$100 and petitioned the state court for collection of the fines. Asserting that the fines and the suit to the court for collection was an unfair labor practice violating section 8(b)(1)(A), which restricts unions from coercing employees in exercising their section 7 rights of not participating in concerted activity, P filed charges against D. The Board refused to uphold P's allegation, ruling that whether or not D's

imposition of fines violated section 8(b)(1)(A), its action was legal under a proviso to section 8(b)(1) giving a union the authority "to prescribe rules with respect to the acquisition or retention of membership therein." Upon reversal by the court of appeals, the Board appeals.

2) **Issue.** Is a union barred under section 8(b)(1) from levying fines and asking for court enforcement of the fines against full members of the union who fail to honor an authorized strike?

3) **Held.** No. Judgment reversed.

   a) The court of appeals deemed that the assessment of fines against strike breakers was a "correction" within the literal terms of section 8(b)(1)(A). To say that Congress in 1947 intended to strip unions of their disciplinary powers is to attribute an intent to regulate unions more stringently than did the later Landrum-Griffin amendments. Expulsion is permitted expressly, and the lesser action of fines and penalties serve the needs of the union, especially a weaker one.

   b) The legislative history contains no reference of intent that internal disciplinary fines should come within the ambit of the section's imprecise words. On the contrary, there were a number of assurances that the section was not meant to regulate internal union affairs.

   c) Therefore, under the proviso, the assessment of the fines was not improper. We do not pass on whether the proviso prohibits enforcement of fines by court action.

   d) The legislative history reveals that Congress assumed that unions had the power to fine, expel, or otherwise discipline their members.

4) **Dissent** (Black, Douglas, Harlan, Stewart, JJ.). The majority's decision is based upon the logic that weak unions need disciplinary power and that fines and the court enforcement of them are less severe punishment than expulsion from the union. Judicial enforcement gives the union an economic weapon that could be more coercive than expulsion.

5) **Comment.** The NLRB, while it has authority under section 8(b)(1)(A) to review the reasonableness of union rules affecting employment status, does not have the power to test the reasonableness of rules affecting membership status (including fines), unless otherwise prohibited by the NLRA. [NLRB v. Boeing Co., 412 U.S. 67 (1973)] The union must enforce its claim against its member in state courts, and state law regarding reasonableness or unreasonableness will control.

Scofield v. NLRB

c. **Fine for violating union rule--Scofield v. NLRB,** 394 U.S. 423 (1969).

1) **Facts.** Scofield (P) charged his union (D) with unfair labor practices, alleging that D violated section 8(b)(1)(A) by coercing employees in their rights guaranteed by section 7. Employees of the Wisconsin Motor Corporation were paid on a piece rate basis; however, they were guaranteed a minimum "machine" rate. Pursuant to the union rule in question here, a union member could only draw pay up to a ceiling rate. Additional production above the ceiling rate was "banked" by the company; that is,

wages due in excess of the ceiling rate were retained by the company and paid out to the employee for days in which his production ceiling had not been met. If the employee demanded payment in full, the company would comply but the employee then became subject to fines by D ranging from $1 to $100 for each violation. D had checked the company's books, found that P and others were in violation of its rule, and fined them $50 to $100. When P refused to pay, D brought suit in state courts to collect the fine. P filed the charge noted above. The trial examiner, the Board, and the court of appeals all found for D.

2) **Issue.** May a union fine its members for violating a union rule forbidding the drawing of pay beyond a given ceiling rate?

3) **Held.** Yes. Judgment affirmed.

   a) If a union rule invades or frustrates an overriding policy of the labor laws the rule may not be enforced, even by fine or expulsion, without violating section 8(b)(1). The rule must also reflect a legitimate union interest.

   b) Here, there has been no showing that the fines were unreasonable, the mere fiat of a union leader, that P was involuntarily a member of the union, or that they were improperly enforced. Thus, this inquiry must focus on the legitimacy of the union interest vindicated by the rule.

   c) The trial examiner found that the rule was intended to reduce competitive pressures between employees, *e.g.*, to prevent the lowering of the piece-work rate so that high-output employees were earning little more than they did before.

   d) Here, the ceiling rate was important in negotiating the minimum hourly rate, determining hourly rate raises, etc.

   e) There is no merit to P's contention that the rule impedes collective bargaining and encourages featherbedding. If the company wants to require more work of its employees, the company should strike for a better bargain.

4) **Dissent** (Black, J.). I dissent for the same reasons discussed in my *Allis-Chalmers* dissent, *supra*.

5) **Comments.**

   a) The "machine" rate was based on the hourly work product of the average competent employee. Allowances were made for setting up machines, fatigue, cleaning tools, and personal needs.

   b) In another case, a union fined picket-line-crossing employees in amounts that in some instances exceeded their base pay by more than four times. It sued some in state court to collect unpaid amounts and attorney fees. The company filed section 8(b)(1)(A) charges and the Board ruled that Congress did not give it authority to regulate the size of union fines or to establish standards for testing their reasonableness. The Supreme Court agreed with the Board. It found no basis for any congressional desire to build upon the Board's expertise or attain uniformity. [NLRB v. Boeing Co., *supra*]

d. **Resignation from union.** If a member effectively resigns from the union before committing an act that is contrary to a union punitive rule, it is a violation of section 8(b)(1) for the union to impose fines and attempt to collect them in state proceedings. [NLRB v. Granite State Joint Board, Textile Workers Local 1029, 409 U.S. 213 (1972)]

e. **Fine for attempting to resign--Pattern Makers' League of North America v. NLRB,** 473 U.S. 95 (1985).

   1) **Facts.** The constitution of the Pattern Makers' (D) provides that a member may not resign from the union while a strike is going on or is imminent. D fined 10 members who attempted to resign during a strike. The Board held these fines to be in violation of section 8(b)(1)(a). The court of appeals enforced the order, and the Supreme Court granted certiorari.

   2) **Issue.** Does the Act preclude a union from fining members who attempt to resign while a concerted action is being conducted against an employer?

   3) **Held.** Yes. Order enforced.

      a) Such a union restriction restrains an employee's section 7 right to refrain from concerted activities. The Board's construction is consistent with *Allis-Chalmers, supra.*

      b) Congressional protection of unions' control over their own internal affairs does not go so far as to authorize restrictions on the right to resign from membership. Such would curtail freedoms of choice protected by the Act. Full union membership can no longer be a requirement of employment.

      c) Even a union security provision lawful under the Act will not prevent a member from resigning. The proviso to section 8(b)(1)(A) does not go that far.

   4) **Dissent** (Blackmun, Brennan, Marshall, JJ.). Neither the words of the Act nor the legislative history support the Board's construction. Unions are permitted to establish their own reasonable membership rules. The rule in issue was designed to permit the union to effectively pursue collective goals. The Court should not defer to the Board's construction.

f. **Union discipline of supervisory members.** In the construction industry particularly, supervisors are, and remain, members of the union which is the bargaining representative at a particular construction site. On the next job, the supervisor may well work as a nonsupervisor. If a union improperly expels or disciplines a supervisor in his or her membership capacity, neither the supervisor nor the employer have standing under section 8(b)(1)(A). However, a charge may be brought against the union under section 8(b)(1)(B) for interference with the company's selection of its own bargaining representatives. For many years, the application was confined to supervisor-members who were engaged in negotiations or the processing of grievances. In the late 1960s, the Board broadened its application. [*See* San Francisco-Oakland Mailers' Union 18, 172 N.L.R.B. 2173 (1968)] The Supreme Court has generally held that direct union disciplinary action which "may adversely" affect supervisors' bargaining or grievance functions may be covered. Union discipline is improper for supervisors who cross a picket line to perform their supervisory duties, when it might affect supervisors' "willingness" to serve as grievance processors or bargainers. [*See* Florida Power & Light Co. v. Electrical Workers, 417 U.S. 790 (1974)] More recently, the Court held that union discipline was not barred for supervisors who worked for employers who did not have a bargaining relationship with the union, rejecting the Board's "reservoir" doctrine as being too broad a restriction on the capacity to discipline its own members. [NLRB v. IBEW, Local 340 (Royal Electric), 481 U.S. 573 (1987)]

G. JUDICIAL SUPERVISION OF UNION DISCIPLINE

1. **Limitations on Union Discipline.**

   a. **Background.** At common law and under the original NLRA (1935), unions had sweeping disciplinary powers over their members. This right of self-rule could be abused in union government. The LMRDA —the so-called "Landrum-Griffin Act"—was passed in 1959 to protect more fully the rights of union members, curb abuses of union power, and promote internal union democracy.

   b. **LMRDA Title I—"labor's bill of rights."** Title I of Landrum-Griffin (29 U.S.C. section 411 et seq.) was passed to guarantee union members certain basic rights necessary to insure democracy within unions.

   1) **Equal rights.** Section 101(a)(1) gives members "equal rights and privileges" to nominate candidates, vote on internal matters, and attend and participate in membership meetings, "subject to reasonable rules and regulations in the organization's constitution and by-laws."

      a) **Union jobs protection under the LMRDA--Finnegan v. Leu,** 456 U.S. 431 (1982).   Finnegan v. Leu

         (1) **Facts.** In a local union election, Finnegan and other business agents (Ps) supported the loser. Leu (D), the winner, fired Ps, who had been appointed by the loser, saying he felt they were not loyal to him and would be unable to implement his policies and programs. Ps sued D for violating the LMRDA. The courts below ruled that the Act did not protect the business agents from discharge.

         (2) **Issue.** Is it a violation of the LMRDA for a successful candidate for union office to replace business agents who supported the opponent?

(3) Held. No. Judgment affirmed.

(a) The LMRDA amendments were added to insure that unions would be democratically governed and to protect union members in the expression of their views. The LMRDA was not intended to protect union officers as such.

(b) Ps had a dual status. As members they had a right to campaign for the candidate of their choice, but as appointed officers they were not immune from discharge by the new president.

(c) The action here did not amount to "discipline" under the Act, which contemplates punitive actions such as fines, suspensions, or expulsions. The actions taken here did not affect P's membership status.

(d) The new union leadership should be in a position to choose a staff whose views are compatible with its own.

2) **Removals of union elected officers--Sheet Metal Workers' International Association v. Lynn,** 488 U.S. 347 (1989).

a) **Facts.** Lynn (P) was elected to a three-year term as business agent of Local 75, which was affiliated with Sheet Metal Workers (D). The local was experiencing financial difficulties. P unsuccessfully urged the local's officers to reduce their expenses before raising dues. D subsequently took over the local in trusteeship. Shortly afterward, the appointed trustee recommended a dues increase and directed P to support it. P refused, and campaigned against it. The local voted against the increase and the trustee removed P from his office because of his opposition. After exhausting intra-union procedures, P brought action in federal district court claiming that his removal violated his free speech rights under section 101(a)(2) of the LMRDA. The district court dismissed, saying that the right to speak out about union affairs did not protect P against removal as agent. The court of appeals reversed, and the Supreme Court granted certiorari.

b) **Issue.** Is the removal of an elected union business agent in retaliation for statements made at a union meeting a violation of the LMRDA?

c) **Held.** Yes. Judgment affirmed.

(1) In *Finnegan v. Leu, supra*, we held that the free speech provisions did not prevent the removal of *appointed* union officials because of their speech activities. That was done in recognition of the overriding objective of democratic union governance which would allow victorious candidates to select their own staff. That case did not involve the question of an *elected* official.

(2) It is true that P was able to address the meeting, but he did so at the price of removal. The consequences of removing an elected official are much different from removing an appointee. The chilling effect is compounded. It discourages not only the official but also the

members who elected him. The existence of a lawful trusteeship does not impair the right to speak out or the protection of the Act.

3) **Freedom of speech and assembly.** Under section 102, union members are guaranteed the basic rights of free speech (the right to "assemble freely" and the right to "express any views, arguments, and opinions").

- a) **Responsibility of members toward the union.** At the same time, however, section 101(a)(2) permits unions to adopt and enforce reasonable rules concerning the responsibility of every member toward the union as an institution and toward refraining from conduct that would interfere with the union's performance of its legal and contractual obligations (*e.g.*, advocating "wildcat" strikes).

- b) **Replacement of union officials.** Appointed union officials, such as business agents, have the right to run for office and support or oppose candidates on policies without being penalized; however, it is not improper for a successful faction in an election to replace those who opposed them or their policies if their retention would prevent the successful faction from implementing its program. [Wambles v. International Brotherhood of Teamsters, 488 F.2d 888 (5th Cir. 1974)]

- c) **Balancing.** The courts must consider in each case to determine where the member's rights of free speech end and the union's legitimate interests begin.

    (1) **Statements made when no union interest at stake.** Where there is no clear union interest at stake, a union member may freely express his opinions about union officers and their policies—even if his statements are false and libelous.

    (2) **Accusations against union officers--Salzhandler v. Caputo,** 316 F.2d 445 (2d Cir. 1963). *Salzhandler v. Caputo*

    - (a) **Facts.** The financial secretary (P) of Local 442, Brotherhood of Painters, Decorators, and Paperhangers of America (D), spread leaflets among fellow union workers that accused the union's president of misconduct, including the misuse and siphoning off of union funds. D's president, Webman, charged P before a union trial board with violation of the union constitution by libeling a union officer. P was found guilty of misconduct in his duty as a member or officer of D. P was removed from office and was suspended from union activities for five years. While his internal appeal was pending, P brought suit in federal district court under section 101(a)(2) of the LMRDA, which gives union members the right to freely express any opinion involving union affairs. The district court ruled that the allegations concerning Webman were libelous and that the LMRDA does not give union members the license to slander officers of the union. Thus, the complaint was dismissed. P appeals.

Labor Law - 203

(b) **Issue.** Is a union member protected under the LMRDA from union discipline for alleged libel in accusing union officers of misconduct?

(c) **Held.** Yes. Judgment reversed.

1] The LMRDA guarantees freedom of speech among union members, so that even slanderous statements do not merit disciplinary action. By passing the LMRDA, Congress sought to keep union officers from misusing their authority against criticism by union members.

2] The only exceptions to the guarantee of freedom of speech in the LMRDA, interference with the union's legal or contractual duties and violation of a member's obligation to the union as an institution (not the union's officers), do not apply in this case. If P's statements were libelous, a civil suit might be brought against him, but not disciplinary action by the union.

c. **Judicial review of union disciplinary proceedings.** Common law courts did not hesitate to require unions to adhere to the due process provisions of the union's own constitution and by-laws, and to require (as a matter of public policy) that such provisions measure up to judicial notions of fairness. The courts have applied the same principles in reviewing union disciplinary procedures under LMRDA section 101(a)(5).

1) **Scope of judicial review.** Thus, for example, a court may order reinstatement of a union member expelled after a hearing in which it was determined that the member had engaged in "fraudulent activities," where it did not appear that the member had been accorded a "full and fair hearing."

2) **Federal courts and judicial review--International Brotherhood of Boilermakers v. Hardeman,** 401 U.S. 233 (1971).

a) **Facts.** Two employees (Ps) engaged in an altercation with their union business agent. They were tried and found guilty of violating the union's constitution and the local's by-laws. They were then expelled from the union (D). Ps brought suit alleging that they had been denied a full and fair hearing. The trial court awarded damages after determining that D had used the wrong standard to evaluate the conduct, and the court of appeals affirmed. D appeals.

b) **Issues.**

(1) Do federal courts have jurisdiction to review union decisions involving breaches of the union constitution?

(2) Should federal courts adopt a different standard of review than that used by the union tribunal?

c) **Held.** (1) Yes. (2) No. Judgment reversed.

(1) The suit is not preempted by the jurisdiction of the NLRB.

(2) Judicial review of the findings of a union tribunal is *limited* and the courts will *not* "retry" the evidence or substitute their judgment for that of the union tribunal. The only question is whether there was a full and fair hearing.

(3) However, a "full and fair hearing" requires that there be *some* evidence to support the union determination. To this end, a court may examine the record to insure that the union findings are not totally without basis in the evidence.

(4) Ps were served with specific charges in writing as required by section 101(2)(5)(A) and there was sufficient evidence to support the charges.

d) **Comment.** Separation of functions is not mandated by union due process, and the Fourth Circuit Court of Appeals has held that a union tribunal may be both prosecutor and judge. A hearing would be inadequate under section 101(a)(5) if the accused member is not allowed to confront and cross-examine witnesses against him. The right to be represented by counsel is not essential to a fair hearing.

3) **Dues, initiation fees, and assessments.** Section 101(a)(3) provides that assessments or increases in dues or fees must be voted upon by the membership at large.

4) **Protection of the right to sue.** Section 101(a)(4) protects the right of union members to sue and testify against the union or its officers in administrative or judicial proceedings, and to participate in legislative proceedings.

a) **Limitation against employer interference.** The employer is prohibited from encouraging actions against the union that are otherwise protected by the section. However, precluding a right-to-work group from financing suits against unions because the group is funded by contributions from interested employers has been held an unconstitutional infringement upon the group's First Amendment rights.

5) **Due process safeguards against improper disciplinary actions.** The Landrum-Griffin Act guarantees union members certain basic rights of due process in union disciplinary hearings (section 101(a)(5)). Except for nonpayment of dues, no member of any labor organization may be fined, suspended, expelled, or otherwise disciplined unless such member has been:

a) Served with specific charges in writing;

b) Given a reasonable time to prepare a defense; and

c) Afforded a full and fair hearing.

6) **The common law and disciplinary actions--Mitchell v. International Association of Machinists,** 196 Cal. App. 2d 796 (1961).

Mitchell v. International Association of Machinists

a) **Facts.** This is a suit for reinstatement into a union. Mitchell (P) and another were expelled from the International Association of Machinists (D) for openly supporting, in speeches and television appearances, Proposition 18 (a "right-to-work" law). The measure was defeated and P was expelled from the union for "conduct unbecoming a member." P's writ of mandate was denied, and P appeals.

b) **Issue.** May a union member be disciplined by a union for openly supporting a political cause to which the union is opposed if the political cause is not patently in conflict with the union's best interests?

c) **Held.** No. Judgment reversed.

(1) A trade union is not, in reality, a strictly voluntary organization. The union has been given great power. Whether a union can discipline a member for engaging in a political activity depends on: (i) the interest of the community and the individual in the individual's union membership; (ii) the importance to the community of the individual's right to express himself on political issues; (iii) the interest of the union in excluding obnoxious members; (iv) the interest of the union in speaking with one voice; and (v) the nature of the political activity and the manner of its conduct.

(2) Applying the above test to the facts in this case yield the following conclusions:

(a) The individual has a financial stake in the strike fund, and perhaps a pension fund, and she loses the right to participate in the union's "government" upon expulsion.

(b) Full and free exercise of the individual's right to speak on the conduct of government is not only his right—it is his duty.

(c) Unions are not composed of like-thinking individuals. Only when dissident views have a possibility of acceptance do the individuals become "undesirable." In this instance, discipline serves only to intimidate those who remain.

(d) Where the union's activity is directly designed to attain economic goals (*e.g.*, decisions to strike, etc.), the courts' solicitude has been demonstrated. However, where, as here, the individual member purports only to represent himself, not his union, the union's public position is not diluted.

(e) One can believe in right-to-work laws and remain a good trade unionist. The issue here is not whether the union is justified in its opinion, but whether the point is sufficiently debatable so that society's interest in the debate, together with the individual's right to free speech, outweighs the union's interest. On that point there can be no doubt—P's rights here are more important than the union's.

7) **Exhaustion of internal remedies required.** Section 101(a)(4) provides that before he may institute any judicial or administrative action against the union, a

union member has to exhaust the union's internal hearing procedures, if he can do so within four months.

a) **Common law exceptions.** The "exhaustion of remedies" rule, however, is subject to numerous common law exceptions. Thus, actions by union members against the union will not be dismissed, even though union internal procedures have not been complied with, under the following circumstances: (i) where no adequate union remedy exists; (ii) where union procedures or bias among union officials preclude a fair hearing or appeal; (iii) where the appellate procedures within the union are "unreasonably burdensome"; *or* (iv) where the injury to the employee is either irreparable or difficult to calculate, and immediate action is therefore required.

b) **"May" rather than "must" exhaust.** Section 101(a)(4) has been interpreted to mean only that union members "may" (as opposed to "must") be required to exhaust internal union remedies.

c) **Exhausting internal remedies--Falsetti v. Local Union No. 2026, United Mine Workers,** 161 A.2d 882 (Pa. 1960).

   (1) **Facts.** Falsetti (P) filed a bill in equity seeking restoration of his membership in the United Mine Workers (D) and reinstatement in his employment (from which he had been discharged). P alleged that D and his employer had unlawfully conspired against him and that as a result, he was fired from his job and kicked out of D. D contended that P had not exhausted the internal remedies and that hence his suit was not ripe for adjudication by the courts. P contended that he had exhausted his remedies and that, even if he had not, such an attempt would be useless. The lower court dismissed the bill, and P appeals.

   (2) **Issue.** Must a member, having a claim against a union, exhaust his internal union remedies before bringing a court action against the union?

   (3) **Held.** Yes. Judgment affirmed.

      (a) There is an overriding public interest in promoting well managed autonomous associations which are able to perform their functions effectively and still provide for the fair treatment of individual members who must be disciplined. For this reason, we adopt the exhaustion rule. The justifications of this rule are: (i) it benefits the union by preventing its "dirty linen" from being washed in public; (ii) it also benefits the majority of association members for the same reason; (iii) courts would not be burdened by premature suits; and (iv) the union appeal is less expensive than a lawsuit for all parties.

      (b) This rule should not, however, ignore the rights and interests of an occasional member who, with good cause, does not follow the union's internal procedure. For example, the rule should not be followed where: (i) the associational appeals cannot, in fact, yield remedies; (ii) union officials have by their own action precluded the member from having a fair or effective trial or appeal (*e.g.*, obvious bias against the member); (iii) the appellate procedure would be unreasonably burdensome (*e.g.*, the appellate board will not meet for several years); or (iv) the exhaustion of remedies rule would subject the member to an injury that is, in a practical sense, irreparable.

(c) Here, P has not sought help beyond the local level and his allegation of futility is not supported by evidence. P has not shown that the intra-union remedy is not effective. Thus, the lower court is affirmed.

d) **The federal courts and exhaustion--Kowaleviocz v. Local 333, International Longshoremen's Association,** 942 F.2d 285 (4th Cir. 1991).

(1) **Facts.** Kowaleviocz (P), a local union member, had a long-running dispute with the officer of the local union (D) over a dues increase. The two had numerous verbal exchanges at union meetings. Finally, in December 1984, the officer moved and the membership approved that P be fined $100 and be suspended from all union rights and privileges, except work, for 10 years. P appealed this action and the District Council of the union overturned the punishment as being too harsh. In January, the officer filed charges against P for using profanity. This charge was dismissed. In August, the officer appealed this dismissal to a meeting of the general membership. P attended the meeting, but had no notice that the appeal had been made. Over his objections, the meeting reversed the dismissal but made no decision as to penalty. In September, P was notified that he had been fined $100 and suspended for 10 years. P then appealed the action within 30 days of notice of the penalty, but it was rejected as untimely. P then filed this action in federal district court. The district court granted summary judgment against P for failure to exhaust internal union remedies and held that the failure was not excused by union illegal action or protection of P's speech rights. P appeals.

(2) **Issue.** Were D's actions in disciplining P so illegal or void as to excuse the exhaustion of internal union remedies?

(3) **Held.** Yes. Judgment reversed.

(a) P's appeal is brought under Subchapter II of the LMRDA, the members' "Bill of Rights," which was designed to protect union members' rights to freely discuss and criticize union management and officers. It does so by assuring procedural due process. Section 411(a)(4) requires exhaustion of reasonable internal union hearing procedures before bringing an action in federal court.

(b) Exhaustion is not mandatory, and the decision to require exhaustion is a matter for the courts. If the court finds that the disciplinary action is "indisputably illegal or void," exhaustion may be excused. An action will be void if no notice was given, if the tribunal is biased, if the offense is not included in the union constitution, where there are other substantial jurisdictional defects, or where there is lack of fundamental fairness.

(c) Here, the union's constitution requires that appeals must be in writing, state the facts and grounds for appeal, and be filed with the secretary. The union officers' appeal was certainly in violation of these requirements. The district court was wrong not to determine that this was "indisputably illegal" conduct by the union.

    (d) The district court was also wrong not to determine that P's speech rights were involved. Regardless of personal animosity, it is clear that P had a history of opposing certain official actions that had been taken. Disciplinary action taken to inhibit criticism of local leadership is a serious violation of a union member's rights under the statute. The union action was void, and P's need to exhaust was excused.

(4) Comment. The exhaustion of internal remedies doctrine has been dispensed with where union disciplinary action was "void" since it was based on an offense not specified in the union constitution. [Simmons v. Textile Workers Local 713, 350 F.2d 1012 (4th Cir. 1965)]

H. ELECTION OF UNION OFFICERS

1. Common Law Background.

    a. **Refusal to hear complaints.** Most courts at common law refused to hear complaints about the election of union officers for several reasons.

        1) Unions were regarded as private, voluntary associations whose election procedures were left to private ordering.

        2) Former procedures in equity limited actions to the protection of "property rights", and the courts found no "property" rights in union elections.

        3) There was no basis for measuring damage to union members.

        4) If the complaint was made after an election had been conducted, the courts were ill-equipped to provide the remedy—a new election—because: (i) they lacked poll watchers, counters, and similar officials (some courts, however, appointed a "master" to oversee an election (*see infra*)); (ii) a new election involved appointing new election officials subject to the same pressures and prejudices as the old union officials; and (iii) the details of union election procedures were considered overwhelming.

    b. **Limited jurisdiction.** Some courts *did* assume jurisdiction of complaints involving union elections. Relief, however, was usually confined to the following situations:

        1) Where the complaint alleged that the union had failed to follow its own constitution or by-laws in nominating or voting for officials;

2) Where those provisions were "contrary to public policy"; or

3) Where judicial intervention could be effective (for example, before the election took place).

2. **Landrum-Griffin, Title IV.** It became clear that federal legislation was needed to guarantee fair union elections. Federal law had given union officials very broad powers and discretion to negotiate conditions of employment and to process grievances. To insure that such officials would be responsive to their constituents, Congress set out minimum requirements for conducting free and democratic union elections.

   a. **Rights of union members under Title IV.** Landrum-Griffin provides the following rules and procedures for nominating and electing union officials:

   1) **Voting.** All members in good standing are allowed to vote, and each member has the right to one vote. [§401(e)]

   2) **Frequency of elections.** Local officers must be elected at least every three years; international officers every five years. [§§401(a), (b)]

   3) **Secret ballot.** Union officers must be elected by secret ballot. [§401(e)]

   4) **Nomination.** Reasonable opportunity must be given for the nomination of candidates. [§401(e)]

   5) **Eligibility for candidacy.** Every member in good standing is eligible to be a candidate, subject to "reasonable qualifications uniformly imposed." [§401(e)]

   6) **Notice of election.** Members must be notified of the election at least 15 days prior to the election. [§401(e)]

   7) **Dissemination of campaign literature.** If campaign literature is distributed by the union, it must be done at the expense of the candidates and without discrimination between or among candidates. [§401(c)]

   8) **Membership lists.** A union whose contract requires membership in the union as a condition of employment is required to maintain membership lists and to make such lists available for inspection by bona fide candidates. [§401(c)]

   9) **Observers at the polls.** "Adequate safeguards" must be provided for the election itself, including the right of any candidate to have observers at the polls and at the counting of ballots.

   10) **Election expenses.** Candidates may not use union funds to finance their campaigns, but nondiscriminatory use of such money (as in nonpartisan statements of issues) is permitted. [§401(g)]

   11) **Compliance with union constitution and by-laws.** The union must comply with its own constitution and by-laws respecting election

requirements, provided that the latter are not inconsistent with the provisions of Title IV. [§403]

b. **Enforcement provisions.** Title IV of the Landrum-Griffin Act confers upon the Secretary of Labor and the courts the power to protect the right of union members in connection with union elections.

   1) **No preelection remedy.** The Landrum-Griffin Act provides that the Secretary of Labor has exclusive authority to institute proceedings to enforce the provisions of Title IV, but this authority commences after the election has been conducted. Thus, even though some union rule or act clearly violates the election provisions of the 1959 Act, the Secretary of Labor cannot intervene until the election and exhaustion have taken place.

c. **District court jurisdiction--Calhoon v. Harvey,** 379 U.S. 134 (1964).

   1) **Facts.** Three members (Ps) of the National Marine Engineers Benefit Association District No. 1 (D) filed an action in federal district court alleging a violation of LMRDA section 101(a)(1), Title I. The complaint was that the union's by-laws allowed a member only to nominate himself for a union office, while the national allows only members with five years' tenure who had spent a certain amount of time at sea in specified vessels during the preceding three years. The district court dismissed, holding that even if true, the facts did not constitute a violation of section 101; although a violation of section 401(e) of Title IV might have been found, the court would not have jurisdiction. The court of appeals reversed, holding that the facts did constitute a section 101 violation. The union appeals.

   2) **Issue.** Can a district court, under section 102, exercise jurisdiction over an action which is in substance a violation of Title IV?

   3) **Held.** No. Judgment reversed.

      a) Section 101 protects union members from discrimination against individual rights to nominate or vote for anyone in disregard of union rules.

      b) Title IV deals with eligibility standards for union elections, and suits involving such violations must follow the mandatory procedure of section 403.

   4) **Concurrence** (Stewart, Harlan, JJ.). This ruling might allow unions to hide discrimination under eligibility standards.

   5) **Comment.** The purpose is to prevent individuals from blocking union elections. Thus, not even a violation of Title IV itself can be used as the basis for suit (under Title I of the Act) to obtain preelection judicial review.

d. **Requirement of reasonable qualifications--Local 3489, United Steelworkers of America v. Usery,** 429 U.S. 305 (1977).

1) **Facts.** United Steelworkers of America's (D's) International Constitution, applicable to local elections, required that to be eligible for local office, a member must have attended at least one-half of the regular meetings of the local for the past three years. The Secretary of Labor (P) brought an LMRDA action under section 402(b) to invalidate the requirement. The district court dismissed, and the court of appeals reversed.

2) **Issue.** Is an attendance rule that renders a substantial number of members in a local ineligible for office invalid under section 402(b) of the LMRDA?

3) **Held.** Yes. Judgment affirmed.

   a) Application of the rule in this case renders 96% of the members ineligible for holding office. The Act does not prohibit the imposition of "reasonable" qualifications, but a rule that "substantially deplete[s] the ranks of those who might run in opposition to incumbents" can hardly be reasonable.

   b) Even though a member has personal control over the criterion for eligibility, it is still too restrictive because it impairs the general membership's freedom to oust incumbents by requiring that a member must decide 18 months in advance of the election.

   c) It is not necessary for the Secretary to show that the rule has had the effect of entrenching the incumbent faction. As an attendance device it is a failure, and that objective fails to make the requirement a reasonable one.

4) **Dissent** (Powell, Stewart, Rehnquist, JJ.). The members have it within their control to qualify themselves and have chosen not to. The majority has come near to adopting a per se "effects" rule.

e. **Mootness.** In *Wirtz v. Local 153, Glass Bottle Blowers Association*, 389 U.S. 463 (1968), the Court refused to declare a case moot because the election in issue had been succeeded by a new election pending the appeal. The Act is not designed to protect the right to run for a particular office at a particular election; the public interest "transcends" such a narrow interest.

f. **Procedure.** In order to contest an election, a member must file a complaint with the Secretary of Labor.

   1) **Finding of "probable cause" as prerequisite to lawsuit.** If, upon investigating the member's complaint, the Secretary of Labor finds "probable cause" to believe that the Act has been violated, he or she must bring suit in federal court within 60 days of filing of the complaint to set aside the election. [§402(b)]

      a) **Statement of reasons for not suing.** Where the Secretary decides not to bring suit to set aside the election, a defeated candidate may seek judicial review of the decision. The Secretary must provide a statement of reasons for not suing, which are subject to review on a "not arbitrary or capricious" standard. [Dunlop v. Backowski, 421 U.S. 560 (1975)]

2) **New elections.** The federal court will determine whether the Act has been violated (*see* below), and if it finds a violation, it will order that new elections be held. The Secretary of Labor is empowered to supervise the new election and to certify to the court the names of the winners. [§402 (b)]

3) **Judicial power to invalidate elections—the "nexus" requirement.** In any suit filed by the Secretary of Labor to set aside a union election, the federal court may declare the election void and order a new election only upon a finding based on a "preponderance of the evidence" that (i) some provision of section 401 has been violated and (ii) the violation "may have affected the outcome of the election." [§402(c)(1), (2)]

   a) **Effect.** It is not enough merely to show irregularity and the outcome.

   b) **Burden of proof.** Proximate cause may be difficult to establish, since any contentions as to the factor which did or did not affect the outcome of the election are necessarily speculative. Recognizing this, the Supreme Court has held that the Secretary of Labor need establish only a "reasonable possibility" that the violation affected the outcome of the election. This is sufficient to demonstrate a prima facie case under Title IV. The burden of going forward with the evidence then shifts to the union, which must establish that the illegal act or conduct did not affect the outcome. [Wirtz v. Hotel, Motel & Club Employees' Union, Local 6, 391 U.S. 492 (1968)]

g. **External financial support--United Steelworkers of America v. Sadlowski, 457 U.S. 102 (1982).** *United Steelworkers of America v. Sadlowski*

   1) **Facts.** United Steelworkers of America (D) amended its constitution to prohibit certain candidates for union office from receiving financial assistance from nonmembers. Sadlowski (P), who had received such assistance, brought suit to invalidate this provision. The district court, finding the rule invalid, granted summary judgment for P, and the court of appeals affirmed. The case was taken to the Supreme Court.

   2) **Issue.** Is a union rule that prohibits candidates for union office from receiving contributions from persons who are not members of the union invalid under the LMRDA?

   3) **Held.** No. Judgment reversed and case remanded.

      a) Section 101(a)(2) of the LMRDA does not incorporate the entire body of First Amendment law. Under the statute, a restrictive union rule will be valid if it is reasonable.

      b) The union's outsider rule may have some impact on the interests protected by section 101(a)(2), but as a practical matter the impact may not be substantial and the rule does not prohibit outsider solicitation for other purposes, such as litigation.

      c) The outsider rule serves to avoid undue influence upon union affairs by nonmembers, a purpose clearly contemplated by the Act.

4) **Dissent** (White, Brennan, Blackmun, JJ., Burger, C.J.). In asserting their right to run for office in a large union, union members may need access to outside financial assistance in order to overcome the built-in advantage that incumbent leadership enjoys.

I. CORRUPTION IN UNIONS—LANDRUM-GRIFFIN TITLES II, III, AND V

1. **Title II of the Landrum-Griffin Act—Reporting and Disclosure Provisions.** LMRDA Title II is based on the assumption that availability of information concerning union activities, coupled with democratic procedures within the union (Titles I and IV, *supra*), will be an effective means of controlling corruption. The significant provisions of Title II are:

   a. **Basic union information.** Sections 201(a)-(c) require that the union disclose certain basic information (*e.g.*, names of officers, various procedures, fiscal condition) and that all such information be available to members. The Secretary of Labor is authorized, in the case of smaller unions, to reduce and simplify the amount of paperwork that the Act requires.

   b. **Financial transactions by officials.** Union officers and union employees are required to disclose financial transactions with the employer or any associated business. [§202(a)]

   c. **Reporting by employers.** Employers are required to report certain expenditures to, or agreements with, union officials, union employees, or managerial employees. [§203]

   d. **Criminal penalties and civil remedies.** Willful violation of the reporting provisions of Title II is punishable by a fine of up to $10,000 or imprisonment for not more than one year. [§209] Section 210 authorizes the Secretary of Labor to initiate civil actions, and section 601 gives her the right to inspect union records and to question such persons as deemed necessary in order to determine whether possible violations of Title II have occurred.

2. **Limitations on Union Officials—Title V.** Title V, entitled "Safeguards for Labor Organizations," is intended to aid union members in ridding their organizations of corrupt union officials. It does so, in conformity with common law practice, by placing union officers, agents, shop stewards, and other union representatives and employees in a trustee relationship vis-a-vis the union and its members (*i.e.*, by imposing fiduciary duties on union officers). Title V does not spell out such duties in detail, but leaves the task of formulating substantive law on this subject to the courts.

   Highway Truck Drivers & Helpers Local 107 v. Cohen

   a. **Defraying legal costs of officers--Highway Truck Drivers & Helpers Local 107 v. Cohen,** 182 F. Supp. 608 (E.D. Pa. 1960), *aff'd*, 284 F.2d 162 (3d Cir. 1960).

   1) **Facts.** Section 501(a) of the LMRDA, which charges union officials with a federal duty to uphold their fiduciary duties to their union members and disallows exculpatory union provi-

sions, took effect on September 14, 1959. On September 30, 1959, nine members of a Teamsters local (Ps) filed against their officers (Ds) under the new law, accusing them of conspiracy and fraud from 1954 on. Simultaneously, a criminal action was brought against Ds. Members of the local voted to cover Ds' expenses in the civil and criminal suits. Ds argued that the law was prospective only and sought dismissal. Ps asked for an injunction against the use of any union funds for Ds' legal expenses.

2) **Issue.** May a union pass a resolution to defray the legal costs of their officers in criminal and civil cases alleging fraud against the union?

3) **Held.** No.

   a) Section 501(a) is not retroactive. However, union funds may not be used to defend officers accused of fraud. Neither the union constitution nor its ancillary powers can lend validity to a resolution to reimburse union officers for a suit against them for fraud against the union.

4) **Comment.** A union official accused of wrongdoing may not resort to the protective resources of the union to defend himself, even if it will not involve out-of-pocket expenses to the union. Use of such resources might be approved by a court upon a showing of likelihood of success and if there is no conflict with the union. The union, however, may reimburse the official for trial expenses if exonerated.

3. **Disclosure of Information.** The LMRDA requires the filing of certain information with the Secretary of Labor. Included is information about the organization, membership requirements, selection of officers, assets and liabilities, emoluments received by officers, loans to officers, and other loans and disbursements. The information must also be made available to members. Officers and certain employees must also file information with the Secretary. Employers must also file information about certain expenditures.

4. **"Trusteeships"—Landrum-Griffin, Title III.** The term "trusteeship", as used in the Landrum-Griffin Act, is defined as "a method of supervision or control whereby a labor organization suspends the autonomy otherwise available to a subordinate body under its constitution or by-laws."

   a. **Background.** Before the passage of the Landrum-Griffin Act in 1959, trusteeships had been praised as an effective means of preserving the integrity and stability of labor organizations by empowering officers of the international union to govern local unions in which serious misconduct was found. However, trusteeships were frequently used by union officials as a means of plundering the treasuries of local unions, perpetuating their own power, and preserving the power of international officers by removing "unfriendly" people at the local level and controlling the selection of delegates to international conventions. Congress therefore incorporated Title III into the Landrum-Griffin Act to regulate the means for imposing and maintaining trusteeships.

b. **Requirements for trusteeships.** Title III, section 302 of the Landrum-Griffin Act provides that trusteeships may be established and administered only in accordance with the constitution and by-laws of the labor organization imposing the trusteeship, and then only if the aim is:

1) To correct corruption;

2) To prevent misappropriation of assets;

3) To assure performance of the union's contractual and bargaining representative duties;

4) To restore democratic procedures; and/or

5) To carry out "the legitimate objects of [the] labor organization."

TABLE OF CASES

(Page numbers of briefed cases in bold)

A-1 King Size Sandwiches, Inc., NLRB v. - **74**
Abraham Grossman d/b/a Bruckner Nursing Home - **42**
Acme Industrial Co., NLRB v. - 75, 150
Adkins Transfer Co., NLRB v. - **46**
Air Line Pilots Association, International v. O'Neil - **185**
Air Master Corp., NLRB v. - 43
Alba-Waldensian, Inc. - 73
Alexander v. Gardner-Denver Co. - 152, 156
Allen Bradley Co. v. Local Union No. 3, IBEW - 165, 166
Allied Chemical & Alkali Workers v. Pittsburgh Plate Glass Co. - 79, 81, **86**
Allis-Chalmers Manufacturing Co. - **133**
Allis-Chalmers Manufacturing Co., NLRB v. - **197**, 199, 200
Allis-Chalmers v. Lueck - 176, 178, 179
Amalgamated Association of Street, Electric Railway & Motor Coach Employees v. Lockridge - 170
Amalgamated Food Employees Union Local 590 v. Logan Valley Plaza, Inc. - 106
American Federation of Musicians v. Carroll - 168
American Hospital Association v. NLRB - **57**
American National Insurance Co., NLRB v. - **80**
American Newspaper Publishers Association v. NLRB - 126
American Seating Co. - 54
American Shipbuilding Co. v. NLRB - **97**
Apex Hosiery Co. v. Leader - **9**, 165
Atkinson v. Sinclair Refining Co. - 148
Automotive Technologies - 24
Avco Corp. v. Lodge 735 IAM - 147

Babcock & Wilcox Co. v. NLRB - 26, 27, 28, 106
Barrentine v. Arkansas-Best Freight System, Inc. - 152
Bartenders Association - 65

Beasley v. Food Fair of North Carolina, Inc. - 180
Belknap, Inc. v. Hale - **177**
Bell Aerospace Co., NLRB v. - 29
Best Products, NLRB v. - 33
Beth Israel Hospital v. NLRB - 25
Bildisco & Bildisco, NLRB v. - 160
Bill Johnson's Restaurants, Inc. v. NLRB - 179
Blue Flash Express, Inc. - 35
Boeing Co., NLRB v. - 198, 199
Boire v. Greyhound Corp. - 61
Charles D. Bonanno Linen Service, Inc. v. NLRB - **58**
Bowen v. United States Postal Service - 189
Boys Markets, Inc. v. Retail Clerks Union, Local 770 - **147**, 148, 150
Breininger v. Sheet Metal Workers, Local 6 - 189
Brooks v. NLRB - **64**
Brotherhood of Railroad Trainmen v. Howard - 72, 183
Brown v. Hotel & Restaurant Employees, International Union Local 54 - **174**
Brown v. Pro Football, Inc. - 167
Buffalo Forge Co. v. United Steelworkers of America - 148
Burlington Northern Railroad Co. v. Brotherhood of Maintenance of Way Employees - **11**
Burnip & Simms, NLRB v. - 46
Burns International Security Services, Inc., NLRB v. - 144, 164

C. & C. Plywood Co., NLRB v. - 150
C.S. Smith Metropolitan Market Co. v. Lyons - 108
Calhoon v. Harvey - **211**
California Saw & Knife Works - 195
Carbide & Carbon Chemicals Co. - 134
Carey v. Westinghouse Electric Corp. - 149, 154
Chamber of Commerce of the United States v. Reich - **96**
Charles D. Bonanno Linen Service,

Labor Law - 217

Inc. v. NLRB - **58**
Chevron U.S.A., Inc. v. Natural Resources Defense Council - 155
Chicago Health & Tennis Clubs, Inc., NLRB v. - **55**
City Disposal Systems, Inc., NLRB v. - **91**
Clayton v. International Union, United Automobile Workers - 190
Collyer Insulated Wire - 92, 153, 154
Communications Workers v. Beck - 194
Complete Auto Transit, Inc. v. Reis - 148
Conley v. Gibson - 183
Connell Construction Co. v. Plumbers & Steamfitters Local Union No. 100 - **167**
Coronado Coal Co. v. United Mine Workers - 5
Cumberland Shoe Corp. - 63
Curtin Matheson Scientific, Inc., NLRB v. - **66**

Dal-Tex Optical Co. - 29
Debs, United States v. - 4
Deena Artware, Inc., NLRB v. - 127
Deklewa v. IABW - 41
DelCostello v. International Brotherhood of Teamsters - 184
Denver Building & Construction Trades Council, NLRB v. - **114**
Detroit Edison Co. v. NLRB - **75**
Diamond Shamrock Co. v. NLRB - 24
Dorchy v. Kansas - 102
Douds v. Metropolitan Federation of Architects - **116**
Dubo Manufacturing Co. - 150
Dunlop v. Backowski - 212
Duplex Printing Press Co. v. Deering - **6**, 12, 121

Eastex, Inc. v. NLRB - **92**
Edward G. Budd Manufacturing Co. v. NLRB - **44**
Edward J. DeBartolo Corp. v. Florida Gulf Coast Building & Construction Trades Council - **104**, 118
Electromation, Inc. - **38**
Elk Lumber Co. - 96
Ellis v. Brotherhood of Railway, Airline & S.S. Clerks - 194
Emporium Capwell Co. v. Western Addition Community Organization - **70**
Enmons, United States v. - 108

Enterprise Association of Steam & General Pipefitters, Local No. 638 (Austin Co.) - 122
Erie Resistor Corp., NLRB v. - **96**
Ex-Cell-O Corp. - **89**
Excelsior Underwear Inc. - **28**, 27
Exchange Parts Co., NLRB v. - **36**

Fall River Dyeing & Finishing Corp. v. NLRB - **162**
Falsetti v. Local Union No. 2026, United Mine Workers - **207**
Farmer v. United Brotherhood of Carpenters & Joiners, Local 25 - **171**
Fiberboard Paper Products Corp. v. NLRB - **82**, 83, 85
Finnegan v. Leu - **201**, 202
First National Maintenance Corp. v. NLRB - **83**, 84, 85
Fleetwood Trailer Co., NLRB v. - 100
Florida Power & Light Co. v. Electrical Workers - 201
Ford Motor Co. v. Huffman - 183
Fort Halifax Packing Co. v. Coyne - 176
Fruit & Vegetable Packers & Warehousemen, Local 760, NLRB v. (Tree Fruits) - **118**, 120, 121

GTE Lenkurt, Inc. - 23, 24
Gamble Enterprises, Inc., NLRB v. - **126**
Gateway Coal v. United Mine Workers - 141
General American Transportation Corp. - 154
General Electric Co. v. NLRB - **59**
General Electric Co., NLRB v. - 111, 118
General Knit of California, Inc. - 32, 37
General Motors Corp., NLRB v. - **192**, 193
General Shoe Corp. - 29
General Stencils, Inc., NLRB v. - 63
Gissel Packing Co., NLRB v. - **30**, 31, 51, 52, **62**
Golden State Bottling Co., NLRB v. - 163
Golub Corp., NLRB v. - 30
Gourmet Foods, Inc. v. Warehouse Employees of St. Paul - 63
Granite State Joint Board, Textile Workers Local 1029, NLRB v. - 200
Graves v. Ring Screw Works - 139
Great Dane Trailers, Inc., NLRB v. - **98**

H.K. Porter Co. v. NLRB - **88**
Hammontree v. NLRB - **155**
Hanna Mining Co. v. District 2, Marine Engineers Beneficial Association - 180
Herman Wilson Lumber Co., NLRB v. - 30
Hershey Foods Corp., NLRB v. - 193
Hertzka & Knowles v. NLRB - 39
Highway Truck Drivers & Helpers Local 107 v. Cohen - **214**
Hod Carriers Local 840 (Blinne Construction Co.) - **109**
Hollywood Ceramics Co. - 32
Howard Johnson Co. v. Detroit Local Joint Executive Board - 144, **163**
Hudgens v. NLRB - **105**
Humphrey v. Moore - 187
Hutcheson, United States v. - **10**, 165

IBEW v. Foust - 183
IBEW, Local 340, NLRB v. (Royal Electric) - 201
ILA v. Allied International Inc. - 111
ILGWU v. Quality Manufacturing Co. - 92
Independent Metal Workers, Local 1 (Hughes Tool Co.) - 184
Insurance Agents' International Union, NLRB v. - **76**
Interborough Contractors, Inc. - 92
International Association of Machinists v. Street - **193**
International Brotherhood of Boilermakers v. Hardeman - **204**
International Brotherhood of Teamsters, Local 695 v. Vogt, Inc. - **104**, 108
International Harvester Co. - 151
International Ladies' Garment Workers v. NLRB (Bernhard-Altmann Texas Corp.) - **40**
International Longshoremen's & Warehousemen's Union, Local No. 50 - 125
International Rice Milling Co., NLRB v. - 112, 114

J.I. Case Co. v. NLRB - **68**
J.J. Newberry Co. - 31
J.P. Stevens & Co. v. NLRB - 49, 51
J. Weingarten, Inc., NLRB v. - 92, 187
Jacobs Manufacturing Co. - **157**
Jean Country - 26, 107
John Wiley & Sons v. Livingston - 142, 144, 161, 164

Johnson-Bateman Co. - **158**
Jones & Laughlin Steel Corp., NLRB v. - 15

K & K Construction Co. v. NLRB - 120
Katz, NLRB v. - **77**, 142
Kowaleviocz c Local 333, International Longshoremen's Association - **208**

L.G. Everist, Inc., NLRB v. - 112
Laidlaw Corp. v. NLRB - **94**, **99**, 100
Land Air Delivery, Inc. v. NLRB - **87**
Lechmere, Inc. v. NLRB - **26**, 107
Leedom v. Kyne - **61**
Lenkurt Electric, NLRB v. - 31
Linden Lumber Division, Summer & Co. v. NLRB - 52, **64**
Lingle v. Norge Division of Magic Chef, Inc. - **178**, 179
Litton Financial Printing Division v. NLRB - **142**
Lividas v. Bradshaw - 179
Livingston Shirt Co. - 27
Local 3, International Brotherhood of Electrical Workers, NLRB v. - **110**
Local 12, United Rubber Workers v. NLRB - 184
Local 24, International Teamsters v. Oliver - **175**
Local 57 Ladies Garment Workers v. NLRB (Garwin Corp.) - 51
Local 174, Teamsters v. Lucas Flour Co. - 138
Local Union No. 189, Amalgamated Meat Cutters v. Jewel Tea Co. - **166**, 167
Local 357, International Brotherhood of Teamsters v. NLRB - **195**
Local 761, International Union of Electrical, Radio & Machine Workers v. NLRB (General Electric Co.) - 111, **117**
Local 900, International Union of Electrical Workers v. NLRB (Gulton Electro-Voice, Inc.) - **196**
Local 1229, IBEW, NLRB v. (Jefferson Standard Broadcasting Co.) - **95**
Local 1976, United Brotherhood of Carpenters & Joiners v. NLRB (Sand Door) - 121
Local 3489, United Steelworkers of America v. Usery - **211**
Local Joint Executive Board of Hotel Employees - 110
Lodge 76, International Association of

Labor Law - 219

Machinists v. Wisconsin Employment Relations Commission - **173**, 177, 178
Loewe v. Lawlor - **5**, 9
Logan Valley - 101
Lorben Corp., NLRB v. - **33**

Mace Food Stores, Inc. - 41
Machinists Local 1743 (J.A. Jones Construction Co.) - 125
Mackay Radio & Telegraph Co., NLRB v. - 94, **96**
Magnavox Co., NLRB v. - 25
Magnesium Casting v. NLRB - 60
Mallinckrodt, Inc. - **131**
Malone v. White Motor Corp. - 175
Marine Engineers Beneficial Association v. Interlake S.S. Co. - 180
Markwell & Hartz, Inc. v. NLRB - 118
Marsh v. Alabama - 106
Meat & Highway Drivers, Local Union No. 710 v. NLRB - **122**
Metropolitan Edison Co. v. NLRB - **100**
Metropolitan Life Insurance Co. v. Commonwealth of Massachusetts - **175**, 176
Midland National Life Insurance Co. v. Local 304A, United Food & Commercial Workers - **32**
Midwest Piping - 42
Milwaukee Spring Division of Illinois Coil Spring Co. - **159**
Miranda Fuel Co., NLRB v. - 184
Mitchell v. International Association of Machinists - **205**
Mueller Brass Co. v. NLRB - **45**

NLRB v. ___ (see opposing party)
National Radio Co. - 154
National Woodwork Manufacturer's Association v. NLRB - **121**
New York Telephone Co. v. New York Department of Labor - **176**
Nolde Brothers, Inc. v. Bakery Workers - 142, 143

Olin Corp. - **151**, 152
Operating Engineers, Local 49 v. NLRB (Struksnes Construction Co.) - **34**
Operating Engineers Local 150 v. Flair Builders, Inc. - 141
Order of Railroad Telegraphers v. Chicago & Northwestern Railway - 83
Order of Railroad Telegraphers v. Railway Express Agency - 68

Otis Elevator Co. (United Technologies) - 84

Parker-Robb Chevrolet, Inc. - 49
Pattern Makers' League of North America v. NLRB - **200**
Peerless Plywood - 27
Phelps Dodge Corp. v. NLRB - 43, **49**
Phillips Petroleum Co. - **134**
Pittsburgh S.S. Co. v. NLRB - 30
Plant v. Woods - **4**
Plasterers' Local Union No. 79, NLRB v. - 125
Plumbers & Pipefitters Local 520 v. NLRB (C-Catalytic, Inc.) - 152
Post Publishing Co., NLRB v. - 41
Pure Oil Co. - **134**

Radio & Television Broadcast Engineers Union, Local 1212, NLRB v. (CBS) - **124**
Radio Officers Union AFL v. NLRB - 193
Railway Employees Department v. Hanson - 194
Raytheon Co. - 151
Republic Aviation Corp. v. NLRB - **24**, 93
Republic Steel Corp. v. Maddox - 137
Retail Store Employees Union, Local 1001, NLRB v. (Safeco Title Insurance Co.) - 120, 121
Roy Robinson, Inc. - 154

Sailors' Union of the Pacific (Moore Dry Dock Co.) - **115**, 117, 118
Salzhandler v. Caputo - **203**
San Diego Building Trades Council v. Garmon - **169**, 173, 178, 180
San Francisco-Oakland Mailers' Union 18 - 201
Savair Manufacturing Co., NLRB v. - 37
Scofield v. NLRB - **198**
Sears, Roebuck & Co. v. San Diego County District Council of Carpenters - 173
Sewell Manufacturing Co. - 33
Sheet Metal Workers, International Association v. Lynn - **202**
Shopping Kart Food Market, Inc. - 32, 37
Simmons v. Textile Workers Local 713 - 209
Sinclair Refining Co. v. Atkinson - 146, 147, 148
Singer Co. - 36

Smith v. Evening News Association - 136, 150
Southwestern Porcelain Steel Corp., NLRB v. - 74
Spielberg Manufacturing Co. - 151, 152
Steele v. Louisville & Nashville Railroad Co. - **71**, 183

T.W.A. v. Independent Federation of Flight Attendants - 100
Teamsters v. Morton - 177
Television Broadcasting Studio Employees Local 804, NLRB v. - 196
Textile Workers Union v. Darlington Manufacturing Co. - 30, 31, **48**
Textile Workers Union v. Lincoln Mills of Alabama - **137**
Thornhill v. Alabama - **12**
Transportation Management Corp., NLRB v. - 46
Truck Drivers Local 449, NLRB v. (Buffalo Linen) - 97
Truck Drivers Local 568 v. NLRB (Red Ball Motor Freight Inc.) - 187
Truitt Manufacturing Co., NLRB v. - 75

UAW v. NLRB (General Motors Corp.) - 83
UFCW, Local 150-A v. NLRB (Dubuque Packing Co.) - **84**
United Brick Workers v. Deena Artware, Inc. - 127
United Furniture Workers, NLRB v. - 109
United Mine Workers v. Bagwell - 127
United Mine Workers of America v. Pennington - **165**
United States v. ___ (see opposing party)
United Paperworkers International Union v. Misco, Inc. - **145**
United Steel Workers, NLRB v. (Nutone & Avondale) - 27
United Steelworkers of America v. American Manufacturing Co. - **139**, 141
United Steelworkers of America v. Enterprise Wheel & Car Corp. - 139, **144**
United Steelworkers of America v. Sadlowski - **213**
United Steelworkers of America v. Warrior & Gulf Navigation Co. - 139, **140**
United Technologies Corp. - **154**
Universal Camera Corp. v. NLRB - 43, 45

Vaca v. Sipes - 171, 184, 186, 187, **188**, 190
Vegelahn v. Guntner - **3**
Walker Manufacturing Co. - **131**
Wallace Corp. v. NLRB - 72
Wambles v. International Brotherhood of Teamsters - 203
Westinghouse Electric Corp. - 83
Westinghouse Electric Corp. - 152
Westinghouse Employees v. Westinghouse Electric Co. - 136
Wirtz v. Hotel, Motel & Club Employees' Union, Local 6 - 213
Wirtz v. Local 153, Glass Bottle Blowers Association - 212
Wooster Division of Borg-Warner Corp., NLRB v. - **81**
Wright Line - 46
Wyman-Gordon, NLRB v. - 28

Legalines™

Editorial Advisors:
Gloria A. Aluise
 Attorney at Law
David H. Barber
 Attorney at Law
Robert A. Wyler
 Attorney at Law

Authors:
Gloria A. Aluise
 Attorney at Law
David H. Barber
 Attorney at Law
Daniel O. Bernstine
 Attorney at Law
D. Steven Brewster
 C.P.A.
Roy L. Brooks
 Professor of Law
Frank L. Bruno
 Attorney at Law
Scott M. Burbank
 C.P.A.
Jonathan C. Carlson
 Professor of Law
Charles N. Carnes
 Professor of Law
Paul S. Dempsey
 Professor of Law
Jerome A. Hoffman
 Professor of Law
Mark R. Lee
 Professor of Law
Jonathan Neville
 Attorney at Law
Laurence C. Nolan
 Professor of Law
Arpiar Saunders
 Attorney at Law
Robert A. Wyler
 Attorney at Law

LABOR LAW

Supplement for Thirteenth Edition of Cox Casebook

By Charles N. Carnes
Professor of Law

THE **barbri**® GROUP

A THOMSON COMPANY

EDITORIAL OFFICES: 111 W. Jackson Blvd., 7th Floor, Chicago, IL 60604
REGIONAL OFFICES: Chicago, Dallas, Los Angeles, New York, Washington, D.C.

SERIES EDITOR
Angel M. Murphy, J.D.
Attorney at Law

PRODUCTION MANAGER
Elizabeth G. Duke

FIRST PRINTING—2003

Copyright © 2003 by The BarBri Group. All rights reserved. No part of this publication may be reproduced or transmitted in any form or by any means, electronic or mechanical, including photocopy, recording, or any information storage and retrieval system, without permission in writing from the publisher. Printed in the United States of America.

LEGALINES
LABOR LAW COX
Supplement for Thirteenth Edition of Casebook

Insert the following as **I. B. 2. b. 2) b) (3)** *at p.* **20:**

(3) **Unit professionals as "supervisors."** In *NLRB v. Kentucky River Community Care, Inc.*, 532 U.S. 706 (2001), the Supreme Court rejected the Board's argument that professional nurses are not supervisors when exercising direction over subordinates in connection with their professional capacities (exclusive of authority to hire, fire, reward, etc.). Justice Scalia said, "The problem . . . is not the soundness of . . . [the Board's] labor policy. . . . It is that the policy cannot be given effect through this statutory text." Four dissenters said too broad an interpretation of "supervisor" would nullify the protection of groups of employees that Congress included in the Act and dealt with specifically.

Insert the following as **II. B. 5. b. 3) and 4)** *at p.* **67:**

3) **Proof of "reasonable doubt" about majority support--Allentown Mack Sales & Service, Inc. v. NLRB,** 522 U.S. 359 (1998).

Allentown Mack Sales & Service, Inc. v. NLRB

a) **Facts.** The service and parts employees of Mack Trucks, Inc. were represented by Local 724 of the International Association of Machinists and Aerospace Workers (P). In late December of 1990, Mack Trucks sold the assets of its Allentown branch to its managers, who operated it as an independent dealer, Allentown Mack Sales & Service (D). The new entity hired 32 of the original 45 Mack Truck employees. Before and immediately after the sale, a number of employees made statements suggesting the union had lost support. During job interviews, eight employees indicated they no longer supported the union, and a shop steward told a manager that if an election were held, the union would lose. A night shift worker said the entire night shift of five or six employees did not want the union.

The union requested recognition and the company refused, saying it had a "good faith doubt" about support by the employees. It conducted a secret poll of employees, supervised by a Roman Catholic priest in February. The union lost 19 to 13 and filed an unfair labor practice charge.

The ALJ concluded that D was a "successor employer" and inherited a duty to bargain and there was a presumption of continuing majority support. The ALJ found no procedural problem with the poll, but concluded that the company did not have an "objective reasonable doubt" about the majority status of the union. The Board agreed and ordered the company to bargain with the union. Before the court of appeals, the company challenged the facial rationality of the Board's test and its application to the facts. The court of appeals enforced the Board's order. The Supreme Court granted certiorari.

b) Issues.

(1) Is the Board's standard for employee polling rational and consistent with the Act?

(2) Are the Board's factual determinations supported by substantial evidence?

c) Held. (1) Yes. (2) No. Judgment reversed and case remanded with instructions to deny enforcement.

(1) Courts must defer to requirements imposed by the Board if "rational and consistent with the Act." The company argues it is irrational to require the same factual showing to justify a poll of employees and for an outright withdrawal of recognition. We do not find the unitary standard so irrational as to be "arbitrary [or] capricious" within the Administrative Procedure Act ("APA"). The Board believes polling is potentially disruptive of established bargaining relationships and unsettling to employees. It has chosen to severely limit the conditions for polling—only when the employer might otherwise withdraw recognition. True, polling is made useless for insulating a withdrawal of recognition from an unfair labor practice charge, but an employer may recognize that an abrupt withdrawal of recognition—even of a minority union—will antagonize union supporters and alienate employees on the fence. Even with a good faith doubt, an employer may wish "conclusive proof that the union *in fact* lacked majority support." The Board's avowed preference for an RM election indicates a reason for a more rigorous standard for polling. The consequences of an election are more severe than for a poll. If it is rational to make the standard higher or lower, it surely is not irrational to split the difference.

(2) The Board said the company had not demonstrated it had a "reasonable doubt, based on objective standards." We must decide whether that conclusion is based on substantial evidence, *i.e.*, whether "it would have been possible for a reasonable jury to reach the Board's conclusion." The Board said the word "doubt" may mean "uncertainty" or "disbelief," and used the meaning in the latter sense. We cannot accept this linguistic revisionism. "Doubt" is uncertainty rather than a "belief in the opposite."

(3) Following the ALJ, the Board found that seven out of the 32 employees, roughly 20%, had made statements acceptable as objective considerations and concluded this alone was not sufficient to create an objective reason-

able doubt of majority support. But, there was much more. The ALJ and the Board disregarded the statements of three other employees. One was deemed a desire for better representation or better performance. This engendered an uncertainty about the speaker's support and could not be entirely ignored. More significant evidence was excluded from consideration. The statement about the entire night shift was ignored because the employee did not testify or explain how he formed that opinion. The fact of disfavor is not the issue, but the existence of a reasonable doubt by the company. In absence of doubt that it had no basis for the opinion or was telling the truth, that statement should have been given considerable weight. Another employee expressed an opinion that in a vote the union would lose in the original unit configuration. It was improper to ignore the relationship between the sentiments of the two workforces. This employee was a steward and in a good position to assess the sentiments of the employees.

(4) Given fair weight to the company's circumstantial evidence, it was quite impossible for a rational factfinder to avoid the conclusion that D had reasonable, good faith grounds to doubt—to be **uncertain about**—the union's retention of majority support.

(5) The company asserts that a reading of the cases reveals that the Board has in practice abandoned the "good faith" branch of its withdrawal of recognition standard in favor of a head count. The Board denies this. The Board could have raised the standard above or below the reasonable doubt and the preponderance levels, but it cannot leave them in its rule and apply them as if they meant something else. The APA requires reasoned decisionmaking. The Board's factfinding is not supported by substantial evidence.

d) **Concurrence and dissent** (Rehnquist, C.J., O'Connor, Kennedy, Thomas, JJ.). I disagree that the Board's standard is rational and consistent with the Act. Its reasoning is short on two counts. First, there is no support in the language of the Act for its treatment of polling. Also, the Board fails to demonstrate how polling, done with the proper procedural safeguard, amounts to overt coercion or threat of retaliation. A poll would protect employee choice. Also, the Board equates polls, RM elections, and unilateral withdrawals of recognition. Treating activities with diametrically different results the same is irrational. The differing consequences suggest that polling should be subject to a lower standard.

e) **Concurrence and dissent** (Breyer, Stevens, Souter, Ginsburg, JJ.).

(1) The majority departs from settled principles allowing agencies broad leeway to interpret their own rules.

(2) The majority also disagrees with the ALJ's failure to count three employee statements. The first employee made his statement during his job

interview. The ALJ properly noted that a prospective employee is likely to say whatever he believes the employer wants to hear. The Board also ruled that statements of dissatisfaction are not the equivalent of a withdrawal of support. This is an exercise of discretionary authority that Congress placed squarely on the Board. The statement about the night shift should not deserve "considerable weight," since the Board views with suspicion statements made "purporting to represent the views of others." This was a highly general conclusion, unsupported, and made in a job interview. It was not improper to ignore it. Finally, the lack of specifics concerning the "union would lose" statement gives some support that it was overstated. It also was a statement about the views of others. The majority fails to mention that the ALJ considered it to be "almost off the cuff." The Board acted well within its authority in making its findings and reaching its conclusions.

4) **New tougher standard.** In *Levitz Furniture Co.*, 333 NLRB No. 105 (2001), a majority of the Board adopted a different and more demanding standard for the withdrawal of recognition. In place of its 50-year-old standard, it adopted the rule that an employer may unilaterally withdraw recognition only when the incumbent union has actually lost majority support in the unit. The company has the burden to counter the presumption of continued majority status. The standard for an RM petition is good faith "uncertainty." Evidence of uncertainty can be anti-union petitions and unverified, but reliable, statements regarding the sentiments of others and expressions of dissatisfaction with the union's bargaining performance.

Insert the following as **III. A. 5. m. and n.** *at p.* **78,** *and reletter subsequent paragraphs accordingly:*

m. **Overall impasse.** In *Duffy Tool & Stamping v. NLRB*, 233 F.3d 995 (7th Cir. 2000), during negotiations following an RM election the company proposed a no-fault attendance point system under which excessive accumulations could result in termination. The union firmly rejected the proposal and the company implemented the plan. Several employees were terminated while negotiations on other matters continued. The Board found a section 8(a)(5) violation because the parties were not deadlocked over all mandatory subjects. The court of appeals held that (i) early removal of items from the bargaining agenda makes it less likely the parties can find a common ground for final agreement, and (ii) by implementing a particular issue on which there is deadlock, the employer is signaling that the union is a paper tiger, which would also impede the overall objective to achieve labor peace. It said finally and conclusively, "there is no such animal as a deadlock on a single issue in a multifaceted negotiation." A "nonnegotiable" demand is likely a bluff and generally a price can be found at which there will be a surrender. An unreasonable demand on an item not central to the employer's business or labor relations may be a sign of "bad faith."

n. **Wage negotiations—merit plans--McClatchy Newspapers, Inc. v. NLRB,** 131 F. 3d 1026 (D.C. Cir. 1997)

McClatchy Newspapers, Inc. v. NLRB

1) **Facts.** McClatchy Newspapers, Inc. (D) operated two newspapers. The CBA for its Sacramento paper contained a merit pay system. Each job started with a minimum salary and had automatic pay increases up to a fixed maximum. After that, any further increases would be based on merit as determined by D. Ninety percent of employees had reached the maximum rate. In negotiations, D proposed a pure merit system and the union (P) proposed to eliminate the merit increments. After impasse, D began granting merit increases without consulting P, allowing only non-binding comment. The CBA provision for the Modesto paper was similar to the original Sacramento system except it provided for an annual performance appraisal. Later after impasse, D implemented its proposed merit plan. In both instances unfair labor practice charges were filed.

In the Sacramento case (which was tried first), the general counsel argued that D had a duty to bargain about wages and that granting increases without consulting with P was a violation of the Act. D contended it could implement its plan after impasse. The Board found a violation, reasoning that D had unilaterally insisted that P "waive" its right to be consulted about wage changes. Upon appeal, a three-judge panel first remanded the case, with one judge suggesting that the Board consider a limited exception to the impasse rule. The Board then adopted this approach, reasoning that implementation is proper "only as a method for breaking the impasse." It noted that once a merit increase was granted, P would be unable to "bargain knowledgeably" or "explain" how the wages were formulated. It said there would be no "fixed, objective status quo" to bargain about and would "disparage" P. The exception was limited to cases where an employer "refused to state any definable objective procedures and criteria." The Modesto case was decided on the same reasoning.

2) **Issue.** Does the Board have authority to modify its impasse rule to limit unilateral wage increases implemented under a standardless merit wage plan?

3) **Held.** Yes. Judgment affirmed.

a) We detect three lines of attack by D: (i) "settled doctrine" allows an employer to implement its last offer after impasse, which the Board has no authority to change; (ii) that the Board treats this pay proposal as a permissive bargaining subject; and (iii) the Board did not adequately set out the boundaries of its exception and reconcile its own precedents. The Supreme Court has recognized the Board's impasse/implementation doctrine. It has never recognized that an employer has a right to implement its final offer, and certainly has never considered whether the Board can carve an exception. It is not clear that the Act prevents it in this case.

b) *NLRB v. Insurance Agents' International Union*, 361 U.S. 477 (1960), prevents the Board from equalizing disparities of bargaining power. Yet *Charles D. Bonanno Linen Service v. NLRB*, 454 U.S. 404 (1982), recognizes that in regulating bargaining, it may appraise conditions that implicate bargaining power. The line between economic neutrality and authority over process is hard to draw. We consider this case closer to *Bonanno Linen*. The impasse rule is designed to break the impasse and encourage further bargaining. The Board, in its expertise, concluded rather than pressuring the union to bend, it might undermine its ability to bargain in the future—it could not negotiate against a standardless "discretionary cloud" and be disparaged by its inability to act in setting terms and conditions of employment.

c) Of course the Board cannot "sit in judgment upon the substantive terms of collective bargaining agreements." D overreads *NLRB v. American National Insurance*, 343 U.S. 395 (1952). Pay is no part of a management functions clause. Bargaining to impasse and implementation after impasse are not equivalents and can be treated differently. The Board's decision does not prevent implementation of a merit plan—provided it defines "merit" with objective criteria. Finally, we think the Board may rely on its expertise to consider wages as of paramount importance in bargaining and are to be set bilaterally.

Insert the following in place of **V. B. 5. a. 9)** *as* **V. B. 5. a. 9), 10), and 11)** *at p.* **145:**

9) **Review of credibility determinations and disposition on the merits.** In *Major League Baseball Players Association v. Garvey*, 532 U.S. 504 (2001), an arbitrator decided that there was no collusion among baseball owners when they failed to offer Garvey a contract for the 1988 and 1989 seasons. The arbitrator refused to give credence to a baseball executive's letter admitting collusion because it was inconsistent with prior denials. The arbitrator dismissed the grievance. Upon appeal, the court of appeals directed the district court to issue a judgment in favor of Garvey for $3 million. Without briefs or oral argument, the Supreme Court summarily reversed as inconsistent with clear principles of judicial review of arbitration awards. It held it was reversible error for the court of appeals to overturn the credibility determination of the arbitrator and dispose on the merits. Even if it were the product of dishonesty or "affirmative misconduct," the court should vacate the award and remand for further proceedings permitted by the CBA. It found no "serious error" on the part of the arbitrator.

10) **Setting aside awards on the basis of public policy--Eastern Associated Coal Corp. v. United Mine Workers, District 17,** 531 U.S. 57 (2000).

Eastern Associated Coal Corp. v. United Mine Workers, District 17

a) **Facts.** Smith was a road crew worker who drove a heavy vehicle on the public highways and was subject to the Department of Transportation random drug testing. In March 1996, he tested positive for marijuana. Eastern Associated Coal Corp. (D) discharged him. The union (P) grieved and took the matter to arbitration. The arbitrator found no "just cause" for discharge and ordered Smith to: (i) accept 30 days suspension without pay; (ii) participate in a substance abuse program; and (iii) to undergo random drug tests for five years. Smith passed four random drug tests in nine months. In July 1997, he again tested positive and was fired. P again went to arbitration. The arbitrator found no just cause in light of Smith's 17 years as a good employee and his moving personal plea that family problems had caused the one-time lapse. The arbitrator assessed: (i) suspension without pay for three months; (ii) reimbursement of costs of both arbitrations; (iii) continuation in the drug abuse program; (iv) continuation of random testing; and (v) presentation to D of an undated letter of resignation to take effect if Smith tested positive in the next five years.

D sought to vacate the award on grounds that it contravened a public policy that prohibits operation of dangerous machinery by workers who test positive for drugs. The district court recognized a strong regulation based on policy, but ruled the award of conditional reinstatement did not violate it. The court of appeals affirmed, and the Supreme Court granted certiorari.

b) **Issue.** Do considerations of public policy require the courts to refuse to enforce the arbitration award?

c) **Held.** No. Judgment affirmed.

(1) We assume the CBA calls for the reinstatement since the parties have given the arbitrator the authority to interpret the contract's language, including "just cause." Even if convinced the arbitrator committed serious error, a court may not overturn the award. There is no claim that the arbitrator acted dishonestly or beyond his authority, so we must determine whether it is unenforceable because the reinstatement is contrary to public policy.

(2) The authority of courts is not limited to instances where the award itself violates public policy. But, the exception is narrow and must satisfy the principles of *W.R. Grace & Co. v. Rubber Workers*, 461 U.S. 757 (1983), and *United Paperworkers International Union v. Misco, Inc.*, 484 U.S. 29 (1987). D argues that a public policy against reinstatement can be found in the regulatory scheme laid down by

Labor Law Supplement - 7

Congress and the regulations against it requiring suspensions of operators' licenses for driving a commercial vehicle under the influence of drugs. D's argument loses much of its force when considering the complex remedial aims that stress rehabilitation and drug treatment and contemplates the employee returning to the job. The award is not contrary to these several policies. It does not condone the conduct; it requires a large forfeiture, payment of arbitration expenses, continued treatment and testing, and assures one more failed test results in discharge. It violates no specific provision of law or regulation. That Smith is a recidivist is not enough to tip the balance. The second lapse is treated more severely. We cannot find "explicit," "well defined," " dominant" public policy to which the award is contrary.

    d)   **Concurrence** (Scalia, Thomas, JJ). I do not endorse the Court's statement "[we] agree, in principle, that courts' authority to invoke the public policy exception is not limited solely to instances where the arbitration award itself violates positive law." Since *Erie Railroad v. Tompkins*, 304 U.S. 64 (1938), we have not refused to enforce an agreement on public policy grounds. After opening the door to "flaccid public policy arguments" of the sort presented here, the Court immediately posts a giant "Do Not Enter" sign. It's hard to imagine how an arbitration award could violate a public policy, identified in this fashion, without actually conflicting with positive law.

11) **Public policy and judicial review of arbitration awards.** In *United Paperworkers International Union v. Misco, Inc.*, 484 U.S. 29 (1987), an employee was fired for possession and use of marijuana. The employee, who worked on dangerous machinery, had been found in the back seat of a co-worker's car with a burning joint in the front ashtray and smoke permeating the vehicle. The matter was grieved and taken to arbitration. Just days before the arbitration hearing both the company and the union learned that on the day of the offense the police had searched the employee's own truck and found gleanings of marijuana in it. The arbitrator sustained the grievance, concluding the evidence was inadequate to prove possession or use, and ordered reinstatement with full back pay. The arbitrator had refused to accept evidence of the police search. In an action to set aside the award, the company challenged the arbitrator's factfinding, interpretation of the CBA, exclusion of evidence, and the reinstatement award as contrary to public policy. The district court set the award aside and the court of appeals affirmed. The Supreme Court unanimously reversed. It ruled the company's claim of public policy was inadequate since it was based only on "general considerations of supposed public interests" and not on a "well defined and dominant" policy reflected in specific laws and legal precedents. It also ruled that it was not for the courts to infer from the gleanings in the truck that the employee was a danger in the workplace and was "under the influence" while there. The Court emphasized the vary narrow role of the judiciary in overturing arbitration awards, saying "The courts are not authorized to reconsider the merits of an award even though the parties may allege that the award rests on errors of fact or on misinterpretation of the contract." It said the parties had contracted to have disputes settled by their own chosen "arbitrator's view" rather than by a judge. The Court also said the courts do not sit as courts of appellate review for factual or legal errors. It said, "If the courts were free to intervene on these grounds, the speedy resolution of grievances by private mechanisms would be greatly undermined." It also ruled that the courts do not have authority to interfere with an arbitrator's honest judgment in respect to the proper remedy or to challenge the arbitrator's exclusion of the police evidence.

Insert the following as V. B. 7. b. 6) e) *at p.* **153;** *and reletter subsequent paragraphs accordingly:*

> e) **Failure to exhaust contractual remedies in ADA cases.** In *Wright v. Universal Maritime Service Corp.*, 525 U.S. 70 (1998), Wright had been injured on the job and settled his claim for permanent disability for $250,000 and attorneys' fees. He also received Social Security disability benefits. Later he was referred by the union hiring hall for work, but the stevedoring companies refused to hire him because he was certified for permanent disability. The union did not grieve or refer the matter to an alternate review plan, but advised Wright to sue in federal court for discrimination under the Americans with Disabilities Act. Both the district court and the court of appeals dismissed for failure to exhaust contractual remedies. A unanimous Supreme Court reversed. The Court recognized some tension between *Gardner-Denver*, *supra*, and *Gilmer, supra*. It refused to determine the validity of a union-negotiated waiver of federal action since none had occurred. Any waiver must be "clear and unmistakable." The CBA here did not explicitly incorporate statutory anti-discriminatory requirements, indeed it had no anti-discriminatory provision. Both the CBA arbitration and the alternate plan were specifically limited to contract disputes. The presumption of arbitrability under section 301 does not go beyond the rationale that justifies it—that arbitrators are in a better position to "interpret the terms of the CBA." The dispute here concerns the meaning of a federal statute.

Insert the following as **X. C. 4.** *at p.* **194***, and renumber subsequent paragraphs accordingly:*

4. **Primary Jurisdiction--Marquez v. Screen Actors Guild, Inc.,** 525 U.S. 33 (1998).   *Marquez v. Screen Actors Guild, Inc.*

    a. **Facts.** The CBA of the Screen Actors Guild (D) contained a security clause requiring "membership." It tracked the language of section 8(a)(3) without explaining the gloss of meaning applied to those words by the Supreme Court. Marquez (P), a part-time actor, applied for a one-line speaking part. The prospective employer required payment of a union fee (around $500) before she could begin work because she had worked in the industry more than 30 days. P tried to negotiate to pay after she had done the work. Later, D withdrew its objection, but was too late and another actor did the work.

P sued both the production company and D, claiming that D had breached its duty of fair representation by negotiating a security clause that could not be enforced because of its failure to explain her right not to join, but only pay for representational activities. She also objected to the 30-day grace period tied to employment in the industry, rather than from the employment being sought. The court of appeals ruled that the district court had no jurisdiction over the case. The Supreme Court granted certiorari to resolve the facial validity of the security clause and to clarify the standards for primary jurisdiction.

b. **Issues.**

1) Is there a breach of the duty of fair representation for a union to negotiate a security clause that tracks the words of section 8(a)(3) without explaining the judicial interpretation of that language?

2) Was the court of appeals correct in ruling the district court had no jurisdiction to decide the breach of fair representation claim in this case?

c. **Held.** 1) No. 2) Yes. Judgment affirmed.

1) As exclusive representative, a union owes a duty "to serve the interests of all members without hostility or discrimination [and] to exercise its discretion with complete good faith and honesty, and to avoid arbitrary conduct." There is no claim of discrimination. A union's conduct will be arbitrary "only if [it] can be fairly characterized as so far outside a wide range of reasonableness" that it is wholly "irrational" or "arbitrary." This gives the union room for a wide range of discretionary decisions and choices, even if the judgment proves wrong or may be a bad deal for the employees. Under this standard, the security clause derived from the NLRA section is far from arbitrary. This clause can be enforced as written because it incorporates all the refinements that have become associated with that language.

2) P also claims that D acted in bad faith because it had no reason to adopt the statutory language except to mislead employees of their rights under *General Motors*, *supra*, and *Beck*, *supra*, even if it always informs employees of their rights and enforces it in conformity with the law. It is difficult to conclude a union acts in bad faith by notifying workers of their rights more effectively and by using a term of art in a contract that the workers are unlikely to read. The court of appeals was correct in rejecting the argument that D breached its duty.

3) The court of appeals correctly refused to exercise jurisdiction over P's challenge to the 30-day grace provision. In *Beck*, we noted than an employee may not circumvent primary jurisdiction by casting statutory claims under the NLRA as breaches of fair representation. A plaintiff must show facts suggesting the union's violation was arbitrary, discriminatory, or in bad faith. P's claim is squarely within the jurisdiction of the NLRB. Her claim is that D used a term in the CBA that was inconsistent with the NLRA.

Insert the following in place of **X. C. 5.** *as* **X. C. 6. and 7.** *at p.* **194:**

6. **Notice and Exercise of *Beck* Rights and Objections.** In *California Saw & Knife Works,* 320 N.L.R.B. 224 (1995), *enf'd sub nom, I.A.M. v. NLRB,* 133 F.3d 1012 (7th Cir. 1998), with approximately 1400 locals and 800,000 members and 12,000 nonmembers covered by 6500-8000 CBAs, the I.A.M. publishes notice of rights to challenge union expenditures and proportionality of dues by sending objections by certified mail (one objection per envelope) either in January or within the first 30 days of becoming subject to a security provision. The general counsel raised several objections to these and related provisions. The Board concluded that the union must give "*Beck* rights notice" to newly hired nonmembers at the time the union seeks to collect dues. The union must meaningfully inform them of their right to object to non-germane activities and inform them of internal union procedures. An objecting employee must be informed of the percentage of the reduction, the basis for calculating it, and of the right to challenge the figures. Failure to do so is arbitrary and in bad faith. Current employees who are to become subject to dues must also be so informed. It ruled that the December notice to members in the union magazine mailed to their last known notice address is adequate. When seeking the discharge of an employee, the union must give reasonable notice of dues delinquency, including the amount due and the method used to calculate the amount. It must inform the employee when to make the payments and that failure will result in discharge. It held limiting escape to only January is an impermissible burden on resignation rights. It is also arbitrary to limit objections one to an envelope. Representational objections are not to be confined to the objector's bargaining unit. It is not necessary to calculate on a unit-by-unit basis and the objector should have the right to arbitrate the allocation. Expenses for germane litigation outside an objector's unit, such as CBA language interpretation and NLRB proceedings, need not be accounted on a unit-by-unit basis. The form of information need only be set forth in "major categories of expenditures" and "mixed" categories may be denoted without more detailed breakdown, but subject to objection. Audits, as understood in the accounting profession, must be supplied. Compilations of information supplied by the union are not adequate. The use of in-house union auditors used to verify district and local expenses is not arbitrary or in bad faith. Such expenses may be proportionately allocated. The consolidation of all dues reductions for an annual arbitration is well within the union's wide

range of reasonableness, as is the requirement that objectors bear their own travel expenses.

7. **Agency Fees—Arbitration or the Courts?** In *Air Line Pilots Association v. Miller*, 523 U.S. 866 (1998), the CBA contained an agency shop clause. In 1992, the union calculated the monthly service charge and allocated 81% of its expenses as germane to collective bargaining functions. One hundred fifty-three pilots challenged the accuracy of the charges in federal court. The union's internal policies and procedures provided that agency fees could be challenged by an American Arbitration Association ("AAA") arbitration. One hundred seventy-four pilots (including more than one-half of the court litigants) invoked arbitration. The district court held that the arbitration process should be exhausted. The court of appeals reversed. In 1986, the Supreme Court, in a public sector case, in *Teachers v. Hudson*, 475 U.S. 292 (1986), had ruled that the First Amendment requires objecting nonunion workers have a "reasonably prompt opportunity to challenge the amount of the fee before an impartial decisionmaker." The Court ruled that ordinarily arbitration is a matter of contract, and that no party should be forced to arbitrate when he has not agreed to do so. Forcing arbitration before access to federal court action would frustrate the objectives announced in *Hudson*. Two dissenters contended that arbitration would facilitate resolution of disputes and would avoid the multiplicity of suits in different forums. Arbitration would aid any later judicial proceeding by narrowing the issues and the handling of complicated financial issues.

SUPPLEMENT TABLE OF CASES
(Page numbers of briefed cases in bold)

Air Line Pilots Association v. Miller - 12
Alexander v. Gardner-Denver Co. - 9
Allentown Mack Sales & Service, Inc. v. NLRB - **1**
American National Insurance, NLRB v. - 6

California Saw & Knife Works - 11
Charles D. Bonanno Linen Service v. NLRB - 6
Communications Workers v. Beck - 10, 11

Duffy Tool & Stamping v. NLRB - 4

Eastern Associated Coal Corp. v. United Mine Workers, District 17 - **7**
Erie Railroad v. Tompkins - 8

General Motors Corp., NLRB v. 10
Gilmer v. Interstate/Johnson Lane Corp. - 9

Insurance Agents' International Union, NLRB v. - 6

Kentucky River Community Care, Inc., NLRB v. - 1

Levitz Furniture Co. - 4

Major League Baseball Players Association v. Garvey - 6
Marquez v. Screen Actors Guild, Inc. - **9**
McClatchy Newspapers, Inc. v. NLRB - **5**

NLRB v. ___ (see opposing party)

Teachers v. Hudson - 12

United Paperworkers International Union v. Misco - 7, 8

W.R. Grace & Co. v. Rubber Workers - 7
Wright v. Universal Maritime Service Corp. - 9

Labor Law Supplement- 13

Notes

Notes

Notes

Notes